D0437285

OPERATION BLUNDERHEAD

OPERATION BLUNDERHEAD

THE INCREDIBLE ADVENTURES OF A DOUBLE AGENT IN NAZI-OCCUPIED EUROPE

DAVID GORDON KIRBY

FOREWORD BY ROGER MOORHOUSE

First published 2015

The History Press
The Mill, Brimscombe Port
Stroud, Gloucestershire, GL5 2QG
www.thehistorypress.co.uk

British Library Cataloguing in Publication Data.
A catalogue record for this book is available from the British Library.

ISBN 978 0 7509 6481 4
Typesetting and origination by The History Press
Printed and bound in Great Britain by TJ International

Contents

Foreword
by Roger Moorhouse

For a long time, when we thought of Britain's wartime Special Operations Executive (SOE), the image that most probably sprang to mind was something akin to James Bond: the cold-eyed, ruthless assassin or saboteur, stalking occupied Europe and striking fear into Nazi hearts. There was something in this, of course. SOE – instructed by Winston Churchill to 'set Europe ablaze' in 1940 – scored some notable successes, most famously assassinating Himmler's deputy Reinhard Heydrich in 1942 and sabotaging German efforts to make 'heavy water' at Vemork in Norway the following year. It even made plans to assassinate Hitler himself.

But, for all their dashing and their derring-do, SOE agents were not all James Bond clones. They were, instead, an eclectic bunch: men and women, drawn from many nationalities and all walks of life, encompassing everyone from safecrackers to bankers, secretaries to princesses. Clearly, the stereotype of the chisel-jawed action hero is one which requires substantial revision.

Yet, even bearing all of that in mind, the story of Ronald Seth is still a remarkable one. Seth, a 31-year-old former schoolteacher, was parachuted into German-occupied Estonia in the autumn of 1942 ostensibly to carry out acts of sabotage in a plan code-named Operation Blunderhead. It was a very rare example of a 'privateer-SOE mission', as the idea had come from Seth himself – then a humble RAF officer – rather than being dreamt up from within SOE. Moreover, unlike the vast majority of SOE missions, Seth had no support network on the ground at his destination; though he knew the country well, he was essentially going in 'blind'. This combination of factors might well account for the peculiar choice of name given to the operation: perhaps someone within SOE was thereby expressing their concern about the mission's feasibility.

In the event, such concerns would be amply borne out. Swiftly captured by local Estonian militiamen and handed over to the Germans, Seth was initially scheduled for execution before persuading his captors that he might be of some use to them. He then embarked on a remarkable odyssey across Europe, surviving on his wits, by turns seducing and frustrating his German captors. Finally, he was sent over the Swiss border, in the dying days of the war, apparently on a mission from Himmler to secure a separate peace with the Western Allies.

Seth's story – full of pseudonyms, mistresses, aristocrats and double dealing – is one that almost seems to have sprung from the fraught imagination of a penny novelist. Yet it is true. Nonetheless, Seth was clearly not above embellishing it, both at the time and in his later memoir. His penchant for spinning a yarn, it seems, was irresistible. He told his German captors, for instance, that he knew Churchill personally, and that he was involved in a movement to restore Edward VIII to the throne.

To some degree, of course, such invention was an essential part of the game of survival that Seth was playing with the Germans. Many prisoners before him had made out that they were well connected so as to save their lives or even just secure better treatment; among them commando Michael Alexander, who claimed upon capture to be related to Field Marshal Harold Alexander, and Red Army soldier Vassili Korkorin, who passed himself off as Molotov's nephew. At first glance, then, it might seem that Seth was merely following in that necessarily mendacious tradition, saving his own neck by making himself appear to be someone who might be of value to Berlin.

Yet, there is more to Seth's story than meets the eye. For one thing, beyond the requirements of self-preservation, he seems to have embellished his own account of his exploits at almost every turn, adding details, vignettes and narratives that he borrowed from others, or else dreamt up for himself. Little wonder, perhaps, that

SOE would later consider him to be royally unreliable, and – tiring of his Walter Mitty-ish excesses – brand him as 'extremely untruthful' and seek to stop the publication of his post-war memoir.

More importantly, perhaps, away from the hyperbole of his later memoir account, it seems that Seth may have played his wartime role of the 'person of interest' rather too well, straying over the line that divides self-preservation from active collaboration. Certainly there were more egregious examples than his own, and there was never sufficient evidence for any legal case against him to be mounted, but nonetheless Seth sailed rather close to the wind. Immediately after his capture, for example, he was already stressing his anti-Soviet credentials and offering to work for the Germans against Moscow. In time, he would inhabit a dubious Gestapo safe house in Paris and act as a stool pigeon in a British POW camp, informing on his fellow prisoners to the German authorities. Finally, he would graduate to the most exalted role of all: that of Himmler's supposed emissary to London.

David Kirby's book is a fascinating examination of this complex, sometimes bewildering story. It is certainly a most impressive tale. Ill-starred as his mission was, it was no mean feat for Seth to have survived his capture in German-occupied Estonia in 1942. The murderous fate that other captured SOE agents suffered, such as Noor Inayat Khan or Violette Szabó showed what treatment he might ordinarily have expected. Yet, what followed – even if one strips away the mythology and half-truths – was truly remarkable.

Beyond telling that fascinating story, the book has additional merits. Firstly, the author – a former professor of history from London University – expertly applies his critical skills, forensically dissecting the myriad layers of exaggeration, secrecy and obfuscation that have enveloped Seth and his tale almost from the beginning, sorting the plausible from the improbable. This is an important task. Historians, like seasoned investigators, always seek corroborating documentary evidence, but in Seth's case it is more vital than ever.

The second merit is that, whilst rigorously applying those formidable investigative skills, Kirby's is nonetheless a sympathetic approach. He views Seth as a curiosity, someone who – though he might have straddled the boundary between dissembler and fantasist

– is nonetheless worthy of serious study and objective assessment. Moreover, as he notes at the end of the book, Seth seems to have had a 'curious persuasive quality', which made one want to believe him, 'even if one is not always quite sure why'.

There are aspects of Seth's story, one fears, that can perhaps never be satisfactorily clarified, but David Kirby's skilful, sober study is a fitting epitaph to one of the most peculiar episodes of the Second World War.

Roger Moorhouse, 2015

Acknowledgements

Following the career of Ronald Seth has led me down a number of interesting byways, and I wish to express my gratitude for their assistance to the following people:

Pekka Erelt, Meelis Maripuu, Malle Kivivӓli, Helga Riibe and Andres Kasekamp for their advice and expert knowledge on matters Estonian; Axel Wittenberg for delving into the Militӓr-archiv in Freiburg; Philip Pattenden, whose information on Seth's undergraduate days was invaluable; Blair Warden and the Literary Estate of Lord Dacre of Glanton for allowing me access to the correspondence between Seth and Hugh Trevor-Roper; Patrick Salmon and Tom Munch-Petersen for long years of friendship and shared expertise on northern Europe; and a special thanks to Laurie Keller, whose genealogical expertise and constant support has both assisted and inspired me.

1 | 'I thank God for one thing: I can still laugh.'

Paris, August 1944

On the afternoon of 28 August 1944, Air Commodore H.A. Jones received a surprise visit in his Paris hotel room. Jones had served with distinction in the Royal Flying Corps during the First World War, and had taken up the role of official historian of the air force in the interwar years. He now held a senior rank in the Air Ministry with responsibility for public relations, and it was in that capacity that he had hastened to the French capital immediately after its liberation from Nazi German control. What the true purpose of his mission was is not clear, though he was soon plunged into the chaos and confusion of a city where thousands were eager to establish their credentials with the liberation forces, and thousands more sought to conceal their past actions.

Amongst those seeking to make contact with the Allied officers now hastily setting up makeshift quarters in the city were agents who had operated for months, even years, behind enemy lines. Air Commodore Jones had already encountered one of these men when he visited the hotel in the rue Scribe that had been commandeered by his staff. As he later described it, a pleasant looking, thick-set young man aged about 28 approached him, claiming that he had been dropped from a Halifax bomber over France in

May, and asking to whom he should now report. It is perhaps a measure of the confusion that prevailed that Jones had to borrow a piece of paper in order to note down the man's details (subsequent efforts in the Air Ministry to trace this man, who gave his name as Taylor, drew a blank).

No doubt relieved to leave behind the uproar at the Hôtel Scribe, Jones returned to his own quarters in the Grand Hotel, and was in discussion with an accompanying squadron leader when there was a knock at the door of his room, and another young man entered, saying that he would like to speak to Air Commodore Jones. This young man was described as dark-haired, thin, with a muddy complexion and rather beaky face. He spoke good English, but was obviously French. In his possession he had certain documents which he wished to hand over to the air commodore for transmission to London. The principal document was a handwritten report, which had been given to an intermediary, known only as 'X'. 'X' had erased all references to himself in the report and had subsequently passed it on to the man who now stood in the air commodore's hotel room. Further enquiry revealed the name of this young man to be Emile Albert Rivière, and his address as 56 avenue de Ceinture, Enghien-les-Bains. The writer of the report, who, according to Rivière, was now in the area of France controlled by the Germans, signed himself 'Blunderhead'.

'Blunderhead' was the code name given by the Special Operations Executive (SOE) to a mission to carry out a sabotage operation in German-occupied Estonia. The sudden reappearance of an agent who had not made contact since he took off for on this mission on 24 October 1942 was to cause some consternation in London, and not a small measure of embarrassment. Only one month before the report written and signed by 'Blunderhead' was handed over to Air Commodore Jones, the War Casualties Accounts Department in London had been informed that 68308 Flight Lieutenant Ronald Seth, reported missing on 21 June 1943, had now been classified as killed on active service on 24 October 1942. The accounts department was to take all action necessary, and was to note that Seth had been paid from other than RAF funds, that for the past five months his wife had received a remittance based on a weekly/monthly marriage allowance of 8 shilling and 6 pence, plus two-sevenths of a flight lieutenant's pay and that payments from other than RAF funds were to cease with effect from 1 August 1944.

The term 'payments from other than RAF funds' is revealing. Seth had in fact been paid out of secret service funds since the end of 1941, when he was taken on by SOE, and he was the man whose report, dated Paris, 7 August 1944, finally landed on the desk of Major Frank Soskice, SOE's Interrogation and Case Officer, some three weeks later.

Soskice, who was to pursue a successful political career after the war, serving as Home Secretary and Lord Privy Seal in Harold Wilson's first government, interviewed Air Commodore Jones on his return from Paris, and managed to produce a succinct overview of the long handwritten report on the same day, 1 September. He concluded that there was no doubt that it had been written by Seth. The style of writing was unmistakeable, and it was in Seth's handwriting. There was moreover a clearly identifiable photograph in the accompanying envelope that contained a letter in which Seth advanced his case for promotion to the rank of acting group captain (unpaid) with retrospective seniority. As for the narrative of events detailed in the report, Soskice was inclined to believe it to be true, though highly coloured and improbable in some of its details. He was clearly not unsympathetic towards a man who, he believed, had undergone many vicissitudes during his months of capture. 'Seth is vainglorious in temperament', was his conclusion 'but it may be wondered whether his sufferings have not slightly unhinged his mind for the time being'.[1]

SOE had not been entirely in the dark about the fate of their agent. They had learnt in April 1943 that he had been captured in Estonia shortly after parachuting in at the end of October 1942, and had subsequently been interrogated by the Germans. A British agent had managed to photograph a number of German documents impounded by the Swiss authorities after two German aircraft had been forced to land in Switzerland, including an extract from this interrogation. From the description of the man under questioning, there could be no doubt that it was Ronald Seth. There was an initial worry that Seth's wireless transmitter might be used to send false information, but surveillance was soon abandoned in view of the lapse of time since his capture. Operation Blunderhead was finally cancelled on 20 May 1943, and proceedings initiated to inform Ronald Seth's wife, Josephine, that he had been killed in action, when the man himself resurfaced in France.

The initial response of SOE was commendably loyal, though there was evidently some uncertainty about what to do with an agent who still remained in German hands. Writing to Colonel T.A. (Tar) Robertson of MI5 on 25 September, John Senter, head of SOE security directorate, confirmed that SOE felt a responsibility to an agent who had undertaken a mission calling for great personal courage, as well as to the Air Ministry which had allowed him as a serving officer to be posted to SOE. Both men agreed that Seth 'should not be treated on his return as a felon but as a British officer who must be invited to explain what had happened when he left this country'.[2]

Unlike certain known targets of interest to the security services such as Harold Cole, an army deserter who was actively collaborating with the Gestapo after betraying the Resistance network he had worked with, Ronald Seth's presence in Paris had passed under the radar. The receipt of his report, written in an SS hospital in the Bois de Boulogne, thus unleashed a series of urgent enquiries about what Seth had been up to over the past eighteen months, and put the security services on alert for any possible attempt by the Germans to use him as an agent. Subsequent letters written by Seth in autumn 1944, after he had been confined to a prisoner-of-war camp in Germany, served only to sow more confusion about his mental health and his relationship with the Germans. The man who ended his long account of his trials and tribulations in various prisons across Europe with the bitter comment that he could thank God for one thing, 'that I can still laugh', was to have even more extraordinary adventures before he finally returned to British soil in the dying days of the war.

❖　❖　❖

What had happened to Seth between the time of his capture in the woods of Estonia in the autumn of 1942 and the liberation of Paris in August 1944, and what adventures he was subsequently to have before the end of the war is a fascinating story, but it is not always easy to establish the truth. His own account, published in 1952 with the title *A Spy has no Friends*, is a highly coloured version of events, and is often at variance with the evidence available in the archives, not least the reports he himself wrote at the time. His boundless self-confidence and lively imagination undoubtedly helped him survive captivity, but they also led him into exaggeration of his own importance and at times into telling downright untruths. He was a man with a heightened sense of his own importance, quite capable of weaving the most elaborate fantasies about his origins and his circle of acquaintances.

Fantastic though his account often is, there is sufficient independent evidence to support the veracity of the basic sequence of events which took him through a succession of prisons on a journey across Europe, to end up on the payroll of the German military secret service, lodged with a dodgy bunch of black marketeers and collaborators on the outskirts of Paris. In researching his story, I have on more than one occasion thought it too fantastic for words, only to be reminded by other sources of the old adage that truth can be stranger than fiction. It is hard to believe, for example, that a British prisoner being treated for scabies in an SS hospital would not only have the opportunity to write a neatly paragraphed and intensely detailed report of his activities on sixty-one foolscap pages, but would also be able to persuade a member of staff to post the document. It is equally difficult to understand why the recipient of the document, and the young man with the muddy complexion who delivered the package to a senior British representative should have willingly taken on this risk in the highly charged atmosphere of the dying days of the German occupation of Paris. The only plausible explanation must be that the Germans were so busy with preparations to leave the city that they had no time to bother about odd folk like Seth, whose credentials as a possible double agent had always been in doubt. It was perhaps Seth's especial talent to sense this. In his ability to play along with the Germans, and their willingness to play along with him, it must also be said, lies the secret of his survival.

Unlike most of the men who ran SOE, Ronald Sydney Seth came from a humble background. His father Frederick was the son of a farm labourer from Northamptonshire who moved to London during the 1860s. If Frederick's father, William, had hoped to better his prospects by moving to the city, these hopes appear to have been dashed. By the time of the 1881 census, the family had returned to the countryside, and William was once more working as an agricultural labourer. Ten years later, his 19-year-old son, Frederick, was living with relatives at Misson in Nottinghamshire, and working on the railways as a platelayer. Working on the railways was a classic way of escaping from the drudgery and impoverishment of farm labour, and Frederick took the opportunity. In 1901 we find him still living in Nottinghamshire, married with a young son, and employed as a railway signalman. Some time during the next ten years, Frederick left the railways and settled in Ely, where in 1911 – the year of Ronald Sydney Seth's birth – he was working in the marine stores. Ronald's mother died in 1916, and his father evidently remarried, for MI5 noted in 1945 that Ronald had a younger half-brother aged about 17 and a married half-sister. Ronald's older brother, Harold Edward, was already working in the marine stores in 1911, and was in the employ of Marks & Spencer in 1942, the year in which his younger brother embarked on his Estonian adventure.

When Frederick died in 1940, aged 67, his occupation was recorded as 'metal merchant'. Apart from a vague reference to some sort of business failure, Ronald did not say much about his father in his various personal statements. There was no inherited wealth, certainly: Ronald had to live on what he could earn. He was a boy chorister in the cathedral choir, and had attended the King's School, Ely, described by one of its former pupils as having been run on a shoestring, with day boys paying only £6 a term.[3] After completing his secondary education, Seth became a schoolmaster, teaching for a couple of years at Belmont House School in Blackheath, London, and for one year at the Bow School in Durham. At Belmont House he seems to have laid the foundation for what would become a further string to his bow in future years, though he gave no hint of this talent in his outline for SOE of his accomplishments. Unless Belmont House was a particularly enlightened and progressive school, the advice and instruction on sexual matters offered by the youthful novice master to his slightly younger charges could only have been given on the quiet.

It is not clear what Seth did after leaving his post at the Bow School. He later claimed to have studied at the Sorbonne, and he told SOE that he had spent a year visiting France, so this may explain the gap, though he replied 'none' when invited to give details of further education since leaving school on his application form for the RAF.

Amongst the details of his career submitted to SOE, Seth claimed that he had read English and theology at Cambridge University between 1933 and 1936. On his application form to join the RAF, he gave the dates of his Tripos examination as June 1933 and June 1938, which is inconsistent with the known record. The academic register of Peterhouse includes a Ronald Sydney Seth, elected in 1933 to a choral exhibition and a Morgan sizarship, and taking up residence at the college in the Michaelmas term of that year. The Morgan sizarship, worth £40 a year, was awarded to those who expressed a wish to be ordained in the Church of England. Ronald Seth's first year seems to have passed uneventfully; he sat Part One of the English Tripos in the summer of 1934, managing a modest third, rowed in the third May boat, and was re-elected to the Morgan sizarship in the Easter term. But things were not going well for him, as is revealed in internal college correspondence from October 1935. He had been very unsettled for some time, and had finally confessed in the Easter term 1935 that he had lost his sense of vocation and would not now be offering himself for ordination. Instead, he was now very interested in social work, and would like to take up a job in that area as soon as possible. It so happened that a man had visited Cambridge to give a talk to undergraduates about the Borstal system, and as a consequence, Seth had successfully applied for the post of housemaster in one of the Borstal institutions. 'We did our best to keep him here for his third year so that he could complete his degree', the unknown tutor writes, 'but he refused to be kept. I understand that he married almost as soon as he went down.'[4]

The writer of the letter was, however, misinformed about Seth's marital status. Ronald Sydney Seth had married a Cumbrian girl, Josephine Franklin, in the summer of 1934. Reading between the lines, it would seem that the necessity of concealing this marriage from the college authorities had been too much for a young man already beset with doubts about his suitability for the church. A letter dated 15 June 1935 from the secretary of the Ely Diocesan Board of Finance to J.C. Burkill, senior tutor at Peterhouse, expressing concern about 'this young fellow and the unhappy developments that have taken place', is a fair indication that the news of his marriage had already reached those who were helping to finance his studies.[5]

What happened to Seth in the months after he went down from the university is unclear, but at the end of November 1935, Mme Anna Tõrvand-Tellmann, the proprietress of the English College in Tallinn, the capital of Estonia, received a letter from Elena Davies of International Holiday and Study Tours, recommending 'a charming young man of good family' for the post of English master. A postscript asked if the post would be available after the new year, as the man in question had been offered a position under the Home Office, but for many reasons he preferred to go abroad chiefly for the experience. Mme Tõrvand-Tellmann, who had been let down by a Mr Blackaby, appeared keen to engage the multi-talented Mr Seth, though she had to admit the salary of £8–9 a month was not of an English standard, even though the cost of living was much cheaper in Estonia. After a further flurry of letters, we find the Seth family, with their 6-week-old son Christopher (who also bore the impressive names John de Witt van der Croote), travelling to Tallinn at the end of February 1936. The three years spent in Estonia were to change their lives in ways none of them could ever have imagined as they set sail on a cold winter's day from Hay's Wharf.[6]

Notes

1. Report on 'Blunderhead', 1 September 1944, HS9/1344.
2. Senter to Robertson, 25 September 1944, HS9/1344.
3. Patrick Collinson, *History of a History Man*, p.44. www.trin.cam. ac.uk/collinson.
4. Unsigned letter of 19 October 1935, Peterhouse Archives. Ansell 1971, p.36. In April 1936, Seth wrote to an unnamed tutor at Peterhouse requesting a certificate of attendance. An unsigned copy of that certificate in the college archive, dated 2 May 1936, gives the dates as October 1933 to June 1935. A copy of the certificate, also unsigned but dated 2 May 1936, in the archives of the English College, Tallinn, gives the dates as October 1932 to June 1935. TLA (Tallinn Town Archives) 52.2.2442.
5. A.P. Dixon to J.C. Burkill, 15 June 1935. Peterhouse Archives. I am indebted to Dr Philip Pattenden of Peterhouse for this information.
6. TLA-148.1.10. Seth himself, in a letter of 30 November, claimed four years' teaching experience and nine months' original research on Daniel Defoe, on which, with typical Seth modesty, he declared himself to be 'an authority'.

2 | 'Circumstances which are both interesting and novel.'

London, October 1941

Had it not been for one unusual quality, Ronald Sydney Seth might well have been ignored or politely turned down for special operations service. A tall, bespectacled fair-haired man of modest physical stature, he looked more fitted for the part of a cheery schoolmaster than that of a saboteur. In September 1939, he had returned to England with his family from Estonia, where he had taught English since 1936. According to his own published account, he spent several weeks job-hunting, and then joined the BBC as a subeditor of the daily digest of foreign broadcasts. Seth claimed that he subsequently went on to help create the Intelligence Information Bureau of the BBC monitoring services, rising to become Chief Intelligence Supervisor (Country). However, he found 'the constant jockeying for advancement' and infighting too much for him, and he resigned. His actual service record paints a rather more modest picture of his short BBC career, in which he advanced from subediting to assistant in the Intelligence Information Bureau, and ending as a supervisor at the monitoring unit based near Evesham. There is no trace of him as 'senior supervisor' (the grade he gave in his personal details submitted for scrutiny by the secret services in 1942), still less as chief supervisor, at the monitoring unit.[1] In February 1941 he resigned from the BBC and volunteered for the RAF. After initial training, he was commissioned in the summer and assigned to intelligence work with Bomber Command. It seems that the rather humdrum routine of low-grade intelligence gathering failed to satisfy his lively mind, for on 28 October 1941, he wrote to Group Captain J. Bradbury at the Air Ministry outlining a proposal to undertake a mission to Estonia.

In his letter, Seth mentioned an unsuccessful approach he had made in March 1941 to the War Office, offering to go to Estonia. It is interesting to note that whereas Estonia in the autumn of 1941 was occupied by the country with which Britain had been at war for two years, namely Germany, in the spring of 1941, it was still at peace, albeit having suffered a forced incorporation into the Union of Soviet Socialist Republics the previous summer. Seth had told the War Office in March 1941 that he wished to go to Estonia to find out what he could about Russian activities there. In the proposal he outlined in October, he was dismissive of the Russians' abilities to set up and direct a resistance movement in Estonia, because they were seen there as potential enemies. Here, as in later correspondence from Seth, there is a strong antipathy to the Soviet Union. In spite of his own admission that his politics were 'vaguely socialist', Seth certainly had no feelings of sympathy with the country that had occupied a land he had come to love, and where he had many friends, some of whom had disappeared during the Soviet occupation.

Far stronger than his dislike of Soviet Russia, however, was Seth's sublime self-belief. 'I cannot say that it is with diffidence that I suggest that the only Englishman who might be successful in carrying out such a plan is myself', he wrote to Bradbury. 'I have the contacts; I know the country, inside out; I speak Estonian fluently.'[2] His plan, though, was little more than a vague proposal to sound out the lie of the land and to try and set up some kind of resistance movement. Seth proposed taking over the identity of an Estonian sailor called Felix Kopti, whose brother Georg had been his former pupil. Seth had apparently been frequently mistaken for Georg during his time in Estonia and as the brothers bore a very strong likeness to one another, he hoped to be able to pass himself off as Felix. From the British authorities, Seth sought assistance in obtaining the necessary papers, a passage to Sweden, and £300; once in Estonia, he claimed, he would be self-supporting.

Seth's proposal was passed on by Group Captain James ('Jack') Easton of Air Intelligence to 64 Baker Street, the home base of the Special Operations Executive (SOE). The recipient noted that it 'read interestingly', and in forwarding the paperwork, asked 'would you like to see the man who seems to have guts, or perhaps a girl friend in Estonia'. Seth was seen on 21 November and approval to employ him, subject to a satisfactory second interview, was sanctioned by the directors on 10 December. The second interview on 13 December was satisfactory, and an application was made to the RAF for his release and promotion to the rank of flight lieutenant, in view of the hazardous nature of the project. On 7 January 1942, he was seconded from the RAF. A salary of £600 a year tax-free, with effect from that date, was proposed, with the possibility of an increase once he proceeded to the field of operations.[3]

The Special Operations Executive (SOE) into which Seth now found himself recruited had come into being some eighteen months earlier, in the immediate aftermath of the disastrous military campaign in the Low Countries and France that had ended with the evacuation from the beaches of Dunkirk. It had not been an easy birth. Within the tightly knit world of the secret service, clandestine operations were regarded with some suspicion. 'Dirty tricks' were somehow felt to be ungentlemanly, a distasteful activity far inferior to the gathering and evaluation of intelligence. Admiral Sir Hugh Sinclair, head of the Secret Intelligence Service (SIS) since 1923, had made a careful distinction between active operations in the field and the often painstaking work of gathering and processing intelligence. The man who succeeded him in 1939, Sir Stewart Menzies, also reasoned that the objectives of special operations (SO) were often at odds with those of secret intelligence (SI). SIS did set up Section IX, or 'D', in 1938 to plan and carry out clandestine operations, including sabotage, but the often grandiose ideas advanced by Laurence Grand, the head of Section IX, and his inability to control operational costs, caused disquiet. Menzies' unwillingness to defend his own head of section at a meeting with Foreign Secretary Lord Halifax at the end of June 1940 opened up the field to others to try their hand at organising sabotage and psychological warfare.

An unlikely but crucial proponent of this kind of warfare was the newly appointed Minister for Economic Warfare, Hugh Dalton. A product of Eton and Cambridge, Dalton had pursued an academic career before entering Parliament in 1924, becoming a junior minister in Ramsay McDonald's ill-fated second government in 1929. An expert in public finance, he was to serve as President of the Board of Trade in the wartime coalition government between 1942 and 1945, and as Chancellor of the Exchequer in Clement Attlee's post-1945 Labour government. Dalton's working life was thus far removed from the world of espionage and secret operations; yet he had had military experience, serving on the French and Italian fronts during the First World War, and earning an Italian military decoration for his actions during the retreat from Caporetto. Some of this fighting spirit clearly inspired him to write to Halifax on 1 July 1940, urging the creation of 'a new organisation', comparable in its activities to Sinn Fein in Ireland or the guerrillas fighting the Japanese in China. Dalton was convinced that such an organisation could not be handled by the ordinary departmental machinery of either the civil service or the military. It would need absolute secrecy, fanatical enthusiasm and a willingness to work with people of different nationalities. Although some of these qualities were to be found in some military men, Dalton was quite clear that the enterprise should not be controlled by what he called 'the War Office machine'.

An organisation created in accordance with these principles was bound to ruffle the feathers of the established bureaucratic order and military intelligence services, and so it proved. The Special Operations Executive (SOE) as outlined in a document handed over to Dalton on 22 July 1940 by the ex-Prime Minister Neville Chamberlain, now Lord President of the Council, was to be outside parliamentary control, secret and inadmissible and all departments were required to assist it. In its six years of existence, SOE lived up to the ideals that inspired its creation, though by failing to put down any firm organisational roots it contributed to its own demise once war had ended. It had no central registry or filing system, and no head office: 64 Baker Street was little more a cover address.

In the dire situation faced by Britain in the months following military withdrawal from Europe, if not exactly setting Europe ablaze, as Churchill urged them to do, SOE did seem to offer a more pugnacious profile than the intelligence-gathering activities of SIS. Lord Selborne, who replaced Dalton in 1942 as Minister for Economic Warfare and as the government's overseer of SOE, felt that, whereas SIS had initially seen SOE as a ridiculous and ineffective bunch of amateurs, they now feared them as dangerous rivals who, if not squashed, would soon squash them.

Although Section IX provided many of the key figures in SOE, others were also drawn in from City firms with strong international connections. There was indeed some suspicion and resentment that SOE recruited heavily through business networks. A not untypical example was George Odomar Wiskeman. Born in Sidcup, Kent, in 1892, and educated at Wellington and Corpus Christi, Cambridge, Wiskeman was a bachelor who had worked for many years in the timber trade. In January 1941, when he was recruited into SOE, he gave as his business address the timber importing firm Price and Pierce, and his residence as 13 Great James Street in Holborn. He claimed to have fluent Swedish and German, and 'rusty' Russian. He had lived for four years in Finland, and five in Russia as consular officer. MI5 described him as naturalised British, query Russian, which may indicate his father was a German-speaking Russian citizen, probably from the Baltic provinces.[4]

Wiskeman was 'S', head of the Scandinavian section of SOE in the autumn of 1941, and he was the man who handled the early stages of Seth's application. Director of operations at SOE ('M') was Colonel Colin McVean Gubbins, KCMG, DSO, MC, a man with considerable experience of covert operations in north-eastern Europe. Gubbins had been a member of the British expeditionary force under General Edmund Ironside, sent to northern Russia at the end of 1918 to offer support to the White Russians fighting the Bolsheviks, and was appointed to the Russian section of the general staff research department of the War Office in 1931. In the late thirties, he undertook a rather secretive mission to the Baltic to investigate the possibility of organising anti-Nazi guerrilla units in the event of war. Gubbins had an extensive network of contacts in north-eastern Europe, and was able to draw upon the knowledge and expertise of a number of men with long-established business links in the area. The Russian revolution and the subsequent establishment of a communist regime had seriously disrupted business, in particular, the timber trade. Many of the leading figures in intelligence-gathering activities concerning Soviet Russia came from a timber trade background. A number of these men also had close links with various anti-communist networks, such as the Promethean League of Nations Subjugated by Moscow, and were involved in anti-Soviet campaigns such as organised in the early 1930s to challenge the import of Russian timber into Britain on the grounds that the use of forced labour in Russia was in contravention of the 1897 Foreign Prison-made Goods Act.[5]

As we have seen, Seth had tried to persuade the War Office to take up his ideas in the spring of 1941, but there is another odd piece of evidence which seems to suggest that he had been thinking as early as the spring of 1940 of trying to get to Estonia. In the course of checking his background for recruitment into SOE, a report from the Metropolitan Police was received by MI5. This stated that in May 1940, Seth had written to A.H. Harkness of Wimpole Street, a leading specialist in the treatment of urological and venereal complaints, 'asking if it was possible to contract psoriasis in the national interest'. Interviewed by the police, Seth explained that the British government was desirous of getting somebody into Estonia, and that contracting this skin complaint would enable him to enter Estonia for treatment by means of the medicinal mud famous for its curative elements.[6]

If the date of Seth's letter to Harkness is correct, then he was already contemplating a return to Estonia before it lost its independence. In the immediate aftermath of the infamous Nazi-Soviet Pact, concluded in August 1939, the three Baltic states had been obliged to conclude non-aggression treaties with the Soviet Union. These permitted the Soviet Union to station troops on Estonian, Latvian and Lithuanian territory. Given that in his approach to the War Office in March 1941 Seth proposed to go to Estonia to investigate Russian activities, there is good reason to suppose that this may also have been his primary purpose a year earlier.[7]

How far was Seth's evident desire to return to Estonia driven by anti-Soviet sentiments? That Seth did entertain such feelings was clear to the MI5 officers who interrogated him after his return to Britain in 1945. But although an urge to spy on Russian activities may have been his principal motive for wishing to go to Estonia before the summer of 1941, it seems less likely to have been the case after the Soviet forces had been driven out of the Baltic States by the end of August 1941 – unless he had in mind the creation of a resistance movement that might equally well operate against a returning Red Army.

As already indicated, there was within SOE a close-knit circle of friends and acquaintances who shared similar anti-Soviet views. These included Colin Gubbins, his close friend Harold Perkins, former owner of a textile mill in Poland, and Ronald Hazell, a former shipbroker with the United Baltic Corporation. Hazell appears as 'Major Larch' in Seth's published account. Hazell was said to have an intimate knowledge of the Baltic States, and was deemed the man most suitable to superintend Seth's training. In July 1941, Hazell had been put in charge of the section of SOE that dealt with Polish minorities, and Poland seems to have been the focal point of his Baltic expertise. Contacts with Estonians seem to have been left almost entirely to Seth to arrange, though Hazell was responsible for training and equipping him in conjunction with the operation orders drawn up by 'S', George Wiskeman. Seth clearly saw him as his friend and mentor;

Hazell, who had to respond to Seth's frequent complaints and enthusiastic suggestions, derived rather less satisfaction from the relationship.[8]

Estonia was not an area with which SOE had hitherto concerned itself, and care was taken to ensure that any operation was cleared with Moscow. SOE had in fact recently concluded an agreement with their Soviet counterparts on cooperation in subversive operations, a circumstance of which the writer of the cipher telegram sent to the British embassy in Moscow at the end of November was mindful. The telegram stated that SOE wished to send an agent to Estonia to carry out 'a particular act of sabotage'. He would be fully instructed on his mission before departure, and would not communicate with London until he came out of Estonia. Since the agreement reached in September with the 'Soviet organisation' (the secret police, or NKVD) precluded British operations in the Baltic States, 'please approach your Soviet colleagues and ask if we can have their permission to send in this man. You should make absolutely clear to them that we would under no circumstances act without their approval'.[9] A week later, Moscow replied, saying that the Soviet side had no objection, and assumed that their assistance would not be required.

Details of the Estonia project were presented in draft form on 15 December. They went a good deal further than the 'particular act of sabotage' that was put up to the Russians as the objective of the mission. The operation was to have three main purposes. The first listed task was to organise and foment disaffection amongst the Estonian population and to promote friction between them and the Germans. The agent was also to carry out acts of sabotage at the shale-oil mines and refineries in the north-east of the country. Although it was recognised that their production levels were small even in European terms, the disruption of output would oblige Germany to supply Estonia with fuel, putting further strains on German transport. Finally, the agent was to carry out any other forms of sabotage, or passive resistance within his capabilities. The proposed date of the operation, which was given the code name 'Blunderhead' in mid-January, was March–April 1942. The operative, to be known in further internal correspondence as 'Ronald', was to be entirely alone, with no arms, equipment or 'toys'. He was to assume the identity of an Estonian seaman. The drafter of the project fully accepted that it was conceivable that within three months, such an operation would no longer be feasible and would have to be abandoned, but at least SOE would have a fully trained operative for possible use in another field.[10]

This is essentially a reworking of Seth's original idea, with rather little material commitment on the part of SOE. Under a false identity, Seth was somehow to make his way by sea to Estonia, and when there, organise a resistance movement and carry out acts of sabotage, presumably securing on his own initiative the necessary explosive and charges and any handy weapons.

The false identity that Seth was to assume was that of Felix Kopti, an Estonian seaman. Born in 1903, Kopti had spent many years on the world's oceans. In April 1940, he had signed on as a seaman on SS *Rugeley*, but had jumped ship at Port Lincoln, South Australia some six months later. He appears as Craftsman Felix Kopti in a photograph taken in 1942 of a group of men of the 106 Independent Brigade Group Workshop, recruited largely amongst Victorians and South Australians, and was still living in Australia after the war.[11]

The bare details of the cover story for Seth, alias Felix Kopti, were in place by the beginning of March 1942. Details of recent shipping movements along the eastern seaboard of South America were gleaned, and in response to Major Hazell's request for information on dockside brothels ('as 90 per cent of a sailor's conversation centres around this particular type of establishment'), names and addresses of choice locations and girls were provided.[12] Having sailed the world for some two decades, most recently off the coast of South America, the fictitious Kopti was supposed to have succumbed to homesickness, and had stowed away on a Swedish ship, landing in Sweden. Stockholm was cabled on 11 March for information on the feasibility of smuggling Seth, masquerading as Kopti, into Estonia, either directly from Sweden, or via Finland. The response was not encouraging. There were no shipping communications between neutral Sweden and occupied Estonia, and the Germans were cutting down on marine communications from Finland.

The legation was also clearly worried about being compromised by seeking to obtain a Swedish visa for a purported Estonian returnee who was in reality a British agent. There had been a crisis in relations with the Swedish authorities in April 1940, when an SIS Section IX team working to sabotage Swedish port facilities handling iron-ore exports to Germany had been broken up and its leaders arrested. Both the minister to Stockholm and the head of the SIS station had taken this very badly, and were in consequence ultra-sensitive to any further involvement in clandestine activities on Swedish soil. Although the men in Stockholm continued to investigate the possibilities, they made little progress, and by the end of April, Baker Street had begun to think of an alternative means of getting Seth into Estonia: by air.

Whilst SOE had been casting around to find the best way to get him into Estonia, Seth had been undergoing training. On 22 April, writing from Morecambe, he reviewed his project in the light of the experiences of the past six months. He assumed he would now be delivered by aircraft, and that in view of the long daylight hours that are a feature of the northern European summer, such an operation would not be feasible until the end of October. He ruled out the possibility of taking supplies with him, since there would be no reception committee, nor any prearranged safe house. Any container dropped by parachute might come down in the middle of the road, and would in any case be too heavy for one man to deal with. The most he could take would be a W/T set and a Colt .32 pistol with sufficient ammunition. In the light of what subsequently happened, with Seth finding himself having to deal with four containers, this seems like a sensible evaluation.

Seth then goes on to re-examine his original plan:

The general principle … was to hold up as many enemy troops as possible so that they could not be diverted to other fronts and to slow down the enemy industrial war machine [underlined and queried in pencil] in the country. This work was to be carried out by:
Rousing the national instincts of the people so that the enemy would [be] doubtful as to the wisdom of weakening the occupying forces. This was to be done:
    by passive resistance
    by minor acts of sabotage
Attacks on rail communication.
Attacks on aircraft.
Attacks on the shale-oil producing plants.

His conclusions now are that he should concentrate on underground propaganda for the first two to three months. If after that time he gauged these activities to have been a success, he would go on to organise passive resistance, forming a band of 50 to 100 saboteurs who would carry out a plan for simultaneous scattered attacks on rail communications, enemy aircraft and shale-oil installations, possibly on high-ranking German officials. This would have the element of surprise, since such attacks would flare up and die out, with no more active sabotage unless circumstances warranted it for at least another six months or so. Sporadic and isolated acts of sabotage, on the other hand, would be of no use, both on account of the small size of the country and the meagre results achieved by such acts.

With the exception of a couple of pencilled queries over details, this part of Seth's letter passed without comment. His concluding pages, however, touched upon a far more sensitive nerve, and provoked a flurry of sharp comments. 'I suggested in the original proposal', Seth writes in a section headed "Policy", 'that so great had been the shocks of the immediate past that the people were in a dazed condition, but that they could be rallied, especially by an Englishman and by me in particular'. The brief period of Soviet rule in 1940–41 had been so brutal and ruthless that Estonians would no longer regard the Russians as preferable to the Germans, as they had before the war. Some 30,000 Estonians, mostly members of the intellectual, political and business elite, had been either murdered or deported by the Russians. The Germans had been a little more sensitive towards Estonian aspirations, permitting the celebration of Independence Day and the flying of the national flag on 24 February, but were as ruthless as the Russians when it suited their book:

> The Estonians are not likely to rally to a cause which would cause a sure amount of present suffering, only to have their country seized by the Russians at the end of the war. And I personally would rather leave them to the Germans than to the Russians.
>
> It is therefore essential for me, personally, to know what policy the Allied nations – I do not count the USSR as an ally – are going to adopt towards the small countries after the war, before I can embark on the proposed action.

He acknowledged that this was a difficult problem which the British Foreign Office would in all probability be unable to answer, but he felt strongly that the issue had to be settled, and he saw no reason why it should not be settled now. The Atlantic Charter, a statement of fundamental principles agreed upon by Churchill and Roosevelt in August 1941, had come out firmly against any territorial changes against the wishes of those peoples concerned. Stalin and Molotov, on the other hand, had demanded that the Soviet Union (which was not a party to the Atlantic Charter) should have strategic frontiers after the war, which as far as the Baltic States were concerned could only mean one thing: loss of independence. Seth goes on to argue that the Baltic States themselves realise that independence as achieved before the war cannot be achieved again, and that they would have to fit into the scheme of foreign policy and economic arrangements dictated by the Great Powers [marginal pencil note – Russia?]. Seth was convinced they would be prepared to accept this, though he is clearly assuming 'Great Powers' to exclude Russia. He is so bold as to say that, whilst it is imperative for the Allies to reach Berlin, it is equally imperative that the Russians should not.

In conclusion, 'Since therefore I cannot betray the Estonians or my own conscience, I feel that I must have assurances that the Baltic States shall not come under direct Russian influence after the war. And those assurances must come either from the Prime Minister or from the Foreign Secretary – I would prefer the former. [pencilled note ; a pious hope!]'. Never lacking in confidence in his abilities, Seth was prepared to lay his case personally before the highest authorities, 'and in fact, if I might suggest it, I think it would be extremely useful if I could lay my points before them orally'.

The letter finished on a more personal note, with a request for promotion to the rank of acting squadron leader (unpaid). For a rookie flight lieutenant, only recently gazetted war substantive flying officer, this was a bold, not to say cheeky, claim. In the margin of the letter is a scribbled comment: 'at this rate one moves up one rank every 3 or 4 months! He hasn't done so badly so far!' Seth justified his claim for promotion on the grounds that in Estonia, where he was regarded as 'a little tin god', his chances of success amongst the natives would be far greater if he had senior officer status; Estonians having 'the Continental love and regard for rank.' Rank should also be commensurate with the task, and he was to be solely responsible for a huge area. The pencilled marginal notes took the position that promotion should be dependent on outcome, and 'most of us have to earn such enjoyment [of being promoted to senior rank] by producing the goods first!'[13]

During the summer months, whilst he was learning how to become an efficient radio operator, Seth's fertile imagination had ample opportunity to explore his role as seaman Kopti. Major Hazell managed rather adroitly to scotch the idea of tattooing, on the grounds that a tattoo would be an irrevocable mark of identity. Obliquely reminding Seth of the original plan for Kopti to pose as a ship's steward he added, 'although many seamen are certainly tattooed, a good many stewards belong to the pansy fraternity and as such object to this type of manly marking'.[14]

Seth also took up once more the business of what he calls 'bodily mutilation'. As we have seen, he had enquired into the possibility of contracting psoriasis as means of providing him with a cover story before he was ever taken up by SOE. He had more recently put up the notion of being bodily mutilated in some way so that he would not be drafted as forced labour in Germany, should he ever be stupid enough to come into serious contact with the German authorities. This idea had been slapped down on grounds that Seth considered ill-conceived and not very reassuring, namely, that he would have to be paid a disability pension after the war. On reflection, he had come to the conclusion that mutilation would affect his ability to carry out his operation, but had in the meantime come up with another idea. Might it not be possible, should danger threaten, temporarily to paralyse his left arm by means of an intravenous injection?

This last suggestion, somewhat surprisingly in view of earlier negative comments, was taken up for further consideration. The substance of Seth's letter, however, seems to have acted as a catalyst for some re-evaluation of the entire project. Was Estonia sufficiently important to warrant 'the setting up of a full-blown SOE network of chief organiser, area organisers, sabotage squads, etc., etc.', or, if not, was it thought desirable to set up a purely 'nuisance post' there, entailing a much smaller organisation operating without explosives or stores, and relying largely on passive resistance?

If the answer to the first question was 'yes', then Seth's requests should receive full consideration in regard to his training. If, however, the answer to the first question was 'no' and 'yes' to the second, this would entail a significant scaling-down of the operation. Seth's training would have to be tailored to meet the particular methods he would be asked to employ. His importance would thus be diminished, and SOE would be able to cut its costs accordingly. For George Wiskeman, now looking after the Swedish arm of SOE operations after the Scandinavian section was broken up into country units, and Seth's controller, 'MPO' (Hazell), the real sticking point was Seth's attitude towards British foreign policy. It was clear to them that the Foreign Office was highly unlikely to give out any statement of policy, and if it did, as Wiskeman frankly admitted, 'it would entail the sale of Estonia to the USSR'. Were Seth to persist in demanding a statement of British policy, SOE might very likely abandon the entire project and assign him to other tasks. Hazell's response was blunt: 'unless R is prepared to carry out total warfare for the sake of his own country and leave the politics of other countries to be solved by wiser heads than his own, then there seems to be no point in sending him to Estonia. He has still to learn the true meaning of the word patriotism.'[15]

This sort of personal politicking was clearly not to the taste of his masters, but it was not untypical of the man. He seems, for example, to have been active in supporting the Abyssinian cause in the autumn of 1935, when that country was invaded by Fascist Italy. He also showed a penchant for writing to the good and the great with advice, or to enlist their support. In 1935, he attempted to persuade the Master of Peterhouse, Field Marshal Sir William Riddell Birdwood, to give his public backing for the Red Cross scheme in aid of Abyssinia, and he pitched in with advice to Lord Halifax during the tripartite talk between France, Britain and the Soviet Union in the summer of 1939.[16]

Seth was nevertheless not a political animal. He declared his politics to be 'vaguely socialist', but what young man in the thirties who claimed to have ideals would have said otherwise? He was essentially driven by a desire to do good, though he lacked the determination and toughness needed to brush aside obstacles and objections, and this meant that his frequent interjections became more a source of annoyance and exasperation than a serious sustained challenge.

What then was the position on Operation Blunderhead as spring turned to summer in 1942, in many ways the most crucial year of the war? At this point, one has to read between the lines, for the files in The National Archives do not record any clear policy decision on what Ronald Seth's mission was intended to achieve. Efforts to secure detailed information on the Estonian shale-oil industry seem to have run into the sand. The hapless individual charged with the task complained that he could find no one who had ever heard of it, other than the suggestion that it might be a racket.

The final plan for Operation Blunderhead was nevertheless approved on 31 August 1942. SOE was now thinking of despatching two men, equipped with a wireless transmitter and a small hand-powered generator, with the area around the town of Rakvere, some 100km east of Tallinn, as a possible landing zone. The month of October would be the latest in which agents could be dropped, since climatic conditions thereafter would leave them in danger of starvation (or more likely, being frozen to death). The objective of the mission was to be the damaging of shale-oil installations, the hindering of German rail communications, and any other actions which, on the spot, might be undertaken to 'annoy the enemy'.

The shale-oil deposits were located in the north-eastern corner of Estonia. From modest beginnings in the 1920s, a sizeable industry had emerged. Production at the four principal refineries had reached around 170,000 tons per annum by 1939, and it was said that the Germans were keen on developing capacity to produce up to 500,000 tons annually. An internal SOE memorandum dated 15 December 1941 admitted that the production of the Estonian refineries was only a very small proportion of world or even European output, but it was used locally, and any serious disruption of fuel supplies would put an additional strain on German resources.

The plan approved at the end of August was somewhat at variance with Seth's own ideas, as outlined in April. Then he had come to the conclusion that he should focus initially on propaganda, and if that yielded favourable results, proceed to more active measures. Seth had had in mind the creation of bands of saboteurs who would carry out a plan of simultaneous but scattered attacks on specific targets. Now, however, he was being sent with the most meagre of supplies, and with no prospect of being rescued from his mission. Special charges for the demolition of shale-oil installations would be supplied, but only if the limited quantity of stores which could be taken allowed for it. The approved plan ended with these less than encouraging words:

> As there will be no reception Committee, these two operators will have to work entirely off their own resources, and the quantity of stores which can be carried will depend upon their physical possibilities of dealing with them after they land. A suitable W/T set has been laid on.[17]

The second man who was to accompany Seth was an Estonian seaman, Arnold Johannes Tedrekin. Tedrekin appears to have been recruited by British security officers based in Sweden. At the end of June, agent 4404 claimed to have unearthed 'a promising Estonian boy' from an internment camp in Sweden. Both MPO and Seth himself were keen to take him on, and have him trained up.

Arnold Tedrekin was fated never to return to Estonia. In 1951, he was working as a motor fitter in Middlesex, where he died on 10 July 1987.[18] In September 1942, however, he was at Stodham Park in Hampshire, learning about the use of explosives preparatory to joining Ronald Seth on the mission to sabotage installations in his native land. Seth joined him at Stodham Park, and reported that the young Estonian showed remarkable aptitude and seemed a promising prospect. He was, however, very restless. Late one evening, returning a little drunk from the pub, he confessed to Seth that he was feeling depressed because of what had happened to his family in Estonia. In Seth's opinion, Tedrekin needed to be given a rigid programme of activities. He himself had not the time to do that, fully engaged as he was in preparing himself for the mission. Within a week, Tedrekin had been quietly dropped from the operation.[19]

As the summer progressed and Seth continued his training, SOE was still desperately trying to gather information, and relevant material. Although Moscow appeared happy for the operation to go ahead, the Russians had failed to provide any papers, such as a passport, that might have facilitated the mission. Rather late in the day, an elaborate plan was concocted for Seth, under the guise of the seaman Felix Kopti, to write to the Estonian consulate in London to obtain a new passport, on the grounds that his old one had been confiscated by the Brazilian port authorities. The Estonian consul-general was, however, wise to this rather half-baked plan, demanding to know when and where the old passport was issued, evidence of identity such as a seaman's certificate and answers to the question of why the Brazilian authorities had seized the passport and how the hapless Estonian seaman had been allowed on shore in England without documents. At the beginning of October, Hazell noted that in view of the questions asked, and the short time that remained before the mission was launched, it would not be possible to go ahead with the idea of obtaining a new passport. There was to be no response to the consul-general's questions.[20]

In the meantime, arrangements for the flight which was to carry Seth to Estonia were being made. Wiskeman noted at the end of September that the Air Ministry had agreed to use a specially modified Halifax flying from Scotland to drop Seth on the Kolga peninsula. This had been identified a week earlier as a desirable dropping point by Hazell, almost certainly on Seth's advice, since this was where he had stayed in a friend's cottage during the summer of 1939. Hazell's memorandum seems, though, to be remarkably hazy about the compass, regretting 'it will not be possible to drop this man further west as there are no communications whatever for non-Germans in Estonia and he has got to find his way in any case to RAKWERE district by foot'. Wiskeman seems to have been equally confused, since he described the Kolga peninsula as 'the most westerly point at which the drop can take place'.[21] Rakvere is in fact to the east of the Kolga peninsula. It is moreover a good 50km from the proposed dropping point, and the footsore Seth would have had to tramp a further 50km from there to the shale-oil fields.

The money to finance the operation was agreed in remarkably short order by the Treasury, within three days of the submission to SOE's director of finance of 'what can best be described as his [Seth's] "pro-forma invoice"'.[22] Seth's estimate of expenses was neatly recorded in a series of sub-headings. He envisaged paying the men he would recruit the sum of 40 Estonian crowns per month, for a period of eight months. The largest grouping, a special organisation of forty men, would receive a grand total of £640. Cells of five men would be paid £80 each for watching and probable action against the ports of Tallinn, Paldiski, Pärnu and the railway junction at Tapa. Other cells were to watch the principal railway lines and the airfields at Rakvere and Viljandi. His own subsistence for a year, at 80 crowns a month, amounted to £50. Seth was to be furnished with £1,000 in five dollar bills, £450 in Swedish crowns, and £50 in gold Russian roubles and German marks.

No one, however, had thought to ensure that Seth had some ready cash for his day-to-day expenses. At the beginning of October, the month designated for the mission, Hazell wrote to SOE's director of finances, stating that they had just received an intelligence report that German small coins and Russian roubles were still current tender in Estonia, and asking if some could be provided so that Seth would have something to tide him over in the first few days of his mission. During his absence, he was to be paid an increased annual salary of £750 per annum, tax-free. For a man who worried constantly about his precarious financial situation, such a sum must have been welcome, though he seems not to have appreciated the full significance of the tax-free bonus.

In his note to SOE's director of finance which recommended approval of Seth's estimates, Hazell added 'so that we, from our side, have done all we can to make the operation a success'.[23] There is in these words a strong undercurrent of resignation, almost of foreboding. From the start, SOE seems not to have moved very far from an initial expression of curiosity. Operation Blunderhead was in all its essentials Seth's own show. His controllers seem to have allowed him to design and cost the project, and left him pretty much to his own devices in making any necessary contacts. His 'invoice' would also suggest that he still envisaged his mission as one of recruitment, rather than straightforward sabotage of the shale-oil installations in north-east Estonia. There is little or no evidence of SOE receiving information from Stockholm about the current military situation in occupied Estonia, in spite of the fact that the SIS Stockholm station regularly received reports from former senior figures in Estonian military intelligence. In a note written in July 1942, regretting the lack of information about Estonia from Moscow, Wiskeman admitted that as they had omitted to ask specifically for such intelligence, 'we have perhaps only ourselves to blame'.[24] All attempts to find how badly the shale-oil industry had been damaged by the retreating Russians, how well was it guarded, or even a detailed layout of its installations seem to have drawn a blank. 'Ronald' was to all intents and purposes about to be put aboard a Halifax bomber and dropped some distance from Rakvere, without any companion, with no reception committee to meet him, and no contact in prospect, other than pre-war acquaintances who might still happen to around in war-torn Estonia. The project first outlined in December 1941 had explicitly ruled out arms, equipment and 'toys', and Seth's long letter written in April had likewise rejected as impracticable the idea of hampering a man on his own by equipping him with heavy supplies. Now, however, this lone agent was supposed to gather up the contents of three containers dropped with him, containing food, camping gear and explosives, plus a wireless transmitter, in a densely wooded area in the middle of the long late October night, with no prospect of assistance from the local population.

Notes

1. Seth, Ronald is recorded as an 'auxiliary' and the starting date of his appointment 19 October 1939 as 'overseas assistant, intelligence', although this has been overwritten in pencil with 'monitoring sub editor'. He is also listed as 'B.A., D.Ph., and M.R.S.L.'. Information kindly supplied by Jessica Hogg of the BBC Written Archives centre. Seth 2008, p.10.

2. Seth to Bradbury, 28 October 1941, HS9/1344.

3. £600 per annum was more than a non-flying junior officer in the RAF would earn, and was comparable to the salary of a university lecturer or a middle-rank civil servant. HS9/1344 for the correspondence with Seth.

4. Personal file of G.O. Wiskeman, HS9/1614/1.
5. Dorril 2000, pp.185–214, 424–9.
6. Metropolitan Police report, 12 November 1941, HS9/1944.
7. HS9/1344 for details of Seth's letters. The in-house history of the Polish minorities section says that Seth 'bombarded the Air Ministry with requests to be sent to Estonia' for a year, HS7/184.
8. Seth 2008, p.12.
9. Telegram to Moscow, 28 November 1941, HS9/1344.
10. Draft project for Operation Blunderhead, 15 December 1941, HS9/1344.
11. www.awm.gov.au for the photograph.
12. Memo from MPO (Hazell), 23 February 1942, HS4/240.
13. Seth's letter of 22 April 1942 and comments, HS9/1344.
14. Hazell to Seth, 13 July 1942, HS4/240.
15. Memo on Operation Blunderhead by '4404' and subsequent comments, HS9/1344.
16. Sir William's politely declined Seth's request on 19 October 1935. Peterhouse College Archives. Seth's letter of 1 June 1939, addressed to the Foreign Secretary Lord Halifax, is in FO371/3356.
17. Memo of 31 August 1942, HS9/1344.
18. *London Gazette*, 17 April 1951, 12 March 1993. There is a passport photograph of the young Arnold at www.snap.ee.
19. Seth's letter of 15/16 September, HS4/240. The official history of the Polish minorities section claimed that Seth did not like Tedrekin and insisted he be removed from the operation, HS7/184.
20. HS4/240.
21. Memo from MPO (Hazell), 22 September and S (Wiskeman), 30 September 1942, HS9/1344.
22. The 'invoice' is in HS9/1344.
23. Memo from MPO, 23 September 1942, HS9/1344.
24. Memo of 17 July 1942, HS4/327.

3 | 'Entirely satisfactory.'

Birkenhead, March 1942

Seth was no sooner signed up by SOE than a programme of training for him was set in motion. On 17 January 1942 Hazell wrote to the head of military training (MT/A1), asking if Seth could proceed in three days' time to the training camp at Arisaig, on the west coast of Scotland. He expressed a wish for Seth to receive special training, though it would be quite in order for him to work with other students where necessary. In particular, Seth should be given a lot of outdoor training in order to toughen him up. As he would be operating entirely on his own, it was essential that his training be thorough.

Arisaig House is today a comfortable hotel looking out over the waters of Loch Nan Uamh, easily accessed by road. Seventy years ago, only a rough single track ran along the shores of the loch; it was its very remoteness that made Arisaig and the cluster of other establishments around the loch so attractive to SOE for the training of its agents. By all accounts, the men were well looked after. One remembered being welcomed with a large glass of whisky, and living very comfortably there for his three-week stay. Others speak of the ample breakfasts, even speaking wistfully of porridge eaten with salt.

The main purpose of the training courses was to toughen up the men physically and to prepare them for the dangers and hardships that would face them in the field. Most found the course beneficial to their physical condition, and enjoyable. Certain exercises, such as rope work, were distinctly challenging. Many found unarmed combat unsettling, and there were several stories of trainees despatching people unfortunate enough to have bumped into them by accident. Other exercises were more fun, especially when it involved setting dummy explosive charges to the local railway line or living off the land, which provided an excellent excuse for poaching salmon or filching lobsters from the locals' lobster pots.

Seth was at Arisaig for three weeks. The final report on his training was encouraging. He proved himself to be a keen student, with a first-class trained mind, making excellent progress in map reading and signalling in Morse code, and showing good leadership qualities. Unfortunately, a knee injury prevented him from completing the physical training course, and it was here that he was less successful. In spite of his determination and enthusiasm, he lacked the physical strength needed for close combat and rope work, as he ruefully admitted in a letter to Hazell. Strengthening exercises and individual tuition did help him improve his shooting ability, but at the end of the course, he remained an indifferent shot. In his summary, the commandant, Lieutenant Colonel Anderson, noted that Seth had made himself competent in the subjects which he considered most useful for his mission. Anderson commended him as 'a very able man who would go through with anything he sets his mind to'.[1]

At this stage, it was clearly intended that Seth was to enter Estonia as a sailor, and by sea. However, as Hazell frankly admitted, the slightly built, bespectacled Seth would cut an unlikely figure as a deck-hand. Hazell therefore came up with the idea of passing him off as a steward, and to this end, he sought to find him a berth for three weeks to a month on board a coaster, either as a mess boy or working in the galley. A berth was found for him aboard SS *Daxhound*, due to sail out of Grangemouth in April, but before then, Seth was to undergo further training at Beaulieu and Station 17. At Beaulieu, the Hampshire home of Lord Montagu, agents were instructed on conditions in the occupied countries to which they were being sent. Not infrequently, they were dragged from their beds to face interrogation from an instructor dressed in Gestapo uniform, a ploy that invariably misfired as the interrogators were usually easy to identify and were generally unconvincing in dress and demeanour.

Station 17 was Brickendonbury manor in Hertfordshire, and taught industrial sabotage.

Agents were also assigned missions. These were varied in nature, from breaking into a house to tailing suspects. At the end of March 1942, Ronald was sent on a surveillance and reconnaissance exercise to Birkenhead. His handwritten report shows his lively imagination at full stretch.

The starting point for his adventures was Woodside Station, a rather grand double-roofed building located next to the ferry terminal for Liverpool and, until its closure in 1967, the Birkenhead terminus for express services from London Paddington. The first thing he noticed on leaving the station was how conspicuous he looked on account of his clothes and shoes, and his height. The few people around on the streets were all poorly dressed and not above 5ft 9 or 10in in height; Seth himself was over 6ft. The fact that he was wearing a collar and tie, and was obviously lost, gave him away to a policeman on point duty in Hamilton Square, and he decided to beat a hasty retreat from the mean streets of Woodside to the central district of Liverpool, where he would be able to find accommodation in a large hotel and be one of a crowd. Having plumped for the comforts of the Adelphi, he spent the evening working out his plan of action for the following day.

His cover story was that he was an RAF officer on leave, who was also a novelist in civilian life. He had come to Liverpool and Birkenhead to gather material for a novel he was writing about the merchant navy. The following morning, he returned to Woodside, where his friend the policeman kindly directed him to the Sea Transport Office. Here, an obliging gentleman occupied himself with a fruitless search for Seth's imaginary friend. Whilst waiting, Seth spotted an attractive woman in her mid-20s, and 'registered the idea that she was the secretary of someone fairly high in authority and if I could contact her I might get some information'. His pick-up technique was original, if rather direct and crude: he bumped into her as she came out into the corridor, knocking her down and laddering her stocking when he trod on her foot. 'Apologising and unable to repair the damage to the stockings, owing to the coupon situation, I asked if I could make up somewhat by asking her to dine and dance that evening. I introduced myself and she said she would love to.'

Having fixed a date for that evening at the Adelphi, Ronald returned to Hamilton Square Station on the Mersey railway, noticing that the same policeman was still on traffic duty. His contact (in SOE parlance, 'the cut-out') finally appeared, and they returned to Liverpool, where they had coffee at Reece's Parker Street restaurant. They arranged a further meeting the next day, and Seth then spent the afternoon in Liverpool Cathedral, and in deciphering his instructions at his hotel.

He got off to a cracking start with his date when she revealed that she had read one of his novels and his book on Estonia, *Baltic Corner*. They were less successful in getting a table in any restaurant that had dinner dances, so they returned to the Adelphi and dined there. At around half-past eleven, Ronald escorted the lady to her lodgings in Prince Alfred Road, Wavertree:

> Her response in the taxi was satisfactory, but as I had the definite idea of being followed (i) outside the hotel and (ii) outside her house where a taxi passed us, stopped lower down the street and discharged its fare. I made my excuses on the grounds there were lights in her lodgings for not going in, and arranged a later rendezvous.

Returning to the hotel, he left his shoes outside his room, but slipped them on again at half-past twelve, and went to the docks. He concluded that by Sunday morning, he had made 'a very satisfactory impression', though whether this referred to the exercise or to his new lady-friend is unclear.

On the Sunday morning, he met up again with the cut-out, who passed on instructions via the medium of a prayer book during the service of Holy Communion. Hoping to keep ahead of the other agents in the field, Seth moved across the Mersey to the Queen's Hotel, Birkenhead. Here he was able to make a useful contact, a Mr Rogers, who claimed the acquaintance of Lord Lever and a managing director of the shipbuilders Cammell Laird. Mr Rogers promised that he would do all he could to help him fulfil his wish to gather material about merchant shipping. An afternoon stroll through Wallasey allowed an opportunity to observe activities in the docks, and also a chance to test reactions. He approached a policeman guarding the dock and pretended to be a German seeking permission to visit the docks. This was treated as a great joke, and he was advised to turn to the Mersey Dock and Harbour Board in person, with his identity card. The evening was rounded off in an 'entirely satisfactory' manner at a thé dansant and dinner in Birkenhead with Mrs Turner, his new lady-friend, who promised to do what she could to get him into one dock at least.

Mrs Turner proved to be as good as her word, though Ronald rather uncharitably suspected a trap at first when she said she could get him into the Morpeth Dock. She was evidently well known at the dock and had no difficulty getting him through the police check. Having seen all he wanted, Seth had no further use for Mrs Turner. Outside the dock once more, he said that he had to return to London and that this was good-bye. He did, however, have the good grace (and manners) to send her a farewell note that evening.

In between times, he had busied himself purchasing sundry items of second-hand clothing suitable for gardening. Adjourning to the gentlemen's lavatory on Woodside station, he completed his disguise as a working man by taking off his collar and tie and begriming his hands and face with dust. In this guise he toured the dockside pubs at lunchtime, gathering more information about the docks. Presumably cleaned up and divested of his disguise, he lunched with Mr Rogers, his contact of the previous day. Later that afternoon, Mr Rogers took him to the Oxton Conservative Club and introduced him to Major Dawson, a local doctor and alderman of the borough. Major Dawson promised to lay on a police car and a visit to the docks the following day. In the evening, Seth changed once more into his old clothes and gleaned more information whilst playing the latest dance hits on rickety pianos in three dockland pubs.

Major Dawson proved as good as his word, providing a police car and a grand tour of the Birkenhead and Wallasey docks. Unfortunately, Mr Rogers, having been liberally plied with drink, fell asleep in his room, and Seth was unable to find the plans of Birkenhead docks he had been promised. He returned to London on an early morning train the following day. Having failed to establish any contact with the leader of the operation, he prepared a three-page report on the docks and rail communication, which mentioned the retired fruit broker Mr Rogers and Major Dawson as useful contacts in the city. Mrs Turner, however, was omitted from the list.[2]

Seth's account of his doings on Merseyside reveals his talent for story-telling. This is not a dry factual statement, but a lively narrative, full of incident and character. Even allowing for his all too evident penchant for exaggerating his own importance, Ronald comes across as a man of considerable charm, able easily to win people's confidence. This much was recognised by the commandant of the Beaulieu 'finishing school', which had set up the Birkenhead exercise. The commandant's report did, however, note a number of disturbing characteristics, and is worth quoting in full as a perceptive assessment of Seth's character and personality:

Intelligent, but an erratic type of brain. Mentally immature. He is intensely enthusiastic, bordering on the fanatic. He appears to possess abundant self-confidence, although he has no illusions as to the possibilities of his being able to carry out the job which he has undertaken to perform. He has a charming personality and is a good mixer but his great weakness is that he is inclined to dramatise nearly everything he does. He is a man who would be best employed alone and he requires a far greater degree of security mindedness and self-discipline if he is to succeed. It is his determination rather than his character that inspires a degree of confidence.[3]

❖ ❖ ❖

With this less than ringing endorsement, Ronald proceeded to his next exercise, on board the SS *Daxhound*, a tanker of 1,128 gross tons, part of a small fleet operated by the Hadley Shipping Company. Seth was able to overcome the reluctance of the ship's master to take him on as anything other than a passenger, and was signed on for the voyage as assistant steward. The skipper's warning that he would find the work rough and the conditions poor were confirmed in far blunter language by the chief steward. When Ronald attempted to tell his cover story, that he was a schoolmaster looking for experience to strengthen his application to join the Navy, the chief steward interjected: 'I know, going to be called up and coming to sea to get out of it like so many other buggers. You'll fucking well wish you'd joined the fucking army before you've been at it long.'

The conditions on board were truly grim. The pots and pans in the galley were filthy, as were the personal habits of the chief steward-cum-cook and his assistants. Although Seth claimed in his report that, after a few days, he was quite enjoying himself, in the next breath he admitted that he was 'rather digging in my teeth to hold out the three of four weeks'. In addition to learning the correct terms for parts of the ship, he also learnt to sleep in his underclothes, to wash only once a day, to make constant use of extremely coarse language, to talk of subjects beloved of sailors and to swill pints of beer.

Daxhound being a coastal steamer, there were plenty of opportunities for boozing in the evenings. Ronald was also exposed to another shoreside temptation in Aberdeen, when he went with the bo'sun to a milk bar for some sandwiches. Two 'smart and presentable' women soon attached themselves to the men. The ladies averred that they were not gold-diggers, and furthermore, they knew of several nice girls, also not gold-diggers, in case the two men had other sailor friends. The bo'sun soon went off with the younger of the two women, and Ronald accompanied the elder, who was a married woman, to her home. Here, they were met by the woman's 16-year-old daughter. After a hurried conversation, Seth promised to return in three-quarters of an hour, when the daughter would be in bed. However, he failed to keep his promise, and returned to the ship.

He had an even more adventurous outing on Tyneside some days later. His shipmates told him that gangs of teenage lads roamed the streets of South Shields and Jarrow with the express purpose of beating up merchant seamen. He was inclined to disbelieve them, but after an evening pub-crawl, he and three other crew members were making their way back to the ship when they were assailed by a gang of around fifteen youths:

> Almost before one knew where one was, the fight was on. I dealt with one with a chin jab, fingers in eyes and knee up, and he was out. Another I caught by the arm, and I think broke his fore-arm, for I heard a crack. I also ran my foot viciously down his leg, and he retired limping, and his arm hanging down by his side. Two of our own people were by this time on the ground and I saw one of the gang about to kick his [sic] head. I rushed up behind him and punched him as hard as I could in the small of his back, at the same time putting my arm round his throat. I applied pressure, he struggled for a little, then in a few seconds went limp and I dropped him. My two companions still on their feet had accounted for four others between them, but we were still outnumbered, three to one.

Seth was about to lay into a fifth youth, when the distant sound of police whistles was heard. Disposing of his opponent with a chin jab, he was just about to tackle a sixth, when he was knocked out cold by a blow to the jaw. Reflecting on the experience afterwards, he felt that it had given him great confidence. Thanks to Captain Sykes (a former member of the Shanghai police force who taught unarmed combat at Arisaig), he had come through with flying colours. 'If one went all out there is absolutely no doubt that one's assailant could be killed every time, quickly and silently.'[4]

Ronald continued his training schedule after his seafaring experience. Whilst at Special Training Station 52, which was located at Thame Park in Oxfordshire and specialised in training wireless operators, he badgered Major Hazell yet again on the matter of promotion. He had recently read a report that spoke of a considerable organisation of guerrillas in existence in Estonia before the German occupation, and if he were to have the opportunity to pick up the threads of this organisation, 'the higher the rank I can have the better it will be'. As before, the men in Baker Street were disinclined to accede to his request. As Wiskeman remarked in a note to Major Hazell, rank could not be of the slightest consequence in Estonia. If Seth ever got in touch with a guerrilla band, 'he can pose as a Field-Marshal or Air Vice-Marshal for all we care'.[5]

The idea of smuggling Seth into Estonia by boat had already been shelved by the end of April, just as he was signing on as assistant steward on board the *Daxhound*. Like all other agents being sent into occupied Europe, Seth had to undergo parachute training at Ringway, Manchester. He was lucky enough to do three of his four his descents from an aircraft; jumps from a tethered balloon were universally feared and disliked. He was rather unfit, and slow to master the ground training, but showed a keen interest, and managed to perform his jumps well without any mistakes.

The parachute training took place at the end of September and beginning of October. A few weeks earlier, Seth had taken part in a series of exercises in Newcastle-upon-Tyne designed to test his skills as an undercover agent. He was highly praised for his work by the men in charge of the programme, Sergeant Ralph Fox and Sergeant Major John Cripps. He was able to pass a message to his contact in a most ingenious manner, without speaking a word. Overall, his performance was rated as flawless, though in concentrating so much on playing out his role, he failed on a couple of occasions to spot that he himself was being tailed. Under rigorous interrogation on his identity, past life and present activities in Newcastle, he was 'superbly self-confident … completely imperturbable, his story was convincing, and no loop-hole was left by which his story could be broken down'.[6]

Taken as a whole, the reports on Seth's training present a positive picture of a man who, despite his physical weaknesses, was enthusiastic, quick to learn, and well equipped with the mental acuity needed for the tasks of an undercover agent. His boundless self-confidence was apparent to all. Indeed, it was probably this belief in his own ability to carry out a solo mission in a remote part of Europe that had not hitherto engaged the attentions of the British secret services that carried him through. Seth's ebullient personality also seems to have persuaded his handlers that he would function best on his own. The attempt to secure an Estonian companion occurred rather late in the day and was quickly abandoned, as much on Seth's own insistence as anything, it would seem. Ronald had set himself up as the unrivalled expert on Estonia, fluent in the language and with a wide circle of contacts. As his own reports on his training exercises amply reveal, he saw himself as a natural leader of men. Whether or not he laid out half-a-dozen toughs in the mean streets of Jarrow is, in a sense, not the issue: what matters is that he himself believed that he had performed this feat. Ronald was the hero of his own imaginings, and his imagination was more than capable of spilling over into reality.

He would need all the self-confidence he could muster for his mission. Those hundreds of men and women sent elsewhere in occupied Europe through the auspices of SOE were at least assured of some contacts and the existence of a resistance network when they landed. When Ronald jumped out of the Halifax, he would be entirely on his own. He could not even know if his pre-war friends and acquaintances were still in Estonia, or indeed, still alive. Even with the benefit of an underground network, his mission would have been difficult. On his own, having to camp out at the onset of a northern winter, making his way across difficult terrain to a target which does not appear to have been closely reconnoitred beforehand, his mission was well-nigh impossible, and his chances of survival abysmally low.

The already slim chances of Operation Blunderhead succeeding were drastically reduced by worrying news, right on the eve of Ronald's departure, about his radio set. There was clearly some difficulty in securing the right kind of equipment, as an exasperated undated memo (in all likelihood drafted at the end of July) makes plain. It was 'out of the question' that, after three years of war, an organisation of the size of SOE could not come up with a simple W/T apparatus. The set would have to be operated 'from the wilds of one of the Baltic provinces [sic]', and there was no possibility of using the local electric current either to work the set or to charge the accumulators. This memo elicited a promise from the technical section on 4 August to deliver an 'A' mark II set, two small batteries and a hand generator to Special Training Station 52 in time for Ronald's training as a wireless operator. The hand generator would probably be of the prime mover type, which would render the batteries superfluous. On 16 August, however, Seth wrote to Hazell complaining that the set could only be worked off the mains and had no battery power pack. A generator and batteries were finally delivered on 11 September, with the promise that a W/T set with a signal plan and crystals would follow.[7] Problems with his radio equipment continued, as is made plain in a note from Wiskeman to Hazell, dated 14 October. Both Seth and his instructor were concerned about the failure of the new set of crystals, and Wiskeman urged Hazell to set down all the failings of the W/T set and have the matter taken up officially.

Whether Major Hazell wrote that statement and what subsequently happened to it is not known, though the problematic crystals were to resurface during MI5's subsequent investigation into Seth's activities. There is, however, prima facie evidence here that an agent was being sent on a dangerous mission, with poor chances of survival, and with patently defective radio equipment. This at the very least puts the men responsible for sending Ronald Seth off at the end of October 1942 in a bad light. This may well have persuaded their successors two years later to give Seth the benefit of the doubt when he resurfaced in France.

In addition to the radio and generator, the lone agent about to be parachuted into German-occupied Estonia was equipped with camping gear, food supplies and explosives, packed into three containers.[8] Seth was to wear a camouflaged canvas siren suit. A spade strapped to his left leg was meant to be used to bury his parachute and the three steel containers. About his person he also carried a torch and knife, a packet of fruit gums, ten small bars of milk chocolate and some Benzedrine tablets, plus a cyanide pill for use in extreme circumstances.

In his book, Seth paid tribute to 'Major Larch' (Hazell) for the care with which he supervised the selection and assembly of his personal kit. In retrospect, he wished Hazell had also superintended the rest of his paraphernalia. One can only endorse his sentiment. Maybe SOE controllers imagined Estonia to be one vast empty wilderness, in which Seth might have time enough to collect his belongings scattered across the forest, but in fact, the place chosen for his landing was close to a coastal road that was regularly patrolled by German and Estonian units. Seth clearly thought he would be able to find shelter with a former pupil who lived in a cottage in the small fishing village of Kiiu Abla, but he did not know if the man still lived there, nor had he considered whether or not he would welcome the sudden unexpected arrival of a British agent with a stock of explosives.

The final piece of the operation to fall into place was the laying on of an aircraft capable of flying the distance to Estonia. For much of its existence, SOE had considerable difficulties with the RAF and Air Ministry, who were not unreasonably reluctant to divert bombers from their principal role in the war. Aircraft could be immobilised for a lengthy period, waiting for the right conditions. The laying on a long-range Halifax bomber for the Blunderhead mission could put it out of bombing action for the whole of the October moon period, as Wiskeman freely admitted. The RAF did, however, accede to the request, and after several days of anxious waiting, Seth received the news on Saturday 24 October that he should be ready for take off any time from noon onwards. He also received a telegram from his wife, saying that she had been awarded a commission, which he took as a good omen.

In his published account, Seth claims that he was taken by 'Major Larch' (Hazell) to say goodbye to Gubbins. Gubbins shook his hand, and told him to take care of himself. 'You are my ewe-lamb in the Baltic. Come and tell me all about it when you get back.'[9] If Gubbins did actually utter such words, one can only marvel at either his disingenuousness or his downright cynicism. No provision was made for Seth to be brought out of Estonia. Rather late in the day, he was given an address in Sweden which he could send a coded message concealed in a seemingly innocent 'aunt Jane is well' type of greeting. Otherwise, he was on his own. This was admittedly his own choice, but it was a choice endorsed by SOE. The 'wiser heads' that Hazell saw fit to evoke to frustrate Seth's attempt to persuade the British government to consider a change of policy with regard to Estonia in the post-war settlement clearly did not think it necessary to pull the plug on Blunderhead, in spite of frequently expressed reservations. Ronald Seth was indeed sent as a lamb to a land of wolves.

RAF Tempsford in Bedfordshire was perhaps the most frequently used base for SOE operations, and it was from this airfield beside the Great North Road that Operation Blunderhead got under way. In view of the distance to be flown, however, the Halifax bomber touched down at RAF Linton-on-Ouse, near York, for refuelling and final checks. Agent Blunderhead was also fuelled up with bacon and eggs, chips, toast and jam before final take-off at 1755 hours. This liberal helping of British stodge, grease and sugar was to be the last he would enjoy for almost three years.

The Halifax W7773 had a Polish crew, two of whom perished in a flight over Norway less than a week later. The plane took a course north-eastwards, flying over the tip of the Skagen peninsula in Denmark and the island of Bornholm to Gotska Sandön, a well-known navigational landmark between Sweden and the Baltic States. The flight was uneventful, and the captain was able to show Seth the proposed landing site, as instructed, in order for him to orientate himself and select a suitable spot for the drop. In Seth's own account, he was able to see the entire Kolga peninsula laid out before him. The huge rock about 200m from the shore on which his friend's cottage was situated was clearly visible. As the plane circled once more, he picked out a field about a mile south of the cottage, skirted on the west by the coast road and on the east by the forest. The captain assured him that he could guarantee to put him down, with his three containers and the heavy package containing his wireless transmitter, without dropping them either in the sea or the woods.[10]

During the flight, Seth had experienced fear and trepidation, but the sight of a landscape where he and his family had been happy sent through him 'a thrill like that of home-coming'.[11] He began final preparations with the aid of the despatcher, who fixed his static line and gave him his final instructions. The three containers and the package containing the W/T set went first; then it was Ronald's turn to drop into the void. He fell alone into the darkness, not knowing what might befall him.

Notes

1. Anderson's report 23 February 1942, HS9/1344. On Arisaig, see Bailey 2009.
2. 'Diary of events, 27.III.42 – 31.III.42', HS9/1344.
3. Report of the commanding office at Beaulieu, HS9/1344.
4. Report of activity of F/Lt R Seth aboard SS *Daxhound*, HS9/1344. Hazell, in his pencilled comment to the report, felt that the seagoing experience seemed to have done some good 'but R. is still as self-confident as ever'.
5. Seth's correspondence, and the responses of his bosses, HS9/1344 and HS4/240.
6. Report of scheme at Newcastle, 4–8 September 1942, HS9/1344.
7. HS9/1344 and HS4/240 for the correspondence on the wireless set.
8. Seth 2008, p.13. The report of Seth's interrogation in Germany notes, however, that the radio and generator were packed together with a sleeping bag, tent, knife, pistol and cash (7,400 Swedish kronor, 1,400 US dollars, 100 Reichmarks and 100 roubles), HS4/240.
9. Seth 2008, p.14.
10. Clark 1999, p.104. An order to carry only one container was apparently ignored.
11. Seth 2008, p.2.

4 | 'A little tin god.'

Tallinn, March 1936

As he floated to the ground on that cold autumn night, Ronald Seth was probably conjuring up pleasanter memories of the country to which he was now returning in such an unusual manner. The account of his stay, published in 1939 with the title *Baltic Corner*, was an affectionate portrait of a small and little-known northern European country and its people. Ronald and his wife, with a 6-week-old baby, had set sail for Estonia some three years earlier, knowing less about their destination than they did about Siberia, in Seth's own words. They were enchanted by their first sight of the medieval city of Tallinn, its towers and spires rising out of the waters of the Baltic, and once they had settled in, they made many friends, toured the country extensively and seemed settled for the duration.

As he made clear in his 1939 book, Ronald Seth was in a state of mental anguish and eager to get away from England.[1] He was, in fact, an overly sensitive young man, as the more perceptive of his trainers during the spring and summer of 1942 noted. As we have already seen in the matter of his departure from the BBC in 1941, Ronald seems to have taken offence very easily at slights or upsets, real or imagined. He also seems to have been adept at putting other's noses out of joint, to judge by the rather sour comments of the British chargé d'affaires in Tallinn, with whom Seth had evidently quarrelled.[2]

The Tõrvand-Tellmann English College, where he was officially confirmed as a teacher in the middle and upper school from the 15 April 1936, had been founded four years earlier. After some early difficulties in finding suitable accommodation, the Seth family, soon to be augmented by the birth of a daughter, Joanna, settled into a comfortable apartment in a leafy district near Kadriorg Park. An Englishman who had attended one of his country's most prestigious universities had a distinct rarity value, and there can be little doubt that his services as a private teacher were sought after. Anglophile sentiments were strong in Estonia, a country with recent unpleasant experiences of Russian and German domination. Seth claimed to have taught a number of the leading figures in Estonian public life, and he also maintained that he was official teacher of English to the Estonian government and the Estonian chamber of private enterprises, inspector of schools for English for the Estonian Ministry of Education, and lecturer in English at Tallinn University. He was to claim later that, before leaving Estonia upon the outbreak of war, the university awarded him an emeritus professorship and the degree of doctor of philosophy 'for services rendered'.[3]

How far do these claims correspond with reality? Ronald Seth is included in an Estonian Ministry of Education list of teachers at the English College for the forthcoming academic year 1939–40, and there is official confirmation that he was released from duties at the school from 5 September 1939. The records of the Tallinn Technical Institute show that Ronald Seth was employed from January 1937 until June 1939, initially on a part-time basis, but from September 1938 as a lecturer with a salary of 113 kroons (a little over £6) a month. There is no evidence of him having been awarded the title of emeritus professor. Furthermore, he was by no means the only British teacher of English in Estonia, nor was the Tõrvand-Tellmann English College the only school in town specialising in the teaching of English. There was a much larger state English college (Riiklik Inglise Kolledz), founded in 1936. Former students of this school have fond memories of Charles Hewer and his successor in 1939, Lionel Billows, who went on to enjoy an international reputation as a pioneering exponent of the teaching of English as a foreign language. Although many transferred to this school from the Tõrvand-Tellmann English College, there is no mention of Ronald Seth in any of their memories of schooldays.[4]

Charles Hewer, who seems to have been in Tallinn at more or less the same time as Seth, is remembered by former pupils as having little more than a couple of words of Estonian; perhaps he was more typical of the English gentleman abroad than Ronald Seth, who claimed to be fluent in Estonian. Contrary to popular belief, Estonian is no more a 'difficult' language to learn than Russian or Italian, but it does belong to a different language family – Finno-Ugrian – with grammatical and structural features that are unfamiliar to speakers of an Indo-European language such as English. There is nonetheless no reason why an Englishman free of the insular prejudices against learning a foreign language and with a willingness and ability to learn, living and working in the country where the language is spoken, should have more difficulties than any other foreigner in acquiring a decent active command of Estonian. Whether Seth was able to acquire sufficient fluency to pass himself off as a native, as he seemed to suggest in his initial approach to SOE, is more debatable. It is perhaps worth noting that he himself, in *A Spy has no Friends*, retells a story about his parachuted re-entry into Estonia in 1942, printed in the Estonian-language supplement of a Swedish newspaper in 1948, which described him as a 'tall, fair man who spoke halting Estonian'.[5] He had spent some time during his training 'brushing up' his Estonian, and he may have been one of those rare individuals with the talent for assuming a persuasive native persona, language, gestures and all. But the cover story concocted at his behest, which made him out to be an Estonian seaman who had spent the past two decades sailing the world's oceans, was flimsy, at best, and seems in any event to have been quietly abandoned. Seth was probably better equipped linguistically than many other British agents employed by SOE – there are too many stories of men parachuted into France with little or no French, for example – but in all probability his sublime self-confidence was greater than his command of Estonian.

The Estonians had been amongst those peoples contemptuously referred to by nineteenth-century liberals and radicals as 'historyless', and in all likelihood fated to disappear. Few in number, occupying a small corner of north-eastern Europe not especially favoured with fertile soil or mineral wealth, their story from the middle ages had been one of subjugation and oppression. Land-hungry petty noblemen from the western German lands, their activities sanctified as a crusade, had colonised the territory between the Gulf of Riga and Lake Peipus during the thirteenth century and imposed a harsh rule upon the native peoples. This Baltic German minority remained dominant throughout the period of Swedish rule in the seventeenth century, and under the Russian empire from 1721 until the revolution of 1917. The condition of the Estonian and Latvian peasantry was likened to that of slaves on the sugar plantations of the West Indies by the social critics who launched the first attack on serfdom at the end of the eighteenth century.

Freedom from servitude in the nineteenth century did little to alter the material conditions of the peasantry. Not until the reforms of the 1860s, which amongst other things finally did away with the landlord's right physically to chastise his peasant-tenants, freed local government from the control of the manorial lords and, above all, enabled peasants to buy the land they farmed, did the situation significantly improve.

Between 1870 and 1917 there was a great deal of change in the Baltic provinces. The land reforms and the growth of markets for farm produce saw the emergence of a class of peasant-farmers who were to become the backbone of the growing Estonian and Latvian national movements. The population of the larger towns expanded massively as workers flooded to the new factories. Where German had been the dominant language in 1850, by 1900 it had become a minority language in all the large cities. The emergence of a politically and culturally conscious Estonian class of property owners did not, however, translate into political power. The hopes of the nationalists of the 1860s and 1870s, that Russia would destroy Baltic German power and thus open the way for Estonians and Latvians to fulfil their ambitions, were not realised. The new generation of national-minded Estonians and Latvians turned increasingly to radical, even revolutionary ideas; they did not make common cause with the Baltic Germans in seeking to resist russification.

The experience of revolution in 1905 fatally widened the gulf between the old Baltic German ruling class and those hitherto dismissively lumped together as *Undeutsche*, non-Germans. A second revolution in 1917 finally swept away the Russian autocracy, and ushered into power a radically different political regime, the Bolsheviks led by Vladimir Ilyich Lenin. As the revolution was being played out in the Russian heartland, the western borderlands of the former empire were overrun by the armed forces of Imperial Germany. It took more than two years of bitter and confused fighting against Russian and German forces for the Estonian people finally to gain independence and recognition. Moreover, the two powers that had threatened to stifle the endeavour, although weakened by war and revolution, were still a danger. The coming to power in 1933 of Adolf Hitler, determined to establish German dominance in Eastern Europe, and the permanent atmosphere of suspicion and mistrust that poisoned any relationship between the small new Baltic states and Soviet Russia, posed serious threats. The situation was not helped either by the inability of the three countries to work together in coordinating foreign and defence policies. In Estonia, there was a persistent belief that, in the event of trouble, the British navy would steam over the horizon once more. It was a cruel illusion, for the appearance of a Royal Navy squadron off the shores of northern Estonia in 1919 had been very much a one-off event, which British policy-makers were determined not to repeat.

By the time the Seth family arrived in Tallinn, the Estonian parliamentary system had been effectively suspended for two years. The regime established by Konstantin Päts, one of the leading figures of the struggle for independence, was authoritarian, but in comparison with those of Nazi Germany and Stalinist Russia, rather mild. Its greatest weakness was that although it stifled political dissent, it failed to put anything positive in its place, and it left the Estonian people with a sense of powerlessness as the dark clouds of war massed on the horizon in the summer of 1939.

The recent political events in Estonia hardly featured in *Baltic Corner*, Seth's account of his stay in Estonia. The book has all the signs of hasty compilation, degenerating into a series of random jottings in the final chapter, and compares poorly with J. Hampden Jackson's *Estonia*, published in 1941. For a man who claimed to have taught English to the highest in the land, Seth seems to have been unusually reticent on the politics of Estonia. He was, however, more than happy to advise the British Foreign Office during the tortuous negotiations between the Soviet Union on the one hand and Britain and France on the other in the summer of 1939.

The sticking point in these negotiations was the unwillingness of the French and British negotiators to accede to the Russian demand for some sort of guarantee against aggression directed against the Soviet Union. The Russians openly proclaimed their doubts about the ability of the Baltic States to defend themselves against German aggression, and were suspicious that the authoritarian governments of these countries were preparing to collude with the Germans. Although the British Foreign Secretary, Lord Halifax, was prepared to accept the idea of guarantees, it would have to be with the consent of the states who would be assisted in the event of aggression. Halifax was also unwilling to go along with the Russian demand for these states to be named in any tripartite agreement.

In his letter to the foreign secretary, written on 1 June 1939, Seth maintained that the reason for the deadlock in the tripartite talks was caused by the desire of the Baltic States to remain neutral, and above all, to avoid provoking Germany. If that potential threat could be removed, Seth felt sure the Baltic States would be willing to accept guarantees. His solution, that Estonia and Latvia should conclude secret alliances with Germany, which would guarantee German assistance, should either be attacked by Russia, was dismissed by the Foreign Office as not being very constructive. Seth was, however, more perceptive about the likely outcome in the event of war: 'Russia would certainly occupy Estonian territory and ports, treaty or no treaty, and both countries are bound to be occupied whatever happens.'[6]

This was indeed the outcome. Unable to reach a satisfactory deal with the British and French, Stalin responded with alacrity to German overtures. Whereas the British negotiators had wended their leisurely way to Russia by boat, the Reich Foreign Minister Joachim von Ribbentrop got in an aeroplane, flew to Moscow, and concluded the non-aggression pact with the Soviet Union within a matter of hours. Beneath the bland text of the published agreement lay the secret clauses dividing north-eastern Europe into spheres of interest: Poland and Lithuania for Germany, Finland, Estonia and Latvia for Russia. Lithuania was subsequently transferred to the Soviet sphere of influence in a second secret arrangement between Germany and the USSR in September. The Estonian government officially voiced its confidence in the pact as a positive measure towards strengthening the security of the Baltic region, a false optimism that was echoed in the press. The Estonian public was thus ill prepared for the crisis that was to erupt a month later.

Having secured the friendly neutrality of the Soviet Union, Hitler now felt free to resolve the next question on his agenda of aggrandisement by invading Poland at the beginning of September. Stalin for his part waited three weeks before applying pressure on Russia's small Baltic neighbours. Estonia was first in line. Within a matter of days, the Estonian government had been battered into submission, and had agreed to a mutual assistance treaty which allowed the Soviet Union to station 25,000 troops on Estonian territory for the duration of the war. Similar treaties were concluded in similar fashion with the two other Baltic States over the next few days.

Stalin's assurances that the Soviet Union would respect Estonia's sovereignty and form of government was small consolation. 'Few people have any illusions that the pacts will remain long in operation' reported the British consul-general to Tallinn on 30 September:

> They believe that it is a matter of weeks, perhaps even days, and also a question of circumstances, or more likely pretexts, before the Red Army marches into Tallinn or a communist rising is fostered inside the country. Many wish their leaders had decided to fight, although most now know that conquest would be a matter of only a couple of days. [7]

The political leadership, however, continued to adhere to an optimistic line, one also followed by most of the press. Whilst it would be unrealistic to expect an openly critical attitude from a press constrained by nationalist impulses as well as by the authoritarian regimes of the three Baltic States, the portrayal of the pacts as resting on firm foundations of mutual respect and guaranteeing peace for the Baltic region in a world at war were a sad indication of the debilitating impact of an authoritarian political system on public opinion. Rumours and anxieties were not assuaged by the bland treatment of the news, for example, of the sudden evacuation to the newly conquered German territories in western Poland of most of Baltic German population in the autumn of 1939. Of the 16,000 Baltic Germans living in Estonia in 1934, barely 1,000 remained, and most of these left in further re-settlements in 1940 and 1941. With his 'call to the homeland', Adolf Hitler brought to an end a German presence in the north-eastern Baltic that had lasted over 700 years.

At the end of November 1939, the Red Army attacked Finland, which had refused to comply with Soviet demands. This put the Estonian government and people under even more pressure, especially as the Soviet Union used its air bases on Estonian soil for sorties over Finland. The British representative to Tallinn did detect a growing hostility towards the Russians amongst not only the populace but even in the press, but he also reported that the head of the press department of the Estonian Foreign Ministry had told him 'whatever might be their real feelings, Estonians had to dissemble'. They were powerless in the grip of Russia and Germany, and the slightest slip would mean that they faced annihilation. [8]

The independence of the three Baltic States lasted a mere nine months from the signing of the mutual assistance treaties with Russia. Taking advantage of the victorious German advance in the West in the early summer of 1940, Moscow demanded the formation of governments capable of fulfilling the terms of the mutual assistance treaties. In mid-June, Red Army units rumbled across the frontier, high-ranking Soviet emissaries were despatched to oversee the creation of governments guaranteed to be friendly towards the Soviet Union, and local communists were encouraged to stage demonstrations. A month later, parliamentary elections were held. Virtually all non-communists were disbarred from standing, and ruthless manipulation of the results ensured victory for candidates willing to vote unanimously for acceptance of their country into the great family of Soviet socialist republics. Estonia was the last of the three states to be incorporated on 8 August 1940.

The events of summer 1940 were presented in Soviet propaganda as a popular revolution, which brought the Estonian people into joyful union with their brothers in the socialist paradise. The reality was very different. A British diplomat from the Moscow embassy visited Tallinn in September 1940, and reported that although the town was still the same tidy and attractive place it always was and the people were well-dressed, prices had shot up and there was a scarcity of commodities such as butter, due in part to peasant hoarding.

The feelings of the Estonian people are at present a mixture of apathetic resignation to their fate, forlorn hope for an ultimate delivery by Great Britain or Germany, fear of the OGPU (the Soviet secret police), contempt for their conquerors, and bitter regret that they did not, like the Finns, make a bid for freedom.[9]

Although the new government was composed mainly of left-wing figures from outside the political circles of the Päts era, communists held the key posts of minister of the interior and head of the secret police. Leading members of the old regime were arrested and imprisoned in Russia even before the formal union with Soviet Russia had taken place. Some 10,000 Estonians were taken to Russia in the mass deportations of mid-June 1941, on the eve of the German attack on the Soviet Union. Over 30,000 Estonian men were additionally drafted into the Red Army. For a nation with a population of a little over one million, such losses were a crippling blow – and worse was to follow.

The massive German assault on the Soviet Union launched on 22 June 1941 swept the Red Army out of Lithuania and Latvia within days. Further German advances in the Baltic were suspended for much of the month of

July, as the main armed forces raced through towards Moscow, and Tallinn did not fall until the end of August. The Estonians thus had more time to organise themselves. Men who had fled conscription into the Red Army constituted the core of the 'forest brothers', guerrilla units that harried the retreating Red Army forces. The last prime minister of independent Estonia, Jüri Uluots, offered to form a government and commit Estonian troops to the fight against the Soviet Union. This offer was not taken up by the Germans, who had their own plans for the Baltic. Only a very limited degree of self-government was permitted. Estonian militia units were strictly subordinated to the German security police. These auxiliary units (Omakaitse) assisted in raids, the arrest of suspected enemy agents and the protection of the shale-oil works against sabotage. A document drawn up in June 1942 effectively defined Omakaitse as a collaborating executive organ with no real police powers. It was not allowed to interrogate, and had powers to arrest only when danger threatened, and even then, prisoners were to be handed over to the Germans.

The massive and rapid expansion of the area of eastern Europe under German control in the summer and autumn of 1941 posed huge problems, not least a severe lack of qualified personnel. The Estonian police units were thus an essential, if strictly subordinate, part of the security apparatus headed by the notorious SS *Standartenführer* Martin Sandberger between July 1941 and September 1943. Sandberger, who had played a key role in the liquidation of the Jewish population in the Baltic during the summer and autumn of 1941, placed great importance on cooperation, and the Estonian police seem to have responded, going into minute detail on all sorts of activities in their weekly reports. The Estonian population at large was urged to be vigilant and to keep a special watch for parachutists, spies and saboteurs, with a reward of 5,000 roubles offered for information, and the threat of the death penalty for concealment of information regarding enemy activity. By January 1942, membership of Omakaitse had reached over 42,000: one in every ten adult males was a member. In the words of one of the Omakaitse commanders 'that is why every single partisan, parachutist or other enemy is quickly spotted … and then liquidated'.[10]

How aware Seth was of the situation in Estonia under German occupation is hard to say. In his published account, he says that he was confident that he could rely upon their hatred of the German invaders as an inducement to the Estonians to help him, and that he had been told that the population would be friendly.[11] But the information received from sources in the Baltic by British intelligence and the Foreign Office told a different story. The hatred and loathing was directed more at the Russians than the Germans, who were careful not to antagonise the Estonians unnecessarily. The relationship with the German occupiers did degenerate, certainly; requisitioning and food shortages were major sources of complaint, and observers were beginning by the autumn of 1942 to report a serious deterioration in the public mood. But it has also to be recognised that British prestige had taken a very bad knock in 1939–40. In the crisis days of June 1940, rumours circulated in Tallinn that, as the British representative reported, 'the Soviet action is in some way connected with the appointment of Sir Stafford Cripps as His Majesty's ambassador to Moscow'.[12] Ten days earlier – just as the Red Army was moving into Estonia – the Estonian president Päts, in a desperate last-minute attempt to get the German government to express in Moscow an interest in the three Baltic States, and thereby stay Stalin's hand, told Hans Frohwein, the German minister to Tallinn, that the Wehrmacht's stunning successes in the Low Countries and France had led the British and French ambassadors to Moscow to urge the Russians to press ahead with the speedy incorporation of the Baltic States 'in the hope that this would drive a wedge between Germany and Russia'. Two days later, the beleaguered president alleged that the commander of the Russian troops now pouring into Estonia was in contact with the British legation in Tallinn.[13]

Rumours of British collusion with the Russians proved invaluable to German propagandists during the occupation. In April 1942, one of the largest Estonian newspapers permitted during the occupation reminded its readers that Cripps had begun his special mission to Moscow on 12 June 1940, only a few days before the Soviet Union presented an ultimatum to Estonia, and concluded that there could be little doubt that the two events were closely connected. An Estonian police report from Rakvere in mid-August 1942 also spoke of a strong reaction to the revelations of Cripps' dealings with Moscow, particularly in light of subsequent Soviet terror in the Baltic lands.[14]

Was there any substance behind these rumours? On 18 June 1940, as Soviet plenipotentiaries were travelling to the three Baltic states in the wake of the Red Army, Andrew Rothstein, the go-between for Ivan Maisky, the Soviet ambassador to London, approached the Foreign Office with a suggestion that the new prime minister Winston Churchill should meet Maisky. Russia was aware that a settling of accounts with Hitler was inevitable, Rothstein said, and the current action being taken in the Baltic States would certainly not be popular in Berlin. The British had been twenty-four hours too late in reaching the Albert Canal in Belgium, Maisky told Hugh Dalton (who was to become SOE boss a month later): 'we do not want to be twenty-four hours too late on the East Prussian frontier'.[15] These heavy hints did not go unnoticed. On 24 June, the left-wing socialist Sir Stafford Cripps, who had been sent in February 1940 to Moscow with the aim of trying to detach the Russians from their agreement with Nazi Germany and who had subsequently been appointed ambassador to Moscow at the end of May, was entrusted by the Foreign Secretary Lord Halifax with the task of bearing a personal message from Churchill to Stalin. 'Should the question of the Baltic States be raised' Cripps was instructed 'you may affect to believe that the Soviet government's recent action was dictated by the imminence and magnitude of the German danger now threatening Russia, in which case the Soviet government may well have been justified in taking in self-defence such measures as might in other circumstances have been open to criticism'.[16]

This kind of circumlocution was not likely to cut much ice with Stalin; nor did it impress Cripps, who felt that the British government should not place unnecessary obstacles in the way of improving relations with Russia. Britain nevertheless managed to avoid being obliged to concede de jure recognition of the Soviet incorporation of the Baltic States in the tortuous negotiations leading up to an agreement in 1942 with the Soviet Union, an ally since June the previous year. Behind the official façade, however, there was little sign of support for the three states. Their ministers were increasingly sidelined, their memoranda on the situation in their homeland politely ignored. The Under-Secretary of State at the Foreign Office, R.A. Butler, rather neatly encapsulated the feelings of his department in a summary of a conversation he had with Maisky in September 1940. If the Soviet Union wished to improve relations with Britain, Butler told the Russian ambassador:

They must understand that we had both a certain sentimental and practical interest in those parts of the world which they had now incorporated. We were not adopting an unreasonable or lachrymose attitude about the passing of these states: but a decent posture at the funeral was surely what he could expect from this country.[17]

This polite dismissal of the Baltic States from the world stage remained hidden from public view, of course. No doubt some Estonians still entertained a belief that Britain had not forgotten them, but amidst the rigours of war, twice occupied in as many years, hungry and demoralised, very few were likely to rally around a lone Englishman carrying a small amount of explosive and a dodgy wireless transmitter. Ill equipped and poorly prepared, Ronald Sydney Seth was about to begin a very different kind of adventure to that he had imagined back in England.

Notes

1. Seth, 1939, p.6.
2. The chargé d'affaires W.H.Gallienne expressed surprise when asked in 1939 to convey to Seth the thanks of the Foreign Office for his help and assistance, not least because 'I have only recently been obliged to give him a dressing down and he may be feeling somewhat disgruntled'. FO371/3356. Seth confirmed this in a letter he wrote in November 1945. His advice on the Anglo-Soviet negotiations of 1939 had been ignored, which he ascribed to the fact that he was *persona non grata* at the consulate, having quarrelled with the chargé d'affaires, HS9/1345.
3. Form C.R.1 19 December 1942, HS9/1344.
4. www.nommeraadio.ee/media/pdf/RRS/riiklikinglisekolledz. I am grateful to Pekka Erelt and Malle Kivivali for providing information about Seth's career in Estonia.
5. 'Inglise langevarjur okupeeritud Eestis', *Stockholms-Tidningen Eestlastele*, 1 May 1948. Seth 2008, p.25.
6. Seth to Lord Halifax, 1 June 1939. FO371/3356
7. Gallienne to Foreign Office, 30 September 1939. FO371/23689.
8. Gallienne to Foreign Office, 8 March 1940. FO371/24762.
9. Memorandum by J.W. Russell of the Moscow embassy on conditions in Estonia, September 1940. FO371/24762.
10. Statiev 2010, p.76. Birn 2006 for details of the cooperation between the German and Estonian security forces.
11. Seth 2008, p.22.
12. Gallienne to Lord Halifax, 26 June 1940. FO419/35.

13. Frohwein to the German Foreign Office, 18 June 1940, 20 June 1940. The despatches are in captured German Foreign Office material held in the National Archives GFM33/319.

14. 'Kaks Kerenskit?'. *Eesti Sõna* 7 March 1942. GFM 33/383. Report of the Rakvere district police. ERA. R-64.1.60.

15. Dalton's memorandum of conversation with Maisky, 18 June 1940. FO371/24844.

16. Lord Halifax to Cripps, 24 June 1940. FO371/24844.

17. Lord Halifax to Cripps, 23 September 1940, quoting from Butler's meeting with Maisky on 4 September. FO371/24845.

5 | 'It seemed to me that the bottom had completely fallen out of things.'

Kiiu Aabla, Estonia, October 1942

Halifax W7773 returned safely to base at 0700 hours, 25 October 1942, after carrying out its night-time mission over northern Estonia. The operation report filed later that day recorded a satisfactory outcome. Seth had jumped without hesitation and well from a height of 800ft, at a location slightly to the south of that originally selected. All parachutes were seen to open by the rear gunner, and the agent was seen to flash his torch upon landing, as previously agreed with the captain.

On the ground, however, things were not going so well. As he drifted to earth, Seth could hear shouting and a dog barking. Looking down, he could see that he was heading straight for some telephone wires, and that a reception party of four or five armed men and a very excited dog were waiting for him. The dog was to be his salvation. As he was about to press the release button to free himself from his harness, which had become entangled in a tree, the sergeant in charge kicked the dog. The dog retaliated by biting his calf and refusing to let go. As the scene rapidly descended into a Keystone Cops farce, with men trying to get the dog off and managing to hit each other instead, the moon disappeared behind a bank of cloud and it began to rain. Amidst the confusion, Seth released himself and began running across a field towards the forest. Here he found a suitable tree and managed to climb some 20–30ft until he found a comfortable fork in which to spend the night.

This is how Seth begins his story in the handwritten account which found its way into the hands of Air Commodore Jones in Paris at the end of August 1944. The veracity of the handwritten account was subsequently challenged by Captain E. Milton of MI5, and we will come to his meticulous analysis of Seth's reports in due course.[1]

First, however, let Seth tell his own story. Having tried but failed to keep awake with the help of a couple of Benzedrine tablets, he awoke at dawn the following day, Sunday 25 October. He heard no sound of his pursuers, and after warming himself with a generous slug of whisky, he climbed down the tree and set off in pursuit of the three containers. On reaching the road, he heard motor-cycles and a lorry, hid in a ditch and watched the containers and the package containing the wireless equipment, which had fallen either on the road or on the side of it, being loaded into the lorry. 'It seemed to me that the bottom had completely fallen out of things', he wrote in 1944, 'and I retreated into the forest to reflect. I did not know the temper of the natives, I was completely without supplies both of explosives and food, and deprived of the means of communicating with my Base.'[2]

In his forest hideout, Seth breakfasted on a couple of clear gums, a square of milk chocolate and a mouthful of whisky. In his published story, he says that his plan now rested upon finding his friend 'Juhan', who had a cottage in the vicinity, and learning from him how conditions were in the country. If these appeared too formidable, he would then attempt to buy or steal a small boat and try to reach Sweden, from whence he would return to England and try again. The cottage in question was located in the hamlet of Kiiu Aabla on the coastal road looking westward into Kolga Bay. The coastal road, never more than a couple of hundred metres from the shoreline, ran northwards to the village of Leesi, joining there the eastern coastal road. The peninsula is some 13km from north to south and 6–8km wide. It is sparsely populated, even today, when it is part of the Lahemaa national park. Beyond the coastal fringe of small fields, with farmhouses and cottages dotted along the road, lies the forest, mostly spruce and pine. The ground is boggy and littered with glacial erratics, boulders dumped at the end of the Ice Age. It was here that Seth spent his first full day on Estonian soil, once more up his tree, hiding from a search party. In 1944, he estimated that some

200 German soldiers, aided by three Fieseler-Storch reconnaissance aircraft, were looking for him; by 1952, the numbers had diminished to a party of soldiers on board three lorries, and one aeroplane.

The search lasted until five in the afternoon, by which time daylight was fading. After the weary soldiers had left, Seth descended from his tree, and set off in search of food. In the 1944 version, he approached one house, whose inhabitants – three women – refused to open the door and give him food. When they imagined he had gone away, two of the women ran to a group of cottages further up the road, and a party of armed Estonian men immediately came out and started firing at the retreating figure. The published version involves rather more people, and Seth is shaken by the hostile attitude of the peasants, which he had not expected – but the end result is the same. Refused food and sustenance, Ronald had to retreat once more to the safety of a tree.

Having tried to fight his hunger pains with whisky (published version; the 1944 account has him taking an opium tablet), Seth strapped himself to the branches and slept until dawn. The first thing he saw when he awoke on Monday 26 October was two men, digging a shallow hole into which they placed a sack. The two men filled the hole, placed a large stone over it, and left. Using his spade, Seth uncovered the sack and found to his amazement that it contained eighteen of the twenty specially prepared explosive charges which had been included at the last moment in one of his containers.

At this point in the story, the narratives diverge. In the published version, Seth shouldered the sack and made his way through the forest to Kiiu Aabla, reaching the cottage in an hour. Here he met the sister of his friend, who told him that 'Juhan' had gone to town and would not be back for some days. Without bothering to ask the sister for some food, Seth remembered that the latch of the kitchen window of the cottage was broken, and he was able to pull the window open and climb in. Nonetheless, a thorough search revealed not a crumb. Further foraging in the days that followed proved equally unsuccessful. Seth took a decision to subsist on a daily ration of two gums, one meat lozenge, one opium pill and three mouthfuls of whisky until his friend returned from the town.

In the 1944 account, however, he did not find the cottage until the early hours of Tuesday 27 October. He spent the rest of the night in a hay-barn, and broke into his friend's house at dusk. He found no food, but slept in his friend's bed that night. The friend is named here as Martin Saarne. The following morning, having judged it prudent to slip out of the house, he met Saarne's sister coming towards the building. As in the published version, she did not recognise him, and she told him that her brother was away and would be back in about a week. The survival plan Seth subsequently devised is more or less the same in both narratives.

What did Seth do with the sack, and what was he doing during the time between its discovery and his night-time trek to Saarne's cottage? Here, the unpublished account differs radically from that which Seth wrote for publication. In 1944, he was clearly eager to show his SOE masters that he had been active in the field. Thus, after unearthing the buried sack, he heard aircraft engines warming up somewhere to the east. He made his way towards the noise, and came across a clearing in the forest with two wooden barrack huts, a possible fuel dump, and three Fieseler-Storch aircraft. A runway had been improvised, running roughly north-east/south-west. Having noted all these details, Seth then turned westwards and managed to reach the coast by 1300 hours. Here, he noted the return of the three aircraft he had seen take off earlier that day, and decided to make an attempt that night to blow them up, using his altimeter switches. Reaching the airfield at around midnight, he managed to place two explosive devices with their altimeter switches in the rear inspection posts of the aircraft. He then returned to the coast to watch what would happen. Shortly after 0800 hours the following day, two of the aircraft took off, and blew up after they had attained a certain height. The third aircraft blew up on the ground, as Seth himself testified when he returned to the airfield.

Having satisfied himself as to the success of his mission, he decided to leave the neighbourhood as quickly as possible. Moving westward, he came upon a kilometre post that told him he was 54km from Tallinn in one direction and 8km from Kiiu Aabla in the other. Avoiding patrols and peasants, and snatching a few hours of afternoon sleep, Seth worked his way northward to Kiiu Aabla. Here, he found no food in his friend's cottage, as already described. The unpublished account now tells of a second daring exploit undertaken by this man, who by his own admission had gone four days without food, subsisting largely on gulps of whisky and opium tablets. He had heard artillery fire the previous day, so he set out to locate the guns, which he found around the middle of the afternoon of the 28th, on the northern tip of the peninsula. He kept the site under observation the rest of the day and night. The following evening, with an explosive package concocted from his remaining fuses, and a spool of wire from Saarne's cottage, he blew up the gun emplacement and for good measure shot the cook who emerged from his hut, dazed by the explosion.

'I removed myself with all possible speed from the locality. My hunger and the slight concussion [from the explosion] made me very sleepy, and I slept intermittently for the rest of the day and throughout the night. The following day (October 30) was my sixth without food, and my whiskey was now almost finished.' Nonetheless, Seth was still not finished with his heroic adventures. By nightfall, he had managed to find the road that ran along the eastern coast of the peninsula and at 2230 hours he came upon four unattended motor-oil transports lined up on the verge. Dipping in petrol strips of oily rag, which he found under the seat of one of the vehicles, he managed to blow all four up. Once again, a handy tree enabled him to watch and observe the satisfactory outcome of his efforts.

Bereft of whisky, which had run out the previous day, and having now gone more than a week without proper food, Seth was, in his own words, 'beginning to feel weak'. He worked his way slowly south and west from the tip of the Kolga peninsula, returning to his friend's cottage in Kiiu Aabla. So far, the weather had been unseasonably mild. On Tuesday, 3 November, the temperature dropped below zero. To make matters worse, Seth fell into a water-filled pit dug for peat. Soaked to the skin and exhausted with the effort of getting out of the pit, suffering from stomach cramps after drinking ditch-water, he crawled into a hut on the shore, burying himself in the hay while his clothes dried out. The night was excessively cold, and his sea stockings and trousers were stiff as boards in the morning. Seth managed to don his frozen clothing, but on leaving the hut he saw an old fisherman coming towards him. Retreating to the cover of the hay, he was compelled to spend most of the day hiding in the hay whilst the old man and his wife prepared sauerkraut.

That night, he finally reached Martin Saarne's cottage. Saarne had still not returned, so he spent the night hidden in the bath-house. At 0700 hours the following morning, Thursday 5 November, he saw Saarne coming out of the cottage. Saarne, who had returned the previous night, gave Seth bread and hot water, 'the first food I had eaten for twelve days'. The printed version has Seth sleeping in a hay-barn, and finding Saarne sitting in his kitchen the following morning.

Saarne had little comfort to offer. He told Seth at once that his mission was hopeless. The older people who were not collaborating with the Germans were lethargic, the younger generation was wholeheartedly on the

German side after the 'disgusting Russian excesses committed during the Red occupation'. At this point in the 1944 narrative, Saarne's sister came in (in the published version, Saarne himself suggests they go to his sister's nearby house, which was some way off the road). Seth and Saarne managed to concoct a cover story out of the sister's hearing, according to which Seth had either been attached to an RAF wing on the Russian front or on a British mission to Russia (1952 version), had been shot down and taken prisoner. He had managed to escape from the prison camp in Riga, and with the help of friends who provided him with clothes and money, had walked to Estonia, where he hoped to find a boat to escape to neutral Sweden.

As the question of procuring a boat was being discussed at the sister's house, her daughter sneaked out to alert the soldiers. The daughter, speaking for some reason in German, had earlier pleaded with Seth to give himself up. Seth had just enough time to escape into the forest:

> Everything had now changed. Hiding myself, I thought things over. Now that my presence was known a cordon would be thrown around the place through which it would be impossible for me to escape in my present physical condition. I could walk only with difficulty, as my feet were beginning to be very painful. Searching, I discovered that I had lost my L-tablet [a cyanide suicide pill, given to all SOE agents]. Attempting to shoot myself, the revolver jammed and I could do nothing about it. After further thought I decided that I would surrender myself to the German authorities. Before I died I might do something to mislead them. My thoughts were not very lucid, and I had no idea of what I might do.[3]

He buried his maps and false identification papers under one stone, Colt pistol, hunting knife, watch and compass, wrapped in a shirt bearing Buenos Aires name-tabs under another. Having shed the incriminating evidence of a sabotage mission and the last traces of Felix Kopti, the homesick sailor from South America, Seth now returned to the sister's cottage. The only person he found there was the elderly husband, lying ill in bed. Scribbling his wife's name and address on a scrap of paper, Seth asked the old man if he would write after the war and let his wife know what had happened to him. He also gave the old man all his money, 4,000 dollars and 7,000 Swedish kronor. This was the equivalent of almost £1,500, a sum which would have purchased a decent three-bedroom house in the Home Counties before the war.

Seth then left the house and walked into the village of Kiiu Aabla, where he was soon surrounded by a group of Estonians waving sticks. One of them, an adolescent boy, threatened him with a rifle. Although Seth does not say so, these men were probably members of the Omakaitse auxiliary police units, and they clearly thought they had captured a Russian saboteur. Seth was only rescued from their wrath by his friend Martin Saarne. Shortly afterwards, two German soldiers came along and he gave himself up to them.[4]

He was taken to a field post not far from Kiiu Aabla, where he feigned ignorance of Estonian and German when questioned in these languages. As luck would have it, one of his captors was the sergeant who had been bitten by the dog on the night of 24 October. Sending everyone else out of the room, and speaking to Seth in broken English, the sergeant promised him food if he agreed not to reveal how he had managed to escape that night. The sergeant was as good as his word, and Seth was able to devour a steaming bowl of meat soup with black bread.

Later that day, he was taken to the local army headquarters a few kilometres along the main road to Tallinn. Here he was questioned further, and taken back by car to the spot where he had landed, and then to Saarne's cottage. In 1944, Seth said that Saarne had then been arrested, and had been shot for helping him, though this had also been denied. In the 1952 version, Seth and his escort moved on to the sister's house, where the old man, very frightened, handed over the money and the scrap of paper with the name and address of Seth's wife. This would of course have enabled the Germans to investigate Seth's true identity. He was well aware that his cover story of having escaped from a prison camp in Riga would not stand up to serious scrutiny, though he hoped it might be enough to save Saarne from the suspicion of having concealed a saboteur.

❖ ❖ ❖

We will follow Seth in the next chapter down the road to Tallinn and incarceration there in the noisome central prison. At this point, let us hand over to Captain E. Milton of MI5 who examined the veracity of Seth's account in 1945.

Had Captain Milton been reliant solely upon Seth's own account, his conclusion that the escape story was 'almost impossible to believe', something invented by Seth 'through vanity and lively imagination', would have been difficult to refute.[5] Fortunately, there is other independent evidence to hand that can be set against Seth's version of events. As we have seen, SOE in London had learnt of his capture in 1943, thanks to the lucky circumstance of a British agent in Switzerland being able secretly to photograph documents from a crashed German plane. This record of Seth's interrogation in February 1943 at Dulag Luft Oberursel confirmed that he had remained at liberty from 24 October to 5 November, and Milton accepted this as true.

The story of the strange Englishman told in the Estonian section of Stockholms-Tidningen in 1948, also seems to confirm that Seth was at large for the best part of two weeks. It does, however, differ from Seth's own account in several particulars. In this version, a farmer and his household were awakened suddenly in the middle of the night by an enormous thump that shook the entire building. Running outside, they discovered a parachute and container full of food and weapons. The authorities were informed, and a few days later, someone was spotted lurking in the nearby woods. A hunt was mounted, but the man evaded capture. Some two weeks later, a tall blonde man knocked on the same farmer's door, and, speaking broken Estonian in a foreign accent, asked for food and shelter. The farmer suspected that he was the wanted parachutist forced out of hiding by the cold and hunger, and alerted the authorities. A detachment of the Omakaitse duly turned up and arrested the hungry and exhausted stranger, who turned out to be not from beyond the river Narva (i.e. a Russian), but a much rarer person who had fallen from the heavens: 'none other than an Englishman, Ronald Seth, who had taught English at a local gymnasium in Tallinn until the outbreak of war.'[6]

There is also a brief note on alleged British parachutists in Estonia in the Seth file HS9/1344, which in all likelihood was based on information channelled via the network of agents run by the former Estonian spy chief, Colonel Saarsen. One of these sources claimed to have heard in February 1943 that the man arrested the previous autumn near Loksa was someone who used to give English lessons in Tallinn, and had spent his summers on the farm where he was arrested. Another also located the farm near Loksa, and claimed that his sudden appearance there in autumn 1942 did not attract any special notice, because he had been such a familiar figure there before the war. This source, a coastguard, thought the young man had turned up in the district at about the same time as a parachutist had come down near the island of Hara, on the east coast of the Kolga peninsula, and had made no attempt to conceal himself. The Germans, however, had connected his reappearance with the parachute drop and had arrested the man. It was not clear if the man was British or Estonian, but he had had connections with the British vice-consul in Tallinn.

As we will see later, there is further archival evidence to confirm that Ronald Seth was indeed at large for the best part of two weeks in northern Estonia. How did he survive? After months of rigorous training, Seth was undoubtedly in good condition, though none of his trainers ever rated him highly in the fitness scale. Faced with danger, men can achieve extraordinary feats as the adrenaline kicks in. Even so, it is hard to imagine how a man with a spade strapped to his leg and stiff from hours of sitting in a cramped aircraft could have managed to run away from five armed (though highly incompetent) men across broken ground, in the dark, and to climb 30ft into a tree. Credulity is stretched still further if Seth had also sprained his ankle in the landing, as he later apparently told Wolfgang Krause-Brandstetter, a German intelligence officer stationed in Paris.

In northern Estonia, coniferous trees predominate, and although Seth never says what species of tree he climbed, it would in all likelihood have been either a pine or a spruce, neither of which is easy to climb, and neither of which affords much cover. An oak or beech tree would have been easier to climb, but at the end of October, would have been leafless. A man lodged in a fork 30ft above the ground would thus have been very exposed to view. If Seth really did hide in a tree for most of the weekend of 24–25 October whilst the manhunt was going on through the forest, one can only attribute his survival to the gross incompetence of the search party.

As Captain Milton pointed out, Seth could hardly have kept going for so long without food. A diet of whisky and opium might have dulled hunger pains and enabled him to sleep through the cold nights, but would also have sapped his capacity for rational thought. Without a copious intake of water to flush the system, the ingestion of these intoxicants would also have been damaging to the internal organs. The only time Seth speaks of drinking water is when it makes him ill, towards the end of his twelve days of freedom. He does not seem to have been equipped with a container in which to gather water from pools and watercourses, or with purification tablets.

The forests of northern Estonia at that time of year have little in the way of food such as nuts or berries to offer. Seth's hunting knife was of little use without the means or knowledge how to trap small mammals, and as he ruefully confessed, even if could successfully stalk a deer, he had only a Colt .32 and thirty rounds of ammunition. Seth also claimed that his attempts to forage for food in isolated farmsteads were fruitless. Most of the chickens had been eaten, and cows seem also to have disappeared. What there was to eat was carefully guarded by the peasantry. Shaken by the hostile reaction to his attempt to procure food from a peasant household on the Sunday evening (25 October) he concluded that he dare not ask for food again. He appears not to have asked Martin Saarne's sister for food, even though he spoke to her, nor does he seem to have wished to reveal his identity to her, even though he claimed that she had known him before the war.

If we are to believe the 1944 version, the lack of food seems not to have affected his strength and ability to carry out not one but three successful sabotage missions, as well as tramping the length and breadth of the Kolga peninsula. Seth would have spent some time trekking around the rugged terrain around Arisaig, but this would hardly have prepared him for the boulders and bogs of the trackless forests of northern Estonia. Walking in these woods all day would tire a fit and well-fed man with knowledge of the terrain. Seth claimed, for example, that on 28 October – his fourth day without food – he walked from Kiiu Aabla to the tip of the peninsula, reconnoitred the gun emplacement, and kept it under observation for the remainder of the day and night. He returned to the cottage on the following afternoon to find some wire with which to make a fuse, and walked back in the evening to carry out his mission. Kiiu Aabla is a good 6km from the tip of the peninsula by road, which means a round journey of 12km in one day on top of six the previous day plus a night of (presumably) watchful vigilance. Seth intimated that the ensuing explosion of 16lb of plastic killed most if not all of the two gun crews, because he fired the charge when both crews were changing shifts in the gun emplacement, and he also claimed that he shot the dazed cook.

On the sabotage missions Captain Milton has a great deal to say, mostly dismissive. In the book published in 1952, Seth is uncharacteristically silent on these activities. Instead, his friend 'Juhan' tells him that he had come at a bad time, because some Russian parachutists dropped in the forests nearby a fortnight earlier were still at large, and were being sought by a sizeable force of soldiers and Omakaitse men. These Russian saboteurs had blown up a gun on the headland, and had burnt some oil transports on the eastern edge of the peninsula. Three aeroplanes kept in the forest to look for submarines had also been blown up mysteriously in the air. 'I smiled', is Seth's Delphic comment: 'I could have told him the truth about these incidents, though I had no proof.'[7]

Captain Milton made the very perceptive point that in subsequent interrogations, no attempt seems to have been made to connect Seth with these acts of sabotage. He argued that, since none of the Russian parachutists had been captured at the time of his interrogation, there was no means of identifying them for certain with the acts of sabotage. The Germans knew Seth was at liberty in the area when the alleged acts took place, and yet they showed no interest in questioning him about them. Milton concluded that the Germans' lack of curiosity was a strong indication that there were in fact no acts of sabotage on the Kolga peninsula at this time.

There is, however, another possible explanation, which is that Seth managed at a very early stage to persuade the Germans that he was a most unlikely saboteur. As the intercepted report on Seth's interrogation in February 1943 at Dulag Luft Oberursel noted, 'the prisoner wished to have nothing further to do with his containers from the moment they were dropped as he had no intention whatsoever of carrying through his mission', and that only fear of cruel treatment instilled in him during his training prevented him surrendering to the 'nearest German authorities'.[8] He therefore decided to stay hidden in the woods, subsisting on the food he had brought with him. As we shall see, this was pretty much the story he told his interrogators in Estonia.

It is possible that Seth did learn of certain acts of sabotage carried out by the Russians, either from his friend Martin Saarne or during his spell in the central prison in Tallinn, and he subsequently refashioned them in 1944 in order to show that he had in fact diligently sought to carry out his mission. He may well have collapsed separate and discrete incidents into one exciting narrative, in which he alone is the hero: we have already seen that he was more than capable of such fantasising in his vivid description of the brawl with the gang of youths on Tyneside. But the more likely reason why the Germans did not press him about the sabotage was not because no such acts occurred, as Captain Milton maintained, but because Seth had already convinced them that his mission had been a failure from start to finish.

Milton's hypothetical explanation of what happened during the twelve days was that Seth hid with Saarne until his money gave out, possibly as a result of fruitless bribes to local fishermen in order to obtain a boat, and subsequently was either denounced or surrendered to the Germans. The story Seth told his captors in Tallinn between 7 and 17 November 1942 and recounted in his handwritten report of 1944 was that, on landing, he made a half-hearted search for his containers in order to find some food. Unable to locate them, he gave up the search after ten minutes, withdrew into the forest where he spent the time drugged with opium and morphine. On 5 November, desperate for food, he left the cover of the woods and wandered along the shore. Suddenly recognising a huge rock out in the bay, he realised that he must be near the house where he had spent the summer of 1939 with his family. He went to the house, found Martin Saarne there, and told him the cover story of having escaped from a prison camp in Riga and his wish to obtain a boat to carry him to Sweden. Saarne told him this was impossible, and he then surrendered to the Germans at 1200 hours. There is no mention of escape from the party of soldiers waiting to capture the man parachuting from the heavens, though that may have been because Seth had agreed with the German sergeant shortly after his surrender at Kiiu Aabla not to reveal his incompetence on that night. The sergeant on the other hand may simply have been a figment of Seth's imagination, as Milton believed.

Did the bottom fall out of Operation Blunderhead as a consequence of the loss of the containers and the wireless transmitter set, combined with the shock of discovering that the natives were not friendly, as Seth seems to suggest in his report, or had he already become, as Milton believed, dismayed by the task he had taken on? Milton's conclusion is that this highly strung man became alarmed at what he took to be SOE's inadequate preparations for his mission, and 'although his vanity stopped him from backing out he went into the field pessimistic'.[9] There is certainly evidence of concern about the inadequacy of preparations, most especially the memo about the failure of the radio set and of the new type of crystal that had been installed in the set, written by the head of the Scandinavian section ten days before Seth took off on his mission. But the general impression of Seth throughout his training was positive. He was enthusiastic, determined and full of self-confidence. The project was very much his own; he had volunteered it, and had played a major part in shaping it. Both the dispatcher and pilot of the Halifax reported that he had seemed happy with the situation, had jumped without hesitation and well. According to the war diary of the Scandinavian section, recording activities during October 1942, 'Ronald was in the best of spirits before and during the trip and made a perfect jump at a point he had agreed with the captain of the aircraft', a little to the south of the point originally decided upon, which was seen to be marshy.[10]

We will never know what did actually happen that night in late October. Was there a reception party waiting for him, complete with excited dog, and was it the flashing of their torches that the rear gunner of the Halifax saw, and not a pre-arranged signal? (Seth claimed in 1952 that he could not flash his torch because of all the excitement going on around him.) Or did being utterly alone in a dark, chilly and unfamiliar landscape, unable to find any of the containers that might at least have offered sustenance and shelter, without immediate contacts and with no certainty that any contacts he might make were still in Estonia or still alive, did all this cause all his enthusiasm and determination to evaporate? Or is there yet another possible explanation, hinted at by Milton, that Seth had imbibed anti-Russian sentiments during his stay in pre-war Estonia, that these feelings had been further inflamed by what had happened during the Soviet occupation when many of his friends had either been killed or had disappeared, and that this hatred of Soviet Russia easily persuaded him to offer his services to the Germans?

Notes

1. Milton wrote three long reports in April–May 1945. The second covers the period up to May 1944; the first, rather confusingly, covers the period thereafter. Both are to be found in KV2/378 and HS9/1345 . The third report is in HS9/1345. Hereafter 'MI5 report 1/2/3'. Seth's handwritten report of 1944 is preserved in almost illegible Photostat copy in KV2/379: the typed version, 'Report of Operation BLUNDERHEAD', is in HS9/1344. Hereafter 'Report 44'. The handwritten report he wrote in London for MI5, which in its essentials differs little from the 1944 report, is in KV2/378.
2. Report 44, p.2.
3. Report 44, pp.2–9. See also Seth 2008, pp.41–3.
4. In his 1945 report for MI5, however, he surrendered to an Estonian coastguard, who escorted him 2km to the nearest German field post; Saarne followed him to the post and tried to convince the Germans of Seth's cover story.
5. MI5 report 3, p.3.

6 | 'Then I fell forward.'

Tallinn Central Prison, November 1942

The capture of a British agent must have come as a complete surprise for the security forces stationed in the northern Estonian county of Harju. Their main task was to look out for fifth columnists and saboteurs and to keep an eye on elements deemed 'untrustworthy'; in other words, for Soviet agents or those suspected of being sympathetic to the Soviet Union. The Estonians had generally welcomed the Germans as liberators, and many thousands joined the Omakaitse defence force during the early months of the occupation, enthusiastically hunting down Red Army soldiers left behind in the retreat and rounding up suspected communists. The occupying forces relied heavily on Estonian co-operation. Estonians outnumbered Germans by over eight to one in the security police. Martin Sandberger, who directed the security forces in Estonia from December 1941 until September 1943, placed particular stress upon the importance of good working relationships between his German officers and their Estonian counterparts. The relationship came under strain, however, as it became apparent that the Germans had no intention of restoring Estonian independence or of reversing the nationalisation measures of the Soviet regime. Food shortages in the winter of 1941–42 further contributed to discontent. But the Estonians were far from organising any sort of resistance to the German occupation. The brief encounter with Soviet rule had only strengthened anti-Russian sentiment. Any Russian unlucky enough to fall into the hands of the Estonian security police rather than the Germans was far more likely to be treated harshly.

Soviet partisan activity in Estonia before 1944 was rather patchy. Those who managed to evade the security forces seem to have preferred to lie low to engaging in acts of sabotage, but most of those parachuted into the country were soon rounded up.

In his own accounts, Seth claims that after a preliminary interrogation at the scene of his arrest, he was driven to Tallinn and lodged in Cell 13 at the Central Prison. According to the Desk Instruction book of Tallinn Central Prison, Roland (sic) Seth was on the orders of the Secret Field Police (Geheime Feldpolizei) held on 5 November. His feet were in very poor condition, and his general health was not good. The date of his admittance to the prison, however, is recorded as 13 November, in other words, eight days after his initial arrest.[1] It is therefore possible that Seth was held elsewhere and questioned by the Geheime Feldpolizei before being delivered to the Central Prison.

Built in the nineteenth century as a barracks, and used as a prison since 1920, this massive fortress-like building by the seashore is now a museum. Today, tourists wander around the dark and dank corridors of a building with a reputation of having being one of the most horrendous jails in Europe. There is an overpowering odour of rotten brickwork and plaster, but nothing to match the stench of an overcrowded, filthy, verminous jail which caused Seth to retch until he thought he had ruptured himself. Conducted down a maze of corridors, Seth tells us that he found himself in a tiny cell with another occupant. Speaking first in Russian, then Estonian and finally, excellent English, the young man revealed himself as a Russian agent called Anton Prokhorov, who had been dropped in southern Estonia six weeks earlier. He had subsequently been captured and sentenced to death, and he was to be executed the following morning.[2]

The two men spent the night talking. Knowing that he was to be executed within a few hours, and believing the same fate awaited Seth, the young Russian confided that Soviet agents were being infiltrated into northern Norway as a preparatory step towards the creation of a Soviet Norwegian state after the war. Seth judged this so important that he noted two years later that 'it has been this simple piece of information which has prompted my every action from the 5 November 1942 to the moment of writing, 4 August 1944'.[3] The sceptical Captain Milton of MI5 dismissed this as an invention by Seth to serve 'as an excuse for any of his subsequent acts with which we might reproach him, and also to justify to his own enormous vanity why he humiliated himself by offering to work for the Germans.'[4] There is no record of a Soviet parachutist called Prokhorov in the list of captured agents and saboteurs published in the 2006 Reports of the Estonian International Commission for the Investigation of Crimes against Humanity, nor is anyone of that name recorded in the Desk Instruction Book of the Central Prison, which adds support to Milton's contention that Seth was making up the whole story. On the other hand, Seth did try in 1944 to send coded messages to London about the threat of Soviet infiltration into Norway, so to that extent he did remain true to his decision to keep his superiors informed about what had been said. What does not seem to have occurred to Seth in writing his 1944 report, or during his interrogation by MI5 in 1945, is that he had been sent to Estonia specifically to carry out sabotage operations calculated to injure Germany, against whom Britain and Russia were jointly fighting. He had not at any time been sent to gather intelligence – this was made perfectly clear by SOE – and certainly not intelligence about the possible political intentions of the Soviet Union in northern Europe. Seth may genuinely have believed himself to be the bearer of vital information, but his political naivety which had already caused raised eyebrows in London simply confirmed him in the eyes of the British secret service as incorrigibly anti-Russian. Being anti-Russian was not necessarily a besetting sin, and in certain circles of the secret service it was an article of faith, but large sums of money had not been expended on Operation Blunderhead in order for the agent to indulge his dislike of the Soviet Union.

Far more seriously, Seth seemed to opt at a very early stage for collaboration with the Germans. On 6 November, having spent one night in captivity, and suffering from frostbite in his feet, he claims that he was taken through the streets of Tallinn for interrogation by two officers of the radio section of the Geheime Feldpolizei. To his astonishment, he discovered that the radio section now occupied the very flat on Veizenberg street where he and his family had lived before the war.

The two principal officers who conducted the interrogation were identified by Seth as an elderly officer, Major Vogl, and *Feldwebel* Nädlinger. Vogl, who had spent time in England in the thirties, seems to have acted as interpreter, whilst Nädlinger was in charge of the interrogation. The questioning, though intense, was courteous and he was not ill-treated in any way. Indeed, he specifically singled out Vogl and Nädlinger as genuinely kind men in his published story.

Some time during this interrogation, Seth was asked if he would be willing to work for Germany by sending messages to England, because in this way his life might be spared:

> Thinking I might so gain an opportunity of sending the Russian information, I said yes. During the questioning, which took place in my former drawing-room, my physical weakness – I was still very hungry – the agony I was in with my feet and former associations caused me to break down, and I wept. This had the effect of gaining for me the real friendship of Vogl and Nädlinger, who conducted my future examination.[5]

So wrote Seth in August 1944. Nine months later, questioned by Captain Milton, he located the matter of collaborating with the Germans at the end of a further eight days of questioning, which might in fact explain the time lag between his arrest on 5 November and his admission to prison on the 13th. Whichever version is correct, the fact remains that Seth had not been subjected to ill treatment before he agreed to work with the Germans. Indeed, in 1945, he told his interrogators in London that he had written from prison to Nädlinger suggesting that he was particularly well qualified to do radio propaganda work for the Germans. His justification for this was that it would enable him to send the 'Russian information' by coded message to London.

Over the next eight days, the interrogation continued at a different address, flat 8, Aia street 5B, with Major Vogl and *Feldwebel* Nädlinger in charge of the questioning. Although nearer the prison than Veizenberg street, the walk still took Seth half an hour of painful hobbling. The interrogation lasted from around nine in the morning to five in the evening, with a lunchtime break, when soup was served. According to Seth, the seventh-floor flat served both as an office and as living quarters for Nädlinger. On the first day of his interrogation, Nädlinger was alone in the flat, and after he had asked a few preliminary questions, he received a telephone call, summoning him to another office to sign some papers. Seth's 1944 account continues the story thus: 'Would I give my word of honour as a soldier not to try to escape if he left me locked in the flat?

He would be gone about 20 minutes. I agreed. While he was gone I examined the papers on his desk.'[6] Interviewed in Bern, after crossing the Swiss frontier in April 1945, Seth also claimed that the papers were on the desk. Under questioning in London in May, however, his story becomes somewhat more elaborate. In this version, Nädlinger locks Seth into his bedroom which communicates with the room in which the interrogation is taking place by a set of glass double doors. Seth discovers that the bolt holding one of the doors is insecure, and by rattling it for a while, is able to open it and re-enter the interrogation room. The papers are not lying on a desk, but after searching around, Seth finds a locked cupboard, and with the aid of a paper clip, manages to force the flimsy lock. On the top shelf of this cupboard is an eight-page questionnaire used for the interrogation of enemy agents. Having examined this questionnaire ('hurriedly', according to the 1945 interrogation), Seth replaces the papers in the cupboard, hoping that Nädlinger would not notice that it had been unlocked, and returns to the bedroom, closing the double doors behind him.[7]

In none of the archived accounts is there a clear indication of what happened next. Nädlinger returned, and the interrogation carried on. In his published account, however, Seth has Nädlinger returning with Major Vogl, and appearing not to notice that the cupboard has been unlocked. He also tidies up the awkward matter seized upon by the eagle-eyed Captain Milton of Nädlinger having no English, and Seth pretending that he had no German; in the moments before the telephone rings to call the *Feldwebel* away, the two talk in French.

Milton made a great deal of the inconsistencies in Seth's story. He maintained that Seth invented the whole episode to gratify his vanity and so that the British authorities would not wonder how much information he gave away to the Germans. He did not, however, contest the accuracy of the details of the questionnaire nor did he question the names of British agents jotted down in the margin of the questionnaire and recalled by Seth. These included some officers Seth claimed to have known during training, such as Captain Phillips and Captain Angelo, but others not known to him, such as Major Buckmaster. Now, it is likely that Seth had also heard of the other officers he listed in 1944 and again in 1945, such as Maurice Buckmaster, the head of the French section of SOE, and was thus able to come up with a plausible list of names supposedly written down on Nädlinger's copy of the questionnaire. But it is also possible that Nädlinger deliberately let him have sight of this document. The story of the telephone call which necessitated leaving a captured enemy agent alone in a flat with inadequate security does not ring true, and one cannot fault the MI5 team for concluding that it was another of Seth's inventions. On the other hand, it may have been a ploy by the Germans to win over Seth by impressing upon him how much they already knew of the workings of SOE (in his published account, he confesses that he was shocked to find how extensive their knowledge was). They were not revealing any great secrets to him; in allowing him to sneak a peek at a commonly used interrogation document, they might have sought to boost his self-assurance and confidence – and like MI5, they may also have spotted Seth's sense of self-importance, which they might hope later to exploit to their own advantage.

Over the next week of questioning, Seth concocted an elaborate cover story which, according to his published account, he hoped would convince his interrogators of his pro-German credentials and present them with a plausible story which at the same time contained enough false information to mislead and even confuse them. The final version of this story amounted to fifty-six typewritten, single-spaced foolscap pages, each initialled by Seth. In broad detail, the story corresponds to the facts of Seth's training and mission, but it is made to appear that Seth was reluctant to undertake the mission and was in fact virtually blackmailed into doing so. In this story, he is conscripted into the RAF, and whilst stationed at RAF Chipping Warden at the end of March 1942, he is told by his Group Captain to report the following day to a certain Mr Goldman at a fictitious address, 2 Francis Place, Berkeley Square. Goldman 'a typical Jewish type', talked to him about Estonia, but refused to reveal any reason for the interview. A few days later, he was summoned to a second interview with Goldman and another unknown man. Goldman told him that the Russians had falsely claimed to have destroyed the shale-oil mines; the shale-oil installations in north-east Estonia were in fact now producing 300 tons of oil daily for the German forces on the Leningrad front. It had been suggested that Seth should be sent to Estonia to organise the sabotage of these mines and, 'as the Russian intelligence service was supplying false information to H.M. Government, to send home all information possible'. Seth protested that he was 'a married man with a young family, that I was more a scholar than a man of action, and considered myself totally unsuited to the job'. This cut no ice with Goldman, who told him that he was the only man in England who knew Estonia well, and in war, country came before family. A few days later, Seth was summoned to the Air Ministry where a Wing Commander Beeding (real name Redding) bawled him out, threatening to reduce him to the ranks if he continued to refuse to accept the mission. Fearing the scandal for his family that might ensue, Seth wrote to Goldman, agreeing to undertake the mission.

On 5 April, he returned to Francis Place and met a Major Beech (i.e. Hazell) who gave him his instructions. He was to sabotage the shale-oil mines, organise active and passive resistance throughout Estonia, and send all intelligence information possible to England. He was then sent to Station No. 17, where agents were taught how to handle explosives. After that, he received training at Station 52, the wireless school at Thame Park, whose commanding officer was one of the men listed on Nädlinger's questionnaire, Major Phillips, and at the parachute centre in Manchester. There is a farewell meeting at the War Office with a general whose name Seth did not know, who described him as 'our only ewe-lamb in that part of the world', and a programme of very intensive anti-Gestapo propaganda, including photographs of atrocities committed by the Germans. On 24 October, Seth took off from RAF Whitton (Seth's variation of RAF Wyton) in Huntingdonshire, with a refuelling stop at an airbase near York. The drop zone was to have been in the Bay of Kunda, some 100km to the east of the Kolga peninsula, but the captain of the aircraft, a squadron leader, told him to jump short of the target, and he had no option but to obey a superior officer. He made a bad exit from the plane, and was completely lost on landing:

During the course of my training I had become more and more disgusted with the whole business. I could not be provided with papers as the Russian and British secret services were quarrelling and the Russians refused to supply any papers; the maps in possession of G.S.G.S. were so poor as to be useless for my purpose; there was no supply in England of Kreditkassenscheine [German banknotes issued for use by the army], so I was to be supplied with American and Swedish money; I only spoke a few words of the language; I felt that I was being made the victim of Jewish financial interests in the mines; and now I was being dropped in a completely strange place 100 kilometres from my destination. I had made up my mind before leaving England to carry out the operation for the sake of my family, but on landing would surrender to the Germans offering myself for work against the Russians whom I have always hated, and who had murdered three of my best friends in Estonia, including my daughter's god-father.[8]

After a perfunctory search for the three containers in order to get hold of the food, Seth retreated into the forest and spent the time sleeping, drugged with opium and morphine. He did not immediately surrender because the anti-Gestapo propaganda had frightened him. He finally realised where he was on 5 November, when he wandered along the shoreline and recognised Saarne's cottage. Having been told by Saarne that flight to Sweden by boat was impossible he surrendered to the Germans at midday.

What then of the acts of sabotage Seth claimed in his handwritten report of August 1944 that he had committed? They were not mentioned in the interrogation, Seth claimed, because, as Nädlinger told him, a party of five Russians dropped on the Kolga peninsula three days before his arrival had still not been caught. These Russian saboteurs were either a very convenient smokescreen for Seth's own valorous activities, or their own heroic exploits were neatly pinched by Seth for his own purposes – or, as Captain Milton supposed, the entire story of acts of sabotage on the Kolga peninsula was a fiction.

At the end of the interrogation, Nädlinger and Vogl were joined by two other officers, and they adjourned to another room for a discussion, leaving Seth alone. Seeing the pad upon which Major Vogl had noted down his replies, he managed to stuff it into the top of his sea-stockings. On returning to the room, Vogl seemed to be looking for something, but said nothing, and Seth was able to smuggle the notebook back to prison, where he memorised the contents. When asked during his subsequent interrogation in London what had happened to this notebook, Seth replied 'rather hesitatingly' that he thought he had destroyed it on the way to Tallinn airport by tearing it to pieces under his storm jacket and surreptitiously dropping the pieces out of the car window and in the airport building. Captain Milton of course found it 'hard to believe' that any security officers would leave a prisoner alone with their papers, 'hard to credit' that, having done so, they would not check up on their papers once they returned, and 'hard to imagine' that, having noticed the loss of such papers, they would have failed to connect the loss to Seth.[9]

There are other aspects of this interrogation that seem odd. Seth stated that he was questioned by the radio section of the Geheime Feldpolizei, yet the eight days were taken up almost entirely with the rather laborious transcription of his cover story, with Major Vogl translating and writing down *Feldwebel* Nädlinger's questions and Seth's answers. Mention is made of an *Oberleutnant* specialising in radio equipment being present at the preliminary interrogation in Seth's former flat, but he seems not to have played any further part until some time midway through the interrogation in the flat on Aia street, when he reappeared accompanied by a civilian and – in the 1944 account – bringing with them Seth's radio equipment. This civilian was identified by Seth in his MI5 interrogation as a pre-war employee of the German electrical firm of Siemens, and as the man who questioned him about his radio frequencies. In 1952, this civilian is described as the man who sold Seth a radio set, a Reich German who had operated for several years as a Nazi agent in Estonia, so he may well have occupied a rather more important position than that of a civilian brought along as an interpreter. Seth maintained that the attempt to persuade him to divulge his radio frequencies stalled when it became obvious that the crystals were missing, and he claimed in his book that when he broached the matter with MI5, the subject was abruptly changed, which led him to suspect that someone had forgotten to pack the crystals. Captain Milton's comment that 'perhaps some essential part of his wireless set was missing' would seem to bear out Seth's own suspicions. In his 1944 report he concluded that, even had his mission been successful, he would not have been able to communicate with England. The mysterious disappearance of the crystals, coming on top of the anxieties voiced on the eve of Seth's departure about the reliability of his radio equipment, reflects poorly on the thoroughness of preparation. There is other evidence of muddle in SOE operations: a Dutch father and son, agents of the Russian secret service (NKVD) parachuted into the Low Countries, had their bags mixed up, for example.[10]

If Seth believed that the Germans, baffled by the absence of the crystals, would abandon the attempt to persuade him to divulge his transmitting frequencies, he was mistaken. He may also have been misled – or blinded by his own vanity, as Captain Milton would have it – into thinking that the Vogl-Nädlinger interview was the main show. It is certainly curious that the lead man was a mere non-commissioned officer, accompanied by a superannuated major whose task it was to take notes in English. This time-consuming exercise, important though it was to Seth, was in all likelihood of secondary significance to the Germans. The main show, as far as they were concerned, came some days later, when he was taken by car to a location in the upper town, formerly the citadel of the Teutonic Knights. Here he was interrogated about his radio frequencies by two unknown men in civilian clothes. Seth had maintained that he knew only that his crystals were marked A, B and C, and that he did not know their numbers. He was then taken into another room and seated in a chair facing a mirror, with a powerful arc lamp behind him. His head was strapped to a board at the back of the chair, and the reflection of the arc lamp in the mirror was focussed on his eyes. A man seated at a table repeatedly asked him to divulge the frequency numbers. If he closed his eyes, he was beaten on the head. At midday, a tempting plate of bacon, eggs and potatoes was placed before him, with the promise that he could eat if he revealed the numbers. During the ordeal, Seth fainted two or three times and was revived with cold water thrown over him. He believed the interrogation lasted some seventeen hours, and he admitted he was about to give in when his questioners gave up. In 1944, he wrote that he remained totally blind until mid-December, and had had recurring fits of blindness lasting several hours until only a short time ago.

It goes without saying that Captain Milton did not believe he was tortured. Indeed, Milton had never come across any other case in which the Germans used such a torture, which smacked of 'American police third-degree methods', though Milton grudgingly admitted such methods might be peculiar to the Estonian police.[11] Whether or not Seth's account of his ordeal was a product of his 'enormous vanity and brisk imagination', there are good grounds to suppose that he was closely questioned about his radio transmitter, and that the questioning was done by men altogether more professional than the rather genial, bumbling duo who loom large in Seth's own portrayal of events. The use of captured radio transmitters was a key element in the war of deception. It is significant that on learning in April 1943 of Seth's capture, SOE immediately alerted Station 52 that even after this lapse of time, the Germans might be able to repair a possibly damaged radio set and send messages on the proper wavelength and frequencies.

Having failed either to elicit from Seth details of his frequencies, or to find the missing crystals, the Germans now faced the question of what to do with their prisoner. It should be remembered that in October 1942, Hitler had issued an order that anyone caught committing an act of sabotage should be executed, whether wearing a uniform or not. Seth had not been caught in the act, but sabotage had been the main purpose of his mission. He had been caught in a war zone where German security policy was a good deal harsher than in the occupied countries of western and northern Europe. The one thing that stood in his favour was that he had a rarity value, and he seems to have sensed that from the outset. His survival depended upon his ability to convince his captors that he could be of service to them. He later maintained that he had three aims: first and foremost, to stay alive; secondly, to ingratiate himself with the Germans and win their confidence; and thirdly, to persuade them that his broadcasting abilities were not unimportant. If he could do this and gain access to a microphone, he reasoned that he would be able to send coded messages back to Britain.

Seth claimed in 1944 and on subsequent occasions that he had not revealed his letter code (though there is no indication that he was ever asked for such details), and he now sought to use this to send his 'Russian information' back to London. To do this, he had first to obtain writing paper, and here again, we have another episode that stretches credulity. At some stage in his incarceration, 'a curious little peasant' was thrust into his cell. Seth devoted several pages in his published account to this man, Matsve Konjovalev. A poor peasant from Petseri, the easternmost and most backward province of Estonia, he stood accused of collusion with a band of Russian parachutists. On the following Monday, he was taken for interrogation and returned with blood flowing from wounds to his head. The terrified man spent much of the night on his knees invoking the protection of the saints, but was eventually persuaded to sleep. At some stage, Seth was awakened by a noise, and discovered Matsve hanging from a pipe leading to the lavatory cistern. He managed to call the guard, and the two of them cut down Matsve, whom Seth was able to revive. The guard had evidently been asleep on duty, and Seth threatened to reveal this unless the man procured paper and a pencil, which he subsequently did. The unfortunate Matsve and the eighteen parachutists were executed by firing squad.

There is considerable confusion over dates here, which may of course support the veracity of the story, except that for much of the time, Seth claims he was blind. Interrogated in London in 1945, he placed the incident of the suicidal peasant before his ordeal by arc light and mirror, and although this incident is recorded after the details of his blinding experience in 1944, the dates given (27 November for the interrogation in the upper town, 20 November for Matsve's appearance in the cell) would seem to confirm that he was sighted and able to write his letters. In *A Spy has no Friends*, however, Seth explicitly states that Matsve appeared a day or two after the bandages had been removed from his eyes. In 1944, he wrote that he was 'totally blind' until 15 December, and less than a week later he was involved in the most dramatic and potentially life-changing episode of his incarceration to date, so that either his recollection of events was faulty, or, as the redoubtable Captain Milton concluded, the whole story was an invention to gain credit for having attempted to get his intelligence to London.[12]

The story of Matsve and its outcome is all too typical of Seth's exuberant imagination, but this is not to discount entirely the possibility that he did in fact procure paper, and write the eleven letters to his wife, which contained coded information. When Seth first set down on paper what had happened to him between his arrest in autumn 1942 and his sojourn in Paris, he was still in the hands of the Germans, and he remained a prisoner until April 1945. During the autumn of 1944, a series of letters written ostensibly by her brother to Mrs Ronald Seth at her Cumberland address of 5 Wickham's Place, Keswick were intercepted by the British security services. On his return to England, Seth was to claim that he had been sending secretly coded messages in these letters, and subsequent investigation by officers of the security service grudgingly acknowledged this to be the case. This would seem to support his claim to have written similar letters in Tallinn Central Prison, sewing them into the inner pocket of his storm jacket and attaching a note urging the finder to send them on to his wife's family home in Keswick.

Seth's declared willingness to work for the Germans did not stand him in good stead, for on 19 December (21 December in the published version) he was informed out of the blue that he would be executed two days later. When he protested that he had not been tried, he was told that the Vogl-Nädlinger interrogation had yielded enough evidence to hang him, and hanging in public was to be the mode of execution. At 0930 hours on 21 (or 23) December, escorted by a party of six soldiers with arms reversed, Seth hobbled on his frost-bitten feet through the streets of Tallinn to the main station, arriving there a couple of minutes before ten o'clock. In front of the station stood a rough scaffold, a platform raised on trestles with a couple of uprights supporting a cross bar, from which dangled a noose. The platform was about 3½ft from the ground and 5ft wide, and had a metal lever protruding from the right-hand side. It was surrounded by soldiers, and although a train arrived a ten o'clock and disgorged a large number of people, they did not linger.

After a wait of about five minutes, a motor car drew up and out stepped an officer and a couple of non-commissioned officers who had weighed and measured Seth the previous day. The Germans now seemed in a great hurry to get the execution over and done with. Seth was lifted on to the platform, his feet were strapped by the corporal and his arms pinioned by the sergeant, who had been deputed to be his executioner. Having placed the rope around Seth's neck, the sergeant/executioner jumped off the platform and took hold of the lever; the officer in charge nodded to him, and saluted Seth; the sergeant wrenched the lever and the trap-door opened. Seth fell, and then felt his feet striking the trap-door, which had dropped only a few inches and had then stuck. 'Then I fell forward. The rope tightened behind my ears and my eyes were filled with bright lights and then darkness.'[13]

When he came to, he found himself back in Cell 13. That night, he was told by the night-warden that the soldiers detailed to guard the scaffold had been warmed up with libations of vodka – either self-administered or offered to them by some Estonians – and that whilst they were thus enticed away from their duties, a couple of wooden slats were nailed under and across the trap, causing it to fail on the day of the execution. The guards, the executioner and his assistant had all been shot for dereliction of duty. In his published account, Seth has the night-warden say that his execution was meant to be a warning to the Estonians not to trust in 'the Third Possibility', i.e. that the western Allies might somehow liberate Estonia. No such explanation is offered in any of the unpublished accounts.

What are we to make of this episode? Captain Milton dismissed it on two grounds. He had seen photographs of hangings carried out by the Germans, which were generally rudimentary affairs, the victim being pushed from a stool or the back of a vehicle, and could not believe they would resort to such an elaborate, albeit hastily erected, scaffold. Furthermore, he did not feel Estonian patriots would have risked their lives to forestall an execution when they must have thought this would merely postpone an inevitable event. That he did not denounce it as yet another example of Seth's febrile imagination working overtime may be ascribed to weariness rather than anything else.

Execution by hanging in wartime Estonia was rather rare; most of those executed were shot. A public execution, staged in front of a busy railway station in the capital, must surely have attracted considerable attention, yet there seems to be no mention of it in the reports gathered by Colonel Saarsen's intelligence network, nor is there any note of it in the prison records. This event must surely have taken place in Seth's head, rather than in reality. Yet, it does point up the question of what the Germans intended to do with an enemy agent in a part of the world where captured partisans and saboteurs were invariably shot.

Having narrowly escaped death – real or imagined – and with the execution postponed until after the holidays, Seth was now given a Christmas present in the shape of a salacious French book. Inside his book on the exotic delights of love in the Orient – which Seth rather primly thought was not very suitable literature for those in prison – he found a slip of rice-paper. On this he scribbled a message: 'On and after April 10 1943 listen on A frequency every day at 1700 GMT and 0100 GMT for fifteen minutes. Do not reply this is most important'. Seth then rubbed the paper in the dirt, crumpled it up and stuffed it into his storm jacket pocket.[14]

This scruffy slip of paper was to have consequences even more momentous in Seth's adventures than his narrow escape from death. For the time being, however, it failed to attract much attention. Seth's attempts to persuade the Estonian prison authorities to let him see the German authorities were unsuccessful. When he was eventually summoned back to Aia street on 29 December, Nädlinger seemed uninterested in his piece of paper, telling him to keep it until they returned to Tallinn. Instead, Nädlinger informed him, they were about to fly to Riga for another round of questioning, on the orders of the general officer commanding the Baltic front. The two drove to the airport – Seth surreptitiously tearing up Major Vogl's notebook on the way – and boarded a Lufthansa flight to the Latvian capital. Poor Nädlinger, on his first flight, was violently airsick, and Seth paints an amusing picture of a German *Feldwebel* being supported by a filthy and unkempt man dressed in tattered, stinking clothes, much to the consternation of the German businessmen and their well-dressed secretaries on board this regular airline flight.

Notes

1. ERA. R– 294.1.170. I am grateful to Meelis Maripuu for providing this information.
2. Seth 2008 pp.51–2.
3. Report 44, p.10.
4. MI5 report 3, p.5.
5. Report 44. p.11.
6. Report 44, p.11. If Nädlinger did actually leave Seth alone, he was in gross violation of the rules for security personnel in Estonia. The rules are in ERA.R–64.1.46.

7. MI5 report 2, p.14. An Estonian version of this questionnaire is in ERA.R-64.1.46. Clearly geared towards the interrogation of Soviet parachutists, it is in two sections: personal details and training.
8. Report 44, p.14. MI5 report 2, pp.15–8 for the account given under interrogation in London.
9. MI5 report 3, p.9.
10. MI5 report 3, p.22, O'Sullivan 2010, p.126.
11. MI5 report 3, p.7.
12. Seth 2008, p.94. Report 44, pp.15–6.
13. Seth 2008, p.108. Report 44, pp.16–7.
14. Report 44, p.17. A slightly different version is in Seth 2008, p.114.

7 | 'I'm afraid they don't like you.'

Gestapo Headquarters, Frankfurt-am-Main, February 1943

In Riga, according to Seth's account, he was lodged in an even older prison, built by the Russians in 1725, and now rejoicing in the title of *Kriegswehrmachthaftanstalt*, or War Forces Arrest Prison. Although Cell number 10 in which Seth was housed was no great improvement on Cell 13 in Tallinn Central Prison – the walls were filthy and the floor smeared with dried excrement — the food was a vast improvement. As this was a military prison, army rations were served. In Tallinn, Seth had subsisted on cold, watery soup and hard chunks of black bread. In two months of imprisonment, he had lost over 20kg. Now he was served bread and jam for breakfast, a variety of thick soups at lunch, with bread, cheese, sausage or fish in the evening, washed down with mugs of ersatz coffee. Seth was able to befriend the cook, an army deserter banged up in the cell next door, and managed to procure extra helpings.

His material circumstances were also significantly improved on the orders of the commander of the German Air Fleet One (Luftflotte 1), General Alfred Keller. Keller, a veteran flyer of the First World War, had played a crucial role in the air campaigns in Poland, Norway, France and Britain. Air Fleet One supported Army Group North during the German invasion

95

of Russia in 1941, and continued to operate in the Baltic region. It is not clear why such a senior figure should have wished to see a captured British agent, or why he instigated the transfer from Tallinn to Riga. Seth's junior rank in the RAF could hardly have been an inducement. Perhaps, like the inmates of the military prison, the air force general was simply curious about a lone Englishman in the Baltic. In any event, the intervention of a senior Luftwaffe commander proved to be crucial in transferring Seth from the attentions of the security forces in Estonia to those of German air force intelligence.

Seth was taken to the Luftwaffe headquarters on Wallstrasse on the day after his arrival in Riga. Here, he had a fifteen-minute interview with Keller and his chief of general staff, described by Seth as a colonel wearing the Knight's Cross of the Iron Cross. This unnamed man was in all likelihood lieutenant-general of the air force, Herbert Rieckhoff, chief of general staff to Air Fleet One between October 1941 and February 1943. Keller was courteous, asking about conditions in England and morale, and ordering that Seth be bathed, shaved and well fed.

On his return to Cell 10, Seth found a thick palliasse and two blankets on his bed, and within minutes, a sergeant appeared with tobacco and cigarette papers. He was later able to procure from the same sergeant a pen and writing paper with which to write a message to the chief of general staff. The purport of this missive was to explain how Seth came into possession of the crumpled scrap of rice-paper on which he had scribbled the message urging him to listen to his radio at stated times on and after 10 April. As he was about to board the aircraft that was to fly him to Estonia, Seth wrote, he had been handed a letter from 'Major Beech' containing this message. As there was no time to learn by heart the instructions, he had written it down on a piece of cigarette paper and stuffed it into his pocket, where it had lain forgotten until he had discovered it in jail in Tallinn.

Having had the message translated, the chief of staff asked Seth what he thought it meant. Seth replied that he thought it might indicate a possible Russian offensive on the Leningrad front in the spring, and that he was to be in readiness to receive a message to undertake sabotage activities on the railway line from northern Estonia to Leningrad. His interrogator made no comment on this and appears to have been more interested in Seth as a possible double agent. Dismissing the guard and interpreter at a second interview, he addressed Seth in French, asking if he was really sincere in offering to work against the Russians. When Seth replied in the affirmative, he was told that General Keller had informed the local commander in Tallinn that he had decided to send him to Berlin on the grounds that he would be more use to Germany alive than dead. Who this local commander was is unclear, but he had apparently been bombarding the Luftwaffe headquarters in Riga with telegrams demanding Seth's return for execution.

Seth expressed his willingness to work 'against the Jews and Bolsheviks', as he puts in 1952, and the Luftwaffe seem prepared to take him up on that offer. Seth also claimed that he wrote three pamphlets in his cell which he suggested might be dropped over Britain. Coded messages about his fate and the Russian information were incorporated into these pamphlets using the letter code whose indicator was a common Estonian way of writing the date (day, month and year, with the month written vertically in Roman numerals).

In the event, there is no indication that his ideas or writings were taken up. Indeed, as the sergeant in charge of him during his spell in the military prison in Riga reminded him, his execution had merely been postponed and could be carried out at any time. The next phase of incarceration would clearly demonstrate that the Germans were a long way from believing Seth was a man they could trust.

Seth claimed that he spent a little over two weeks in Riga. Tallinn prison records, however, show that Unit 713 of the Geheime Feldpolizei had ordered his removal to a prisoner-of-war camp on 11 January 1943.[1] It may be of course that Seth was transferred to Riga 'on loan', and Keller's intervention on his behalf saved him from a return to custody and possible execution. His stay in Riga was otherwise of short duration, for on Thursday, 14 January, he was told that he was to depart that evening for Frankfurt-am-Main. After the usual form-filling, he arrived at the station accompanied by two Luftwaffe sergeants. The station was crowded with soldiers going home on leave, and his escort had to demand that an extra carriage be added to the train so that they could have a compartment for themselves and their prisoner. Without lighting because of the blackout, the carriage was also without heating, and the party had to endure a thirteen-hour night journey to the Lithuanian-Prussian frontier in sub-zero temperatures. At the frontier, everyone was ordered off the train and into the delousing station. Seth was suitably impressed by the efficiency with which some two thousand men were deloused and served hot soup and coffee, but it was not until the late afternoon that their journey was resumed. A well-heated German train with soup kitchen attached took them through East Prussia, depositing them in

Berlin the following morning. Here Seth and his two escorts spent the day at an army transit canteen on the Friedrichstrasse railway station, continuing their journey that evening to Frankfurt-am-Main, where they finally arrived at four in the morning of Sunday, 17 January 1943. Their marathon railway journey across Central Europe was not yet at an end, however, for they had to wait for the first local train to take them to Oberursel. From there they took a tram to the Durchgangslager der Luftwaffe, (Dulag Luft), the transit camp at which captured Allied airmen were initially interrogated.[2]

Dulag Luft was one of the busiest interrogation centres in Germany, and its interrogators had a fearsome reputation for extracting valuable information from captured RAF and USAAF personnel. The main camp consisted of four wooden barracks, an administrative centre and an interrogation block, with single-cell accommodation for up to 200 prisoners. As the camp handled around a thousand prisoners a month in 1943 (and double that amount in 1944), conditions could be cramped, with up to five men sharing a single narrow cell. Prisoners were held in solitary confinement for up to twenty-eight days, the maximum period allowed by the Geneva Convention. Seth described his cell as dirty and ill-ventilated. The glass chamber-pot he was provided with was cracked and leaked, and was not replaced for three days. Rations were meagre, and prisoners could be deprived of cigarettes and reading material for refusing to co-operate with their interrogators.[3]

After three months without hearing another English voice, Seth was relieved to hear a fellow prisoner berating one of the bovine guards in a broad Yorkshire accent: 'When I say I fucking-well want to shave, I fucking-well mean I fucking-well want to shave.'[4] His stay at Dulag Luft, however, was brief, and a huge disappointment after Riga. He was subjected to a merciless and hostile interrogation over a three-day period, and not allowed to smoke, read or shave, but – according to his MI5 interrogation – he was not maltreated. In his book, however, the interrogation lasts for five days, he is made to stand to attention for hours during questioning and is reprimanded for the slightest movement, and at one stage has a heavy paperweight thrown at him, causing a blinding pain in the groin. He is also dragged naked from his overheated cell and dumped on the snowy ground for a time before being returned, not to his cell, but to the interrogation centre.

From the start it was made plain that his story was not believed. Seth was surprised to discover how much his interrogators knew about the

RAF in general, and about him in particular. He was also thrown by being questioned in English, rather than through the medium of translation from German, since this gave him far less time to think. His questioners used the dossier compiled during his sojourn in Tallinn, but chose questions at random instead of following events chronologically. Seth believed he managed to outfox them when he was able to draw an accurate map of the shale-oil region in northern Estonia, thereby substantiating his assertion that he knew the region so well that he did not need maps. He was sufficiently familiar with the functions and duties of a junior administrative RAF officer (which he claimed to have been) to be able to describe them fully when challenged to do so, though this did nothing to blunt the Germans' suspicions that he was in fact an intelligence officer. The Germans had already discovered the eleven letters to his wife that he had concealed in his storm-jacket, though they do not appear to have questioned Seth on their content or possible coded messages.

Captain Milton's verdict on the Oberursel interrogation was that it was unlikely that the Germans possessed British Air Ministry lists of RAF personnel as Seth had claimed, but that it was significant that they knew he was an intelligence officer. This implied that Seth had given them information on Bomber Command which he had learned during his time as a junior intelligence officer at RAF Pershore and Chipping Warden. Milton had clearly not seen the summary of the interrogation that had fallen into Allied hands as a result of a fortuitous air accident over Switzerland, though he expressed an interest in doing so. But the captured digest of the interrogation does in fact substantiate Seth's claim that he was questioned at length on his Tallinn dossier. He is described without qualification as having been trained as an administrative officer, in which capacity he served until May 1942, when he was summoned to meet Mr Goldman at the Air Ministry. Goldman told him that he was the only man with the knowledge necessary to obtain information on the spot about the oil wells at Narva, but he declined the mission on the grounds that it was too dangerous and he was not sufficiently qualified. A few days later, he was summoned to the Air Ministry by a Wing Commander, who reminded him of an officer's duty to accept orders without question and warned him of the alternative of court martial and 'degradation'. 'Degradation' would have meant for the prisoner a severe loss of income, and since he had lost his property, two houses, as a result of bombing, he and his family were now utterly dependent on his earnings. He therefore agreed to the mission and underwent training in the use of demolition materials, radio transmission and parachuting before being parachuted into Estonia on 24 October 1942.[5]

Although there are some differences in detail between this report and Seth's own accounts of his cover story, the basic story of his recruitment into SOE is consistent. It is of course perfectly possible that Seth may have been pressed to reveal information about the RAF, though it is rather unlikely that a new and very junior officer, stationed as he was at officer training units, would have known very much of interest to the Luftwaffe. On the evidence of the captured extract of his interrogation, therefore, it would seem that it was Seth as an agent with a mission, rather than as a source of intelligence about Bomber Command, that was of primary interest.

Most prisoners interrogated at Dulag Luft were subsequently transferred to other prisoner-of-war camps: the camp commander seems on several occasions to have actively opposed the transfer of prisoners to the authority of the Gestapo. Seth's destiny was to be rather different, which suggests that he was being treated as an enemy agent, rather than as a captured airman who might have useful technical information. On the fourth or fifth day of his stay at Dulag Luft, he was visited in his cell by an unpleasant-looking man dressed in civilian clothes.[6] This gentleman turned out to be assistant criminal commissar Fischer of the Frankfurt Gestapo. Seth repeated his story from recruitment into SOE to his arrival in Estonia, with Luftwaffe captain (*Hauptmann der Flieger*) Wierck as his interpreter.[7] At the end of this recital, Fischer observed coldly '*Ich glaube nicht, mein Liebe*' ('I don't believe it, my friend').[8] The prospect of being transferred to the tender care of the Gestapo, which was announced by Wierck on Friday 22 January, filled Seth with dread. As he later wrote, the arduous journey from Riga, lack of food and the rigorous interrogation he had endured had reduced him to a nervous condition, and he now felt that the limit of his endurance had been reached. To make matters worse, his storm-jacket, which had been such a comfort to him in jail, had been ripped part in the search for incriminating concealed material, and the seams of his trousers has burst apart whilst he had been roaming the woods of Estonia. On that score he was rescued by a kindly elderly guard, who gave him a pair of RAF uniform trousers.

Seth was transferred on 22 January from Dulag Luft to the Frankfurt Remand Prison (*Untersuchungsgefängnis*). This building, located in the centre of the town opposite the court house, housed a variety of prisoners of conscience and political prisoners as well as captured Allied personnel. The prison was clean, and the prisoners were expected to keep themselves clean and properly dressed. Seth, as a remand prisoner, was allowed the privilege of wearing his own clothes, including a leather belt given to him in prison in Riga by a Norwegian inmate. Captain Milton had great difficulty in understanding why the Norwegian gave him such an odd present, with *dux femina facti* (a woman as leader of the endeavour: Virgil's *Aeneid*, I, line 364) and 'Good luck England!' scratched on the inside, nor could he understand why a SOE agent should go into the field on a carefully prepared mission with his trousers held up with a piece of string, as Seth claimed he had done.

Milton was also puzzled why the prison authorities had not taken the belt away from the prisoner, and he was disinclined in consequence to believe Seth's attempted suicide. This occurred on his first night in the remand prison, but his attempt to secure the belt to his window bars preparatory to hanging himself aroused the attention of a kindly elderly guard, who managed to comfort him and give him courage to overcome his fears of further interrogation.

The remand prison was to be Seth's home for the next ten months. His daily routine varied little. Prisoners rose at 0600 hours, cleaned their cells and did their ablutions before breakfast was served: a bowl of watery ersatz coffee and 50g of black bread, with jam every other day. From 0745 hours to midday, and from 1300 to 1745 hours, prisoners were given work to do. Seth was initially given the task of folding advertisements for Dr Scholl's Bath and Foot Salts and making these up into packs of fifty, but was eventually moved on to making paper bags. Although monotonous, the work served to occupy his mind and helped him recover from the deep depression that had affected him. The midday meal alternated between a litre of soup and boiled potatoes with vegetables. The evening meal served at 1800 hours usually included a bowl of rosehip tea, black bread, a little fat and sausage, occasionally replaced with cheese or fish paste. Although Seth admitted that for a man in a good state of health this diet might be sufficient, he was already malnourished. In common with the other prisoners, he complained of constant hunger: food became almost an obsession, a craving which dominated the prisoner's existence.

The prisoners had access to a hot shower for a maximum of three minutes once a fortnight, and were shaved once a week. They were allowed exercise once a day for twenty minutes. For intellectual enjoyment, prisoners were given a book every Sunday, and Seth was able to improve his knowledge of the works of lesser Victorian novelists with which the prison library seemed to be well stocked. Since he had given out that he knew no German, he felt unable to attend services in the prison chapel for fear of revealing that he did in fact understand the language.

On the whole, he had no complaints about the treatment he received, apart from at the hands of a couple of warders, both of whom seem to have had personal reasons for hating the British. The trusties were kind, and would slip him extra rations whenever they could. The worst aspect of prison was the isolation. Not knowing the time was particularly upsetting, though on sunny days Seth was able to calculate the time by the length of the shadows on the building opposite his cell window. He was of course unable to communicate with the outside world, or to receive news of his family. He learnt that there were at least three other British prisoners in the prison, and caught a glimpse of one of them, Captain Louis Lee-Graham, captured in France in 1942, but did not succeed in making contact with any of them.

Seth had been in the prison for about a week before he was driven from the prison to Gestapo headquarters on Lindenstrasse, a large house in the leafy Westend suburb of Frankfurt-am-Main. After being kept waiting in handcuffs in an anteroom, he was ushered into a room in which there were three criminal investigators who conducted the examination, a secretary and an interpreter. According to Seth's own account, the interpreter was SS *Standartenführer* Walter Schmitt, in civilian life a manufacturer of jewellery in the town of Pforzheim. Schmitt had been badly wounded at Dunkirk, and had subsequently been delegated as a fluent English-speaker to work for the Gestapo. In Seth's account, Schmitt becomes almost an ally, a wise counsellor and friend. He had most to fear from assistant criminal commissar Fischer, whom he had already encountered at Dulag Luft, but he soon realised that there was a deep antagonism between Fischer and his superior, criminal commissar Hans Büth. A man of between 35 and 40 with a plump, rosy-cheeked face and delicate manicured hands, Büth (spelled 'Bütt' by Seth) held the rank of SS *Obersturmbannführer*. Hans Büth had moved from Cologne to Frankfurt in 1942. Originally assigned to department IV/2, he was soon moved to IV/3, which dealt mainly with those suspected of espionage. Seth presents Büth as a decent fellow, but other witnesses were later to accuse him of having taken part in the physical abuse of prisoners and the theft of Jewish property. He also had 'intimate relations' with female employees. His underling, SS *Untersturmbannführer* Heinrich Fischer, was a veteran policeman, who had moved from the uniformed police force (*Schutzpolizei*) to the Gestapo in the mid-1930s.

The head of IV/3 was SS *Hauptsturmbannführer* Ernst Schmidt, but the man with whom Seth came into contact was clearly Walter Schmidt. Schmidt, who bore the title of *Kommandierter der Waffen-SS*, which was given to those on a temporary assignment, had joined the Frankfurt Gestapo from the Waffen-SS in 1940–41 (which would seem to confirm Seth's account), and had subsequently been transferred to IV/3, where he worked mainly on matters concerning downed airmen. Walter Schmidt is specifically named as an English speaker.[9] The third policeman, variously known as Philips or Phipps, was Fischer's assistant and appears to have played little part in the interrogation.

The interrogation began with questions that followed the same pro forma document used by the Geheime Feldpolizei in Tallinn. All went well until they came to the reasons why Seth had agreed to undertake his mission. He sensed that he would have to change his story, so he admitted that he had not told the truth earlier because he had been too ashamed to do so. As the story was rather complicated, he asked permission to write it down in his cell. Permission was granted, and Seth concocted a new version to explain why he had supposedly been coerced into undertaking the mission to Estonia.

In this new version of events, Seth is obliged to leave his money behind in Estonia because of currency restrictions on his return to England. His father was unable to help him out as he was in financial difficulties because of the war, and he was obliged to borrow money from friends. His BBC salary of £6 10s a week was insufficient to cover the high cost of living, including rented accommodation for a family of four, and to repay the money owed. So far, the story is a true one, Seth wrote later. Money worries run through the Seth story throughout the war years, and there can be little doubt that a man with a young family suddenly obliged to give up a comfortable flat and reasonably secure employment and return to look for work and accommodation amidst all the uncertainties of war would be haunted by the prospect of indebtedness. Seth had contracted a heavy debt whilst in Estonia. In November 1937, he authorised his employer to withhold from his monthly salary and to pay into the account of the British vice consul J.E.B. Leslie the sum of 120 crowns until the debt of 1,059 crowns had been paid.[10] Indeed, anxiety about money may well have been a strong motive for Seth's volunteering his services to SOE: £600 a year tax-free was considerably more than he had been earning at the BBC or as a junior RAF officer.

Thereafter the story descends into fantasy. Seth claims that they were bombed out of two rented properties in Croydon in the spring of 1940. Transferred to the BBC Evesham station in July (in reality, at the beginning of April), Seth found himself in further need of funds to furnish a flat and borrowed yet more money from a friend. That friend got into financial difficulties and in order to repay him, Seth borrowed from a Jewish moneylender against the security of some furniture lent to him by an uncle:

> When I joined the RAF and my wife took a job and we sent the children to a school, at my wits' end, I foolishly sold the furniture, which I had no right to do. My pay as a P/O (Pilot Officer) only sufficed to pay my mess-bills, and I got more into debt, being unable to keep up the payments of interest to the Jew. He then began to press me and in a wild attempt to gain time I gave him a cheque for £120, which was dishonoured. This was in February 1942.

The moneylender threatened to inform the Air Ministry, but Seth heard nothing more until his interview by Wing Commander Beeding. Beeding produced the bounced cheque and said that if Seth refused to undertake the mission put to him by Goldman, he would be dismissed the service and tried for uttering a false cheque, an offence for which he might expect five years' imprisonment. Were he to accept the task, his debts would be paid and nothing more would be said. Faced with the prospect of disgrace for himself and his family, Seth consented.

The veracity of this story received support from Schmidt, who before the war had spent considerable periods of time on business in England. Schmidt confirmed that the uttering of a false cheque was considered a serious crime in England. Fischer was sceptical, which automatically made Büth believe him too. Fischer was also driven into a furious rage when Seth continued to deny that he had ever been given maps of Estonia. Büth, however, merely winked at Seth, and directed the secretary to write down Seth's negative answer. Seth was not pressed on his radio frequencies: his interrogators presumed that he had lost his equipment, since they had managed to find most of it intact. The acts of sabotage were attributed to a party of Russians that had been landed on the Kolga peninsula some time before him, and who had not been captured.

According to Seth, his interrogation lasted for eight days, or forty-eight hours in total. His interrogators were thorough, but he felt confident that he had managed to stick to his story and also to persuade them of his anti-Russian credentials. The Jewish moneylender and the mysterious Mr Goldman were in all likelihood invented to play upon the Gestapo's visceral anti-Semitism, though it is unlikely that they added much weight to Seth's story. Seth felt that the Gestapo was keen to convey the impression that they were 'humane, understanding, highly intelligent and cultured people', and he did his best to keep them on this road by flattering them. Unfortunately, he rather spoilt the effect by insisting that he had been tortured by the Gestapo in Tallinn. His interrogators hotly denied this, insisting that his torturers were members of the former Estonian secret police whom the Gestapo had recruited.[11]

A week after the interrogation had concluded, Schmidt visited Seth in prison. He told him that he had been given the job of preparing Seth's case for consideration in Berlin, that he had compared his two statements and could find no discrepancies, and that Seth either had a phenomenally good memory or was telling the truth. Seth insisted that he was telling the truth. Schmidt said that he was inclined to believe him, and wanted to help him; was there not anything Seth himself could add that would convince Berlin of the sincerity of his offer to do anything against the Russians? He handed over a sheaf of paper and writing materials, and said he would return again after the weekend.

Seth now busied himself with what he did best, the spinning of fantasies. He concocted a description of a fictitious Convoy Timing Department at the Admiralty, claiming as his source an old Cambridge friend Charles Fletcher-Cooke, who was actually in Naval Intelligence; a description of the construction of invasion barges on the Forth, which were subsequently dismantled and reassembled in South coast ports in order to deceive reconnaissance aircraft; and a character study of Churchill in private life, drawn from Seth's claimed personal acquaintance with the Prime Minister.

'When I had finished these accounts, I still had one foolscap page left over. Being loath to return a blank sheet, I wrote something like the following.'[12] The tale he now spun really hit the high spots. It begins in the Dorchester Hotel, where Seth, being at a loose end, attended a Sunday afternoon thé dansant. Here he got into conversation about the war with some other RAF officers at the bar, and was heard to say that, had Edward remained king, there would have been no war. A few minutes later, he was approached by an unknown man who invited him to dine with him at his chambers in Gray's Inn the following Tuesday. Taking this for normal hospitality towards a member of the armed forces, Seth accepted the invitation.

The only other guest at the dinner party is named as Admiral Usborne, the inventor of the paravane and the pom-pom gun. This must be Vice Admiral Cecil Vivian Usborne (1880–1951), an expert in gunnery who invented an early version of the paravane and rapid-fire pom-pom anti-aircraft gun. Usborne was appointed Director of Naval Intelligence in 1931, but was obliged to resign from that post in the aftermath of the Invergordon mutiny. In 1941, he was recalled from retirement for 'special services' at the Admiralty; in other words, he was working in naval intelligence.

Seth claimed that his host was Charles Fearnley-Whittingstall, KC. The only King's Counsel of that name was William (Bill) Arthur Fearnley-Whittingstall, who, according to an obituary notice in 1959, had joined up in 1939 at the age of 37, in spite of a debilitating lameness, and had spent some four years in the Far East with his regiment.[13] Seth was clearly following the advice given during training to base any story on real events or people; why he should have chosen these two particular individuals is, however, something of a mystery.

During dinner, talk turned to the ex-king, and Seth was asked to explain what he had meant by his utterance at the Dorchester:

> I replied that I believed HRH to be a man of action with great sympathy for the worker, that he was, if one could apply the term to a monarch, a socialist, and it was because he intended to become more than a Constitutional monarch and work to relieve the lot of the worker, that fearing him, the Jewish industrialists had forced him to abdicate.

He had heard that when visiting Germany, 'HRH' had shown sympathy with and appreciation of the National Socialist regime. Had he remained king, Seth believed, the question of colonies could have been readjusted and Britain and Germany could have collaborated economically.

Fearnley-Whittingstall then revealed that he had been making enquiries about Seth since Sunday, and had learnt that his family were traditional pages to the king, and that Seth himself was a personal friend of 'HRH'. This background and the nature of Seth's answers to questions about the Duke of Windsor convinced his host and the admiral that he was a suitable person to enter their secret organisation, and to conduct quiet propaganda amongst his fellow officers in the search for further suitable members. The purpose of the organisation was to prepare the way for a British republic. When the time was ripe, there would be a coup, King George VI would be forced to abdicate, and his brother would return in triumph as president of this new republic.

Seth accepted the invitation, and during 1942 attended various meetings of the League at Fearnley-Whittingstall's chambers at which various luminaries were present, including Sir Stafford Cripps, Dingle Foot MP, Lord Brabazon of Tara, the former Under-Secretary of State for Air, and Field Marshal Lord Birdwood. The latter is the only person for whom there is evidence of personal acquaintance with Seth. Field Marshal Birdwood was Master of Peterhouse between 1931 and 1938, and wrote in 1935 a kindly letter to the departed undergraduate wishing him luck with his new career under the Home Office.[14]

In his book, Seth frankly admitted that the Republican League was a complete fabrication and he offered the famous men he named a sincere apology. In the unpublished accounts, the secret organisation is called the Windsor League, and its aim is unambiguously the restoration of the Duke of Windsor as head of state. By 1952, the duke had been prudently airbrushed out of the picture once Seth had said his piece at the Dorchester.[15]

Why did Seth concoct such a story? He had been out of England during the abdication crisis, and seems not to have mixed much in the kind of circles where gossip about the duke's alleged pro-Nazi sympathies might circulate. The persons named as members of the League were in all likelihood plucked from the air; none as far as I can ascertain had any close association with the duke, or any desire to see the monarchy overthrown. The answer may well lie in Seth's response to Captain Milton in 1945: he had had no long-term plan, but the story could not be checked and was likely to interest the Germans. Seth clearly thought that the Germans were innate snobs, and that the best way to worm his way into their confidence was to make out that he had close connections in high places. By his own account, Schmidt maintained that he had been able to make a 'good thing' of the Windsor story. Yet nothing seems to have come of this. As Milton drily observed, the lack of any further detailed interrogation on the League which 'if it were true ... would give them a superb opportunity for fifth-column activities' would suggest that Seth invented 'the whole incident for our benefit'.[16]

Seth was in fact left hanging in limbo after his interrogation. Visits from the sympathetic Schmidt became infrequent and then suddenly ceased. Seth's pleas to be made use of became increasingly desperate. At one stage, he tells us, imprisonment and hunger affected his mental state to such an extent that he wrote to Schmidt offering him two wireless codes he had invented in exchange for cream cakes. His physical condition was also deteriorating. During the summer, his toes damaged by frostbite in Estonia started to fester and his legs swelled up. No sooner had the swelling abated in September than he was afflicted by an outbreak of carbuncles on his right leg.

To make matters worse, the sentence of death hanging over his head was once more revived. There are discrepancies in the dates – 21 June in the 1944 account, late August or early September during his interrogation in 1945, end of July or early August in 1952 – but according to Seth, he was brought before a People's Court and sentenced to death for high treason against the Reich. Suppressing a desire to utter patriotic cries, and suspecting that this might in fact be a Gestapo trick, Seth replied through the interpreter that he had never committed any hostile action against the German people, state or Führer, but had on the contrary offered his services to Germany. This cut no ice with the court, and he was returned to his cell.

It is unlikely that Seth was sentenced to death in such a manner. Although the restoration in 1934 of the legislation governing military justice allowed the Nazi regime to build up a system which in practice offered 'unlimited possibilities' for military lawyers to proceed against internal and external enemies, enemy agents were not generally dealt with by People's Courts.[17] Nor is there much reason to suppose that the Gestapo would stage such an elaborate charade merely to trick their prisoner. Given the poor state of Seth's physical and mental health during the summer of 1943, it is more than likely that the court scene was the product of an overheated imagination.

In the event, nothing more was heard from the court. In early November, Seth received a visit from an army captain, called Dr Gustav Schumann in 1944, but Wilhelm or Walter Gunther in later accounts. The captain told Seth that he was no longer a prisoner of the Gestapo but was being transferred to the Wehrmacht for court martial in Torgau early in 1944. This captain appears to be some sort of defence counsel in the 1944 account, for the two of them discuss the line of defence to be adopted. The captain held out little hope for Seth, whom the high command in Berlin held responsible for the first German retreat from Kharkov in 1943:

> You remember that scrap of paper you gave to the Staff in Riga? We had in the
> Baltic States 2 Infantry Divisions and one Armoured Division, which it was

planned to move to the Charkov sector in preparation for the forthcoming spring offensive. Owing to your scrap of paper and a certain liveliness in Leningrad it was decided to hold these divisions in the Baltic States. The Russians attacked earlier than was expected at Charkov and we had to retreat. Nothing materialised on the Leningrad front. The Staff contends that if these divisions had been on the Charkov sector they would have swayed the balance. I am afraid they don't like you.[18]

This is either the pinnacle of Seth's career as double agent, or a rather fanciful invention by the officer deputed to defend Seth in court – or else it is another tall story out of Seth's inexhaustible locker. The Germans had indeed been compelled to retreat on the Kharkov front early in 1943 before vastly superior Soviet forces. However, the Soviet victory also over-extended their forces, thereby allowing von Manstein to stage a brilliant counter-attack in mid-February, capturing Kharkov in what the Germans termed the Donets campaign. The German victory at this, the third battle of Kharkov, was arguably the last major success of the Wehrmacht on the Eastern Front, a temporary compensation for the recent disaster at Stalingrad.

As it turned out, Seth was not to be executed or sent to Torgau to face trial before the *Reichskriegsgericht*, though a gloomy prison doctor told him that his blood was so bad that only a special diet and fresh air could cure him, and that without these he was unlikely to last until his trial. On 8 or 9 November, however, Schmidt suddenly turned up with good news. A good friend of his in Paris thought he would be able to make use of Seth. After a nail-biting wait of several days – for the trip to the French capital was made conditional on the military authorities not intervening to demand Seth's trial – he was collected from the prison and, accompanied by Commissar Büth and Schmidt, set off by train for Paris.

❖ ❖ ❖

Seth had been imprisoned in the Remand Prison for almost ten months. When he first entered the prison, the battle of Stalingrad was reaching its decisive climax. German forces were about the experience their first major defeat on the continent of Europe. By the time he left for Paris, the tide of war in Europe had begun to turn. The Allied forces had cleared North Africa of German and Italian troops and invaded Sicily in July. Three weeks later, Mussolini was forced to resign. Italy surrendered in September as Allied troops began landing on the Italian mainland. American and British bombers launched massive air raids on major German cities, such as Hamburg, devastated by a firestorm at the end of July. The central districts of Frankfurt-am-Main were attacked at the beginning of October, an event in which Seth found himself wandering around the basement of the jail and discovering an open door leading to the street (the parlous state of his legs and a bomb blast from the street itself put paid to any hopes of escape, however).

Back in London, there had also been significant changes in SOE. The organisation was now much larger, its activities far more diverse. As SOE got into its stride and agents began returning from abroad, security became a matter of great concern. General security, which looked after non-operational issues such as vetting, supervision of training schemes and travel, had already been given a solid administrative structure. Operational security was to encounter rather more difficulties. What became known in 1943 as the Special Security Section, or more colloquially Bayswater on account of its location, constantly ran into difficulties with the country sections of SOE, which defended and protected their agents and were loath to accede to the demand that Bayswater interrogate them first on their return to Britain. Relations with MI5, initially cordial, also became strained. Whereas SOE retained a loyalty to their agents, MI5 tended to regard with suspicion all who returned to Britain in questionable circumstances.[19]

It was to the Security Section that the Air Section of SOE (D/AIR) reported at the end of April 1943 that they were afraid that photographs of impounded German documents from an air crash inside Swiss territory 'concerns us'. The summary of these documents left no doubt that the agent interrogated — a 32-year-old former English teacher in Tallinn, parachuted into Estonia from a Halifax aircraft on 24 October 1942 at around 2330 hours — was Blunderhead. Every effort was now devoted to finding out what Seth might have divulged under interrogation. Stockholm was alerted and warned that the Germans might seek to send false messages to an address in the Swedish capital given to Seth before his departure. Although no signal had been received from the radio set, possibly because it had been damaged, the Germans might still repair it and send messages on the proper wavelengths and frequencies, reported Wiskeman to the Security Section on 3 May. Although an instruction was sent to maintain a permanent listening watch, it soon became clear that Station 52 believed that after such a lapse of time it was very unlikely that the enemy would use the set, even presuming that they had captured the set and Seth's signal plan. The listening watch was finally abandoned a couple of weeks later.

There remained the awkward question of what to tell Seth's wife, and the Air Ministry which had seconded him. SOE did not want Mrs Seth asking embarrassing questions at the Air Ministry, which had not been informed that Seth was a casualty, on the grounds that this would blow the cover of D/AIR's informant. After much humming and hawing, it was felt that the best course of action would be to say nothing at all to the Air Ministry and agree to 'Mrs Blunderhead's request that she may tell her friends that Mr B is missing'.[20] The note was written on Air Ministry paper, and sent to Assistant Section Officer Josephine Seth, stationed at RAF Exeter.

How to deal with the missing agent not only had security implications: salary and possible pension payments were also affected. From mid-October 1942, Seth had been paid £750 a year, tax free. He had been advised by Hazell to have a portion of this paid into a separate bank account, with his wife receiving the rest plus allowances. Wiskeman thought that such an arrangement had been made, but SOE had no knowledge of the precise details. In the midst of SOE discussions about how to handle matters from a security perspective, the D/FIN.A of the Finance Section fired off a rather exasperated letter to D/AIR, complaining that they had paid the full pay beyond the customary twenty-eight days of notification of a casualty, and drawing attention to the usual procedure for the paying of reduced allowances to the wives of missing armed forces personnel, which D/AIR.A now proposed to follow. He asked if the section might be informed before 20 October whether any further casualty action was to be taken with regard to this officer. If not, he would no doubt be presumed killed, and it would then be up to the Air Ministry to take up the matter with the Ministry of Pensions to provide a pension for his widow. This prompted a telephone call from Hazell, in the presence of Wiskeman, and a follow-up letter telling D/AIR.A that payment on the present basis should continue till further notice, certainly until death had been proved, and asking him to make up the balance of the August pay to Mrs Seth.

Although SOE was keen to keep the Air Ministry in the dark, it does appear that there was some liaison with Wing Commander R. Burges of the Casualty Branch, whose loose minute of 21 June invited SOE to consider which parts of a calendared procedure for missing persons, from the Air Council letter of condolence to the Royal message of sympathy, would be appropriate. SOE managed to avoid further awkward questions until the end of 1943, when Burges returned to the matter of procedure. SOE had been unwilling to go beyond informing the wife that her husband was missing and that no further news had been received. Their grounds for doing so were outlined in the response to Burges. Seth was 'not in the ordinary sense an RAF casualty', which meant that the usual channels for ascertaining the fate of a missing airman were not available to SOE. As a consequence, SOE was unable to say with reasonably certainty whether or not a missing agent could be presumed dead.[21]

After the writing of this letter, the Seth case seems to lie on file until the end of July 1944, when Group Captain Burges writes to the War Casualties Department with the information that 68308 Flight Lieutenant Seth, RS has now been reclassified as killed on active service on 24 October 1942. The War Casualties Department is to take any action necessary, noting that Seth had been paid 'from other than RAF funds', and that it was desired to cease payment 'from other than RAF funds' with effect from 1 August. Mrs Seth, now Section Officer at RAF Compton Bassett in Wiltshire, was unofficially told of her husband's demise, but the official notification was not to make any mention of the date of his death. Ronald Hazell, now holding the rank of lieutenant colonel, informed Mrs Seth privately on 19 July of this decision. Mrs Seth, who had been in correspondence with Hazell since October 1942, and who had come to regard him as a friend, replied that although she knew it had to come some time, it was still a shock; however, it did not change her belief that Ronnie was still alive.[22] What lay behind this decision to declare Seth dead is not clear. The captured German documents revealed that he was alive and in captivity at the beginning of 1943. SOE had received no further evidence as to his fate, so the reclassification of Seth as killed in action was either based on an assumption that captured agents were invariably executed, or was simply prompted by a bureaucratic desire to shift the responsibility for payment to another department.

Ironically, the next document in sequence on the file is a letter dated 7 August 1944, just as Mrs Seth was presumably coming to terms with the reported death of her husband. This is the letter that accompanied the handwritten report delivered to Air Commodore Jones in his Paris hotel at the end of August. Addressed to the General Officer Commanding STS HQ, Room 98, Horse Guards, Whitehall, and signed Ronald Seth, it began 'I hope you will forgive my asking this very great favour, but if my operation has so far been successful in your opinion, please could you possibly apply for my promotion to the rank of: Acting Group Captain (unpaid), with seniority retrospective twelve months from the date of this letter?'[23] Seth was making this request so that if anything should happen to him in the succeeding months, his wife and children would at least have a reasonable pension on which to live. Although Major Hazell had assured him that the Organisation would provide £1,000 for his children in the event of his death, £1,000 would not be sufficient to provide the kind of education for his son and daughter that Seth would wish them to have.

Just as SOE had finally agreed to admit that their agent was dead, then, he suddenly reappeared, but in circumstances almost as frustrating and tantalising as his original disappearance, and with the same irritating tendency (in SOE eyes) of asking for promotion. What had Seth been doing in Paris over the past months? And what was he doing now, after the liberation of Paris?

Notes

1. Desk instruction book of Tallinn Central Prison. ERA.R–264.1.167.
2. Camp records, however, have 'Sabotage-Mann' Flight Lieutenant Seth arriving from Riga on 16 January. German Federal Archives, Military Division. BaMa. RL 23/97.
3. Report 44, p.19. Seth 2008, p.139. Seth's description of living conditions and the rations issued conforms to the report of the American Intelligence Service, November 1945. www.486th.org/ Photos/Stammlager/KU3738/DulagLuft.htm.
4. Report 44, p.19.
5. Copies of the intercepted report in HS9/1344 and HS4/240.
6. Seth 2008, p.146.
7. Seth may have misspelled this name. According to the evidence of Emil Kliemann, the man who interrogated him was Wirth, and a *Hauptmann* Wirth is known to have subsequently deserted to Spain via France, KV2/378. Geck 2008, p.139.
8. Report 44, p.19.
9. Seth 2008, pp.160–1. Diamant 1988, pp.310–21 for details of the personnel.

10. TLA. 148/1/10. To put this in perspective, the Seths were paying 85 crowns a month rent, and his salary was around 150 crowns: no wonder he worked sixteen hours a day! Seth 1939, pp.207–8.
11. Report 44, pp.21–2.
12. Seth's Peterhouse contemporary Charles Fletcher-Cooke rose to the rank of lieutenant commander in the RNVR during the war, and entered Parliament in 1951 as Conservative MP for Darwen. Report 44, pp.22–3.
13. Notice by J.F. W-W, *The Times*, 4 November 1959.
14. Letter of 19 October 1935, Peterhouse Archives.
15. Report 44, pp.22–3 for the 'Windsor League', Seth 2008, pp.175–7 for the 'Republican League'.
16. MI5 report 3, p.13.
17. Bauman and Koch 2008, p.145.
18. Report 44, p.26.
19. Murphy 2006, p.97.
20. Memo of 12 June 1943, HS9/1344.
21. Letter to Wing Commander Burges, 13 December 1943, HS9/1344.
22. Josephine Seth to Hazell, 21 July 1943, HS4/240.
23. Personal and confidential, Paris, August 7 1944, HS9/1344.

8 | 'For me, "practical love" is a physical necessity.'

Paris, March 1944

Seth and his two companions arrived at night in Paris. Having spent a year as a prisoner either in Germany or in a part of the world where the natives were less hostile to their current occupiers than to their former ones, he was now in a country with a real resistance movement, which received significant support from SOE. Now entering its fourth year of German occupation, France was no longer a possible springboard for invasion of Britain, but a prime target for an Allied assault, as the war decisively turned against the Axis powers in Europe. Why then had Ronald Seth been plucked from a German prison, where he was apparently languishing under sentence of death, and transferred to Paris?

What his future role was to be was revealed that night of 15 November 1943, when a 'round-shouldered, bleary-eyed man' who had been supposed to meet them was finally rounded up by Commissar Büth and introduced to Seth as Dr Kilburg, deputy chief of the Luftwaffe section of the espionage division of the Abwehr, the German secret service in Paris.[1] Instead of going to prison, Seth and his companions were driven to the Hotel Monsigny, near the Opera, where rooms had been booked for three nights. Some time later, Schmidt told him confidentially that it was Kilburg's intention to train him up and send him to England as an agent. On the afternoon of Wednesday 17 November, Kilburg drove Seth to Neuilly, an outer suburb to the north-west of Paris. Here he was to live, in a rather dilapidated furnished villa, 73 rue de Longchamp, for the next six months.

Hitherto, we have had to rely on Seth's own accounts for details of his story. Now, however, there is other evidence derived from the post-war interrogations of captured German officers and French collaborators. Richard Delidaise, for example, held as a collaborator, told Major Wall-Row of MI5 at the end of September 1944 that on 15 November 1943, the day Seth arrived in Paris, Dr Kilburg had come to see him to ask if he would keep a young British airman whom the Germans were thinking of using. Kilburg promised to provide the airman with an ID card so that he could move freely about the city. Also interrogated in the autumn of 1944, Wolfgang Krause-Brandstetter was able to provide corroborative evidence of the German intention to use Seth as an agent. As a fluent English speaker – Krause-Brandstetter had worked as a representative of the German publishers Tauchnitz in the United States during the 1930s – he was charged with interviewing Seth to sound out his reliability, should German intelligence decide to use him as an agent in England.

Having listened to Seth's story, Krause-Brandstetter was unable to form a clear judgement as to his reliability. He learnt later that Berlin had turned Seth down. As we have seen in the previous chapter, the powers-that-be in Berlin were less enamoured of Seth's abilities than were his interlocutors in Riga and Frankfurt. Why then did people such as Schmidt and his new acquaintance, the dilatory Dr Kilburg, seem to take such trouble over him?

Part of the answer to this question may lie in the convoluted internal politics of the German intelligence service. In a service deeply riven by personal and departmental rivalries, there was ample scope for pet projects in which a precious commodity such as an enemy agent willing to be turned received considerable protection, even against the demands of faraway Berlin. Moreover by 1943 the Abwehr was beginning to put out feelers for a negotiated peace settlement that would involve getting rid of Hitler, the withdrawal of German forces from occupied territories in the West, and an alliance against Russia. A man who boasted of his connections with members of the British establishment – as Seth had done in Frankfurt – and seemed to be eager to offer his services was therefore worth cultivating.

According to Seth's handwritten account, he was passed on to Paris thanks to personal connections within the German military hierarchy.

A certain Captain 'Fritz', whom he had met at Dulag Luft in Oberursel had subsequently been transferred to the Luftwaffe section of the Abwehr in Paris. This man was the Luftwaffe Captain Wierck, or Wirth. Büth got wind of this, contacted 'Fritz', who managed to persuade his chief and close friend to take Seth under his wing. 'Dr Kilburg', however, testified that it was the group leader of the Luftwaffe section within the Abwehr in Berlin, Major Brede, who sent Seth to Paris after his interrogation in Oberursel by a Captain Wirth.

Dr Kilburg was one of several aliases used by Major Emil Kliemann. A Viennese businessman before the war, Kliemann had been posted at the beginning of the occupation to Paris, a city in which he was amply able to indulge his love of women and café life. Seth described him as blotchy faced, a heavy spirits drinker, erratic, excitable and temperamental. A typewritten list of German agents in the Paris region, dated May 1944, notes that Major Emil Kliemann, alias Dr Kilburg, alias von Carstaedt, was believed to have been promoted *Leiter* of the Luftwaffe intelligence section (1L) of the Paris Abwehr in June 1943, and to have been appointed head of the 1L Kommando recently formed as part of the Abwehr's emergency organisation in the West.[2]

According to Richard Delidaise, Kliemann was 'far from being 100 per cent Nazi, rather the reverse, 100 per cent Austrian from the South'.[3] In further support of this assertion, Delidaise claimed that, although Seth had been sent to live with his family for only three weeks, he ended up staying with them in Neuilly, and from April 1944, in Enghien-les-Bains, for seven and a half months, in spite of the fact that the Gestapo in Frankfurt kept demanding his immediate return.

Kliemann seems to have been very much attached to his mistress in Paris, Yvonne Delidaise, with whom he lived in some style at 2 villa Boileau, near the Bois de Boulogne. He admitted to his British interrogators in the autumn of 1944 that he had had no intention of returning to headquarters in Wiesbaden when ordered to do so in August. He set off three times, returning to Yvonne each time, and finally going into hiding with her in Bougival, to the west of the capital, where the couple were eventually picked up by the French security forces set up at the liberation, the FFI (Forces françaises de l'intérieur). Yvonne was the sister of Richard. The children of a French father and German mother, Anna Brening, they spent their early years in Germany, settling in France in 1919. Their father seems to have disappeared from the scene at an early stage. In 1930, the mother married an American, William Stebbins, but that marriage ended in divorce in 1938. By her own account, Yvonne lived mostly in Germany, returning to Paris in August 1939. She was introduced to Kliemann in July 1940 by her brother's wife Louise, nicknamed 'Love', who claimed she had met him by chance in the street. According to Yvonne, Richard became involved with Kliemann after he was demobbed from the army in August 1940.

Richard's version differs from that of his sister in some particulars. He claimed that during the retreat in spring 1940, he was captured by the Germans and used as an interpreter, but then was incarcerated in the notorious Cherche-Midi prison, from which he was rescued by Kliemann, who engaged him as a driver and interpreter. Interrogated by the British, Richard Delidaise said that his mother had been expelled from France in 1938 for not having her papers in order, but was denied work in Germany and accused of spying for France in order to put pressure on him. His decision to work for the Gestapo was partially to facilitate her return to France, as well as to render service to his country by providing information. He learnt Morse and radio construction, and was asked to teach Morse after refusing to go to Spain as a radio agent. In August 1944, he managed successfully to hide from the FFI and find temporary protection with the Americans, though he was eventually handed over to French justice.

The sudden change of circumstances dramatically improved Seth's health. From a weight of 53kg at the time of his arrival in Paris in November, he jumped to 83kg by the beginning of January. He also acquired a mistress. This lady, referred to as 'Thérèse Lupin' in his book, was the sister of Richard Delidaise's wife Louise. 'A strikingly beautiful woman, dark, chic, and not unlike the femme fatale of spy fiction', in Seth's words, a 'woman of loose morals' in the opinion of MI5, Liliane Renggli (as she is known in Seth's unpublished accounts) had a colourful past.[4] Married at the age of 15, and divorced five years later, she had been arrested at the outbreak of the war on suspicion of being a German spy. Released through lack of evidence, she made her way to Paris, where she was drawn into the shady world of the black market. In a British secret service report complied in October 1944, her maiden name is given as Lucienne Liliane Beucherie, living in a flat at 3 rue Lincoln, in a fashionable quarter just off the Champs Elysées. Here she lived with her lover, Jean Soulier, and his mother. The couple were heavily involved in the coffee black market, and when they got into trouble with the authorities, they were helped out by sergeant 'Hubi' Brening, the uncle of Richard and Yvonne Delidaise. The helpful 'Hubi' was according to the report in receipt of Liliane's favours; Seth became 'second string' some time in 1944, and was succeeded by a Spanish barman named Pepito, with whom Liliane was arrested by the FFI, after having been denounced by Mme Soulier. Jean, described as playing the role of 'l'ami complaisant', had managed to join the Free French troops under general Leclerc, though he too was to fall under suspicion as a collaborator.

In his published account Seth says that Kliemann gave him the cover name of Georg Heydt, and warned him never to reveal his true name and nationality, for the resistance would not hesitate to kill him if they learnt he was working for the Germans. Kliemann clearly did not follow his own advice: under interrogation, his mistress, Yvonne Delidaise revealed that he had told her 'Ronny' was a British officer arrested by the Gestapo, and that Kliemann had personally intervened to save him from being shot. According to Yvonne, Seth had been propositioned by the Gestapo in Frankfurt, but had refused to collaborate.[5]

A more elaborate cover story was provided for Seth by Major Kliemann. He was given a new wardrobe and a generous allowance of 2,000 francs a week, and issued with an identity card in the name of Sven Paasikivi. Sven was supposedly a nephew of the Finnish politician (and post-war president) J.K. Paasikivi. His father had been a diplomat in London, and Sven himself had been educated at Cambridge University, which accounted for his strong English accent. This cover story seems to have been just as ineffective as that for 'Georg Heydt', for Seth was generally known as 'Ronny' in the Delidaise ménage, which consisted of Richard and his wife 'Love', the maid Suzanne, her lover and odd-job man Pierre Lapandry and an ancient Italian cook known as 'la vieille Mimi'. An Alsatian bitch called Siegfried (*sic*) and the elderly owners of the house, who lived in the attic, completed the household at 73 rue de Longchamp.

Initially, Seth was not allowed out of the house unaccompanied, but on Christmas Eve, Kliemann announced that he had won his confidence, and could henceforth be treated as a free man. Seth was allowed to travel freely and unaccompanied about the city. A publisher's note to his translation of Ovid's *Ars Amatoria* claimed that Seth had worked as a British agent for the Luftwaffe, and 'to cover certain activities', he let it be known that he was translating this work, and even visited the Bibliothèque Nationale for this purpose.[6] He was supposed to retreat to his room whenever a visitor came to the villa in Neuilly, but even this rule was relaxed.

The laxity with which Seth was guarded reached new heights in the days after Christmas 1943. Kliemann and Richard Delidaise went off to Haute Savoie, ostensibly to check up on agents there, but in all probability to enjoy themselves, for they were accompanied by Yvonne and Louise. The maid and her lover were also given leave to absent themselves, leaving only the old cook. After an hour, she presented herself to Seth, dressed in her outdoor clothes, and declaring she could not stand the house or the people in it any longer, she stormed out. Left alone, apart from the elderly couple in the attic, who seem to have remained out of the way for much of Seth's sojourn, Ronny repaid the hospitality and kindness of his hosts by ransacking the house to see what he could find. In his published account, Seth claimed that this search proved very fruitful, giving him the chance to study Delidaise's radio code books and other secret documents. His August 1944 statement, however, says that everything that might have had significance for a secret agent was locked away, except for a revolver and a box of .22 ammunition. This gave him the idea of shooting a German soldier during the rush hour at the Étoile station. Here, he pressed his small revolver into the back of a suitable victim, fired and vanished into thin air with the crowd, returning five minutes later to find that the man was dead. He then returned to Neuilly, and tried to kill another German soldier, but with less success, for his victim's companion saw him, shouted and fired, hitting him in the right buttock.

Captain Milton, not surprisingly, dismissed this story, and Seth does not relate it in his published version of events – or rather, he tells a different story. Here, he goes to a cinema in Paris and on returning to the Pont de Neuilly metro station, encounters a German soldier who he thought was either mad or drunk. Without the least provocation, the soldier drew his revolver and fired at Seth, who felt a sharp pain in the buttock. Seth managed to run into the rue de Longchamp, and slip into a small café, where he drank a couple of cognacs. When he came to pay, he discovered that his trousers were soaked in blood. Back at the villa, he went into the bathroom to examine his injury, which turned out to be slight, though he was bleeding profusely. As he was sitting on the edge of the bath, or in the bath – his unpublished accounts differ on points of detail – events took a fateful turn. He suddenly heard Liliane, who had presumably come to the villa during his absence, asking him what was the matter:

I said I had had an accident. Unperturbed by my state of complete nakedness, she staunched the flow with eau de cologne and dressed the wound. Then she proceeded [*sic*] me back to the salon. I suddenly remembered my bloody clothes lying on the floor. It was too late to do anything. As Liliane picked up my trousers the revolver fell out. She picked it up and examined the chambers. 'Two,' she said and I was glad she asked me no more questions. She washed my shirt and pants, cleaned and mended my trousers and my overcoat, while I cleaned the revolver and reloaded. I was running a temperature, so she put me to bed and stayed with me the night. Just before I went to sleep, she said: 'There is something, Ronnie. For every German killed like that, the Germans kill ten Frenchmen.' I decided that the price was too dear.[7]

From that moment, Seth told MI5, a relationship grew between him and Liliane. In his earlier, August 1944 account, he felt compelled to justify his 'somewhat unagentlike behaviour'. For him, practical love was a physical necessity; and at that time, he was mentally desperately in need of some 'mondane [sic] contact' to make his world seem real. The strain of playing a role, twenty-four hours a day, when 'the slightest mal-movement, of voice, body or eyes meant, not the hisses of the gods, but the swish of a sword', of having not only to listen to enemy propaganda, but also to agree with it, all told on his nerves. The liaison with Liliane, he asserted, saved his reason and enabled him to go on with his mission. To his credit, Seth went to great lengths to portray Liliane as sincerely attached to the Allied cause, both in the late summer of 1944 and after the war had ended, when Liliane was in trouble with the French authorities.[8]

His liaison, however, aroused much opposition from the Delidaises, especially Louise, who appeared to be intensely jealous of her sister. Elsewhere in his story, Seth indirectly hints that one reason for this hostility was that Louise had attempted to seduce him during one of her husband's absences, but had been rebuffed. Seth found it easy to repel her advances, he says, because he had been told by Suzanne the maid that both the Delidaises were riddled with syphilis. In any event, Louise was offended by his refusal, and forced Seth to sign a written statement that he would never again see Liliane alone. He signed, but did not feel bound by this, seeing Liliane whenever he could at her apartment on rue Lincoln.

Given the murky world in which Liliane moved, Seth's liaison with her can only be described as naïve. He seems to have been aware of this, as his passionate justification of his 'unagentlike behaviour' shows. Although he was given a great deal of freedom to move about Paris, he does not appear to have made any attempt to establish contact with the French resistance (a point noted by the MI5 interrogators). His presence in the city therefore passed unnoticed by SOE or any branch of the secret intelligence service.

In his first days in Paris, Seth claimed that he was visited by his old acquaintance from the interrogation centre at Dulag Luft, Captain Wierck. Wierck (or Wirth) outlined the course of training Ronny, aka Georg Heydt, aka Sven Paasikivi was to receive. He was to be instructed in army, naval and air intelligence, the use of a wireless code, a meteorological code, and of secret ink. After completion of training, he would be put on board a German ship bound for Sweden and would then make his way to the British legation in Stockholm. His cover story would be that he had landed safely in Estonia, had found friends in Tallinn who had got him papers, had been picked up in a raid and sent to work in Germany, and had been put aboard a German ship to work as assistant steward (presumably with false Estonian papers, though this is not clear). The purpose of all this was to place Seth in Britain as a German agent, but there was one big question, how to smuggle a transmitter into Britain? Seth's answer was that, with the knowledge he already had, and supplied with a circuit, he would build one.

The training began in earnest in the new year. 'A very pleasant little Met. man named Kohler', with whom Seth had many long and interesting conversations on international politics and literature, taught him meteorology. The use of secret inks was taught by an irascible Luftwaffe captain, name unknown. Seth also had dealings with a young man of 32, *Oberleutnant der Flieger* Braun, who replaced Wierck at the end of January 1944. Braun claimed to have been up at Caius and Gonville whilst Seth was at Peterhouse, and he took Seth to dine with him at the Hôtel Claridge. 'He obviously intended to make me drunk, so that I would talk. In spite of my various vicissitudes I was glad to find that the hard head which membership of the Peterhouse Rowling [*sic*] Club had not weakened.'[9] After a bottle of red wine, a couple of bottles of champagne and two cognacs, it was Braun who talked. He revealed his real name was Brandstetter of Tauchnitz books, and that he hoped himself to go to England as an agent. Under interrogation by British intelligence officers in September 1944, Wolfgang Krause-Brandstetter (to give him his full name) admitted that he had broken the rules by revealing his real name to Seth when they dined together at the Hôtel Claridge, but he said nothing about training him after this meeting.

In Seth's opinion, Brandstetter was a most unsuitable person for his work. Officially based at the Hôtel Scribe, he also had a private flat at 83 avenue Niel, where he kept a French mistress, an actress named Madeleine. Seth visited him twice in this apartment, where they discussed Seth's mission in the presence of Madeleine, who knew English. Brandstetter also telephoned Neuilly and discussed codes with Seth. He disappeared early in March, and Seth did not see him again.

In March 1944, Richard Delidaise taught him how to transform a radio receiver into a transmitter, and how to wind bobbins to take the place of crystals. According to Delidaise, Seth was already fully trained as a wireless operator, and needed no further instruction in that skill. Seth even boasted in his August 1944 report that German agents were using two radio codes he had devised in prison in Frankfurt, and subsequently had given to the Gestapo.[10]

In April, the Delidaise ménage moved to a furnished villa in Enghien-les-Bains, some 18km north-west of Paris. The villa belonged to Emile Rivière, a young Frenchman who, according to Seth, had been a liaison officer with the British army in 1939–40, had subsequently been taken for compulsory labour in Germany and had been released through the intercession of Richard Delidaise. Rivière had returned to his former post at Radio-Paris. A neighbour in this leafy outer suburb of Paris, M. Carnot Brulin, also worked for Radio-Paris as a director of recording. Originally a commercial radio station, Radio-Paris had been nationalised in 1933, becoming one of three state-owned national radio stations. In 1940, a new Radio-Paris was set up under the control of the Propaganda Abteilung Frankreich. Generously funded, it was able to attract top entertainers such as Tino Rossi and Maurice Chevalier, who helped sugar the pill of propaganda delivered nightly by arch-collaborationists such as the poet Jean-Henri Azèma and the iniquitous Jean-Hérold Paquis.

'Curiously enough,' Seth wrote in April 1945, the Carnot Brulin family were 'noted anglo-philes', and he soon felt able to confide in them and Emile Rivière that he was English, 'because I thought the time might come when I might need assistance'.[11] That time came on 9 June. The Delidaises had gone to Paris, leaving Seth alone with the dog. This time he was successful in his efforts to locate Richard Delidaise's secret papers, thanks to

Richard's wife, who had entrusted him with the key to the cupboard where such documents were kept. Here he found the new radio code that had been issued in February, copied it on to tissue paper, which Mme Brulin helpfully stitched into the lining of his trusty storm jacket.

This code was copied out by Seth during his stay at the SS hospital later in the summer, and it subsequently found its way into the hands of MI5, thanks to Emile Rivière, the beaky-faced young man who appeared at Air Commodore Jones' hotel at the end of August. In a communication to London at the beginning of September, Seth had also stated that he had posted his manuscript to M. Carnot Brulin, but had made a mistake with the Paris post code and was worried that it might not have got through. The fact that the manuscript was delivered to the British authorities – and that these authorities could find nothing to suggest that Rivière at least had been a collaborator – would indicate that Seth had been right to place his trust in people employed by the prime agent of pro-German propaganda in Paris.

MI5 was, however, distinctly sniffy about Seth's account of how he managed to obtain Delidaise's radio code, and about the code itself. Captain Milton commented that, although Richard Delidaise was half-German, his first language was French 'and it is most unlikely that he would have made so many howlers in French when writing out this code. On the other hand, Seth's knowledge of French is very imperfect and the errors in the code seem to me those which an Englishman might make'.[12] Milton concluded that Seth might well have translated into French a code obtained either from the Abwehr for the purposes of his mission, or by transmitting through Delidaise's orders, and passing it off as a brand-new German code in order to obtain credit in London.

Whatever may have been the circumstances in which Seth acquired the code, it seemed at the beginning of May 1944 that he was fated not to make any use of his knowledge. He recounted how one day he was taken aside by Richard Delidaise and told that Kliemann's bosses in Berlin had decided not to use him; he was 'either a fanatic or a very good actor, and neither is any use for this work'.[13] Seth was to be handed back to the Reich military tribunal (*Reichskriegsgericht*), which, he surmised, would mean almost certain death. However, although he could do nothing more for him, Kliemann still had great confidence in his abilities, and had asked a friend in another service to do something for him. A gentleman would come to see him the following day to discuss matters.

This was confirmed by Emil Kliemann himself, though he claimed to have received a letter in January or February from Berlin, saying that Seth was not to be used as an agent as he was considered unsuitable. Kliemann also said that it was the head of the Abwehr in Paris, Colonel Friedrich Rudolph, who had ordered Seth's transfer to the army branch, 1H. Krause-Brandstetter also told his British interrogators that Kliemann had told him that Berlin had rejected Seth as unsuitable material, but that he was hoping that 1H, being less hidebound as Kliemann put it, would be able to make use of him.

The fair, good-looking young man who turned up to interview Seth introduced himself as Gall or Gahl. Seth did not know whether or not that was his real name, but he described him as being a member of the 'Auslands-Gestapo', which was responsible for supporting agents in enemy or occupied countries. Kliemann thought Gall was in fact *Unteroffizier* Schmitt of 1H. Seth may well have been confused over which part of the German secret service the young man belonged to, but there may also be a reason for this. At precisely this time, the Abwehr was in a state of terminal crisis. Long suspected of disloyalty to Hitler, matters came to a head at the end of 1943 with the unmasking of a resistance group in Berlin, the so-called 'Solf circle'. An Abwehr agent with close connections to this anti-Nazi group, fearing the worst if he obeyed the summons to return to Berlin, defected in Istanbul to the British. It was erroneously believed in Berlin that he had also revealed secret codes, and this led to a heated interview between Hitler and the head of the Abwehr, Admiral Canaris, on 14 February 1944. The admiral was dismissed, and later arrested and executed in the aftermath of the July bomb plot against the Führer. The Abwehr was taken over by Amt VI (SD-Ausland) of the SS-dominated Reich Security Head Office (*Reichssicherheitshauptamt*).

The man who came to see Seth, knowing which way the wind was blowing, may therefore very well have introduced himself as an officer of SD-Ausland. In any event, he assured Seth that he would be able to work something out, but that he could do so with absolute certainty if Seth could persuade a relative or friend in France to become a hostage for his good faith once he had reached England. Seth regretted that he knew of no one who might take on this risky burden. A couple of days later, however, much preoccupied with his thoughts, he was persuaded by Liliane to reveal what had happened. Liliane immediately volunteered to be the hostage:

'But,' I answered, 'You don't realise what you are saying. If I go to England it will only be a short time before the Germans find out I am double-crossing them. It means certain death for you. I can't accept'. 'Listen,' she replied, 'there is my side to it. If I do this for you at least and at last I shall have done something useful. I should be happy to die like that. Besides, this information you have – you must get it to England.'[14]

So wrote Seth in 1944. His story of Liliane's dramatic and selfless offer was substantially the same when he retold it to MI5 in the spring of 1945. He continued to have qualms about her safety, though he reasoned that if he could continue to deceive the Germans for at least another month, during which time 'the Organisation' (as he described it in 1944) could either get Liliane out of the country or at least hide her.

On this basis, therefore, Seth told the handsome young man that he had someone prepared to act as hostage. Two days later, he introduced Gall/Schmitt to Liliane. Much to his surprise, the German officer was apparently already acquainted with his lady friend. The two men met in Liliane's flat on the rue Lincoln every other day throughout the rest of May 1944. What they did there is not revealed in any of Seth's accounts. Gall/Schmitt said that his boss in Paris had agreed to accept Liliane as hostage, though she was not to be told of this in case she tried to escape. Seth said nothing to Liliane about any plans to smuggle her out of France, so as not to get her hopes up. But if after he had gone to England a man came up to her and said, '*je veux acheter de l'amour*' (I wish to buy love), this would be a signal that Seth had arrived safely in England. She was to reply, '*Le mien est libre*' (mine is free) and do all that the man told her to do.[15]

Left with this rather dubious password, under surveillance by the Gestapo, 'actively engaged for the cause of England and her Allies', as Seth wrote in his report a few weeks later, Liliane was to become one of the many thousands of Frenchwomen and men who needed all their wits to survive the collapse of the German occupation and the vengeful rafles of the FFI. For, as Gall/Schmitt claimed to be working on the final details of the operation, and that all being well, Seth would be on his way to England in a couple of weeks' time, the Allies landed on the beaches of Normandy.

On the eve of D-Day, Ronald Seth celebrated his 33rd birthday with a luncheon party arranged by Liliane. Chronic disruptions to the power supply meant that the Metro ran only sporadically, and when he attempted to return to Enghien-les-Bains, he was told that the Metro was shut and there would be no more trains out to the north-western suburbs. Still trying to keep his liaison with Liliane a secret, since it had incurred much jealousy and displeasure in the Delidaise household, he telephoned Richard Delidaise to say that he would be staying in Paris overnight with Gall/Schmitt. That evening, he had a brush with Liliane's protector, *Feldwebel* 'Hubi' Brening, and was obliged to turn him out of the apartment on the rue Lincoln. The following day, D-Day, 'Hubi' was back again, morose as ever. There was, however, an air of celebration around the dinner table. Mme Soulier, the mother of Liliane's quondam lover Jean, and an ardent anglophile in Seth's opinion, 'could not restrain her joy' and did not hesitate to express her hopes for liberation. Her indiscreet language must have been infectious, for when she apologised for the lack of oil for the salad dressing, Seth blurted out 'Never mind, when the British and Americans arrive in Paris, everything will be alright'.[16] Seth was later to attribute what happened to him next to his indiscretion, and the jealousy of the Delidaises, particularly 'Love'.

On 7 June, he was finally able to make his way back to Enghien-les-Bains. He seems to have considered joining up with the resistance or escaping back to England via the port of Brest, with the assistance of a French escape organisation, but nothing came of these plans, which Captain Milton described as 'half-hearted' at best. So he remained in the Delidaise household, with the stolen radio codes concealed in the lining of his storm jacket, Liliane his only consolation. On 13 June, two men came to 56 avenue de Ceinture to escort him to Paris. Thinking that Gall/Schmitt had finally managed to find him the flat he had been promised, he got the surprise of his life to find himself once more escorted to prison. Here, he was told that it was impossible to find a flat owing to the military situation, that he would be in prison three days at the most and would then be taken to Germany where final arrangements for his mission to England would be made. In the meantime, he was directed to write to Liliane a farewell letter which maintained the rather threadbare fiction that he was Sven Paasikivi, the Finn, who had been suddenly recalled to his regiment. He was to leave for Helsinki at midday. 'Forgive me, darling', he wrote, 'you know very well that no matter what happens I will return to look for you. I'll write soon and often. Don't worry, darling: I am very sure that everything will turn out as we want. I love you madly, terribly. René.'[17]

The prison in which Seth now found himself stood on a site now occupied by the Fondation Maison des Sciences de l'homme, at the junction of boulevard Raspail and the rue du Cherche-Midi. Built originally as a military prison in the mid-nineteenth century, it was used during the Occupation to house political prisoners. Seth, already a connoisseur of the prisons of Europe, considered the Cherche-Midi to be the worst in Europe. His cell, number 144, was alive with lice as big as the nail on his little finger, and within days, he was being driven mad with scabies. There were no bathing facilities, nor were any clean clothes issued to the prisoners. Rations were meagre in the extreme; watery soup and 200g of bread daily, washed down with ersatz coffee. Food parcels delivered fortnightly by the French Red Cross were a blessing, but consumed within three or four days. Prisoners were held in solitary confinement, though Seth did learn that there were several other Englishmen held there, including one poor unfortunate, an airman who had been there since 1940, who spoke no French or German, and was known, with good reason, as *l'homme oublié*.

Seth's case seemed hopeless once more. He told MI5 that after about a month, Gall/Schmitt came and reported that he could do nothing more for him. He was told he had been denounced to the Gestapo for his incautious remarks over dinner on 7 June, and he presumed that this had been the work of 'Hubi' Brening. Gall/Schmitt left the jail saying that Seth's case had been handed back to Dr Kilburg. Kilburg, or Emil Kliemann, seems also to have fallen out of favour – or perhaps the cloud of suspicion that hung over the Abwehr after its sudden dissolution had prompted the adroit Viennese bon viveur to seek shelter in a less exposed situation, for according to Richard Delidaise, he moved in June 1944 to the Passierscheinstelle, the office responsible for issuing permits and passes, which was located in a disused bank on the Champs Elysées.

Kliemann did eventually turn up at the Cherche-Midi at the end of July, accompanied by Kohler, the man from the Met. with whom Seth had had many long and interesting conversations during the spring. With Kohler acting as interpreter, Kliemann told Seth that for some unknown reason, Gall/Schmitt had cancelled his arrangements and Berlin was demanding Seth's return. He, however, still had faith in Seth, and was trying his very last chance: would Seth be prepared to speak to a gentleman he had brought along with him?

This is Seth's side of the story. Kliemann told a rather different tale. He told his interrogators that after the Allied invasion, 1H had approached him to say they did not want Seth, in whom they had no faith, and in any case, they saw no way in which they could now send him to England. 1H,

Felix Kopti, the Estonian sailor whose identity Seth was to assume. (Estonian State Archives)

The kitchen of Martin Saarne's cottage, Kiiu Aabla. (Author's collection)

Interior corridor, Tallinn Central Prison. (Author's collection)

Opposite top: The cottage of Martin Saarne's sister, Kiiu Aabla.
(Author's collection)

Opposite bottom: The path to the woods at the cottage in Kiiu Aabla.
(Author's collection)

Tallinn Central Prison. (Author's collection)

Opposite top: Former Gestapo Headquarters, Lindenstrasse 27, Frankfurt-am-Main. (Karsten 11)

Opposite bottom: Hotel Adlon, Berlin, where Seth lunched with the Under-Secretary of State at the German Foreign Office in March 1945. (Bundesarchiv)

SS *Oberführer* Walter
Schellenberg. (Bundesarchiv)

The Royal Victoria Patriotic
School, Wandsworth – MI5's
London Reception Centre
where Seth was interrogated in
1945. (Author's collection)

in other words, was trying 'to park the body back on 1L'. Deadlock was only resolved by a Colonel Garthe, who managed to arrange for Seth to be handed over to Christoph, Count Dönhoff.[18] This was the gentleman introduced to Seth by Kliemann, who later claimed that he had only gone to the Cherche-Midi to be present at the official handing over of his quondam agent to Dönhoff. Although sorry for Seth, he told his British interrogators, he was quite relieved to be free of the responsibility of having him on his hands.

Christoph, Count Dönhoff was born in 1906 in the ancestral family home, the castle of Friedrichstein in East Prussia. Trained as a lawyer, he had lived in Kenya for a number of years, and had possibly become active in the Organisation of the Nazi Party Abroad (Auslands-Organisation (AO) der NSDAP) during that time. In 1940, he was working in the colonial section of the AO in Berlin, headed by Michael Neuendorf, a former sheep farmer and Nazi Party activist in South-West Africa. In 1942, Neuendorf became head of the AO in Paris. Dönhoff also moved to the French capital, where he became the head of the section dealing with the registration and return of Germans to the Reich.

Whereas Christoph was a member of the NSDAP from at least the mid-1930s, his younger sister Marion earned a reputation as the 'red countess' in the years before the Nazi seizure of power in Germany. Marion went on to become one of the most celebrated writers of post-war Germany. She was a long-time editor and eventually publisher of the newspaper *Die Zeit*, and her memoirs of a Prussian childhood is a classic of modern German literature.

Despite their political differences, she seems to have been close to her elder brother, with whom she spent some time in Africa. How much he knew of her activities in the resistance to Hitler is an intriguing question. At the time he visited Seth in prison, news of the failed bomb plot against the Führer must have reached him, and he was probably well aware of his sister's involvement. She had been careful not to append her name to any incriminating document, and so was not arrested, but she had been for a long time under suspicion as an enemy of the regime, and that suspicion no doubt extended to members of her family as well.

Why at this fraught moment, with the Allied forces advancing on Paris, and his sister and acquaintances within the East Prussian aristocracy perilously exposed as opponents of the regime, did Dönhoff choose to pick up an enemy agent whom no one else seemed to want? Dönhoff was arrested and interrogated after the war, but attempts to trace his personal file at the National Archives have drawn a blank, and in all probability, it is one of the thousands later destroyed. It seems, however, that he was reluctant to talk about Seth, even claiming that he had had no dealings with him. From other interrogation records, however, it is possible to piece together a picture of his intentions, and of his connections. It seems clear that by the summer of 1944, Dönhoff was one of a growing group in the Nazi hierarchy who believed the war was lost, and that the only way out for Germany was to try and seek some sort of accommodation with the western Allies. Their principal bargaining chip was fear of communism. For an East Prussian aristocrat such as Christoph Dönhoff, his ancestral lands directly in the path of the advancing Red Army, some sort of alliance with the West to halt that advance was worth working for. In Seth, he undoubtedly found a sympathetic listener. The perceived threat of Russia had after all been a far greater driving force for Seth's actions than anything else. The first reason he gave when justifying his decision to work for Dönhoff was that it might afford him the chance to get his 'Russian information' to London by means of his letter code.

Seth was obviously impressed that Dönhoff was an aristocrat, and was no doubt flattered when Dönhoff made great play of honour between gentlemen – though Dönhoff did not fail to remind Seth that if he double-crossed the Germans, they had his lady friend as hostage, or that the alternative to cooperation was to be returned to military justice in Frankfurt. According to Seth, 'he told me that he was a member of the political service, who are anxiously working to try and find some way in which England and Germany can come to a better understanding after the war'. He had recently been interviewing British soldiers captured in Normandy with this end in view, but the men would not talk freely with him, so 'his idea was to put me in British uniform, send me from camp to camp to talk with the men'. After mulling the offer over, Seth agreed to the idea, reasoning that if he did not, some clever German would be assigned the task: he, at least, might be able to mislead the Germans.[19]

Three days later, 30 July, Seth was delivered from prison to the SS hospital overlooking the Bois de Boulogne to receive treatment for scabies and to recuperate from his incarceration. The hospital was housed in a large private house, with a pleasant garden, marred only by the barbed wire and defence works that had been thrown up. Seth paints a bizarre picture of the luxurious treatment he received at the hospital during the final days of the

German occupation of Paris. Dönhoff ensured that he had books, cigarettes, extra rations, and wine with his meals. With the 2,000 francs Dönhoff had given him, he was able to bribe the nurses to bring him extra cigarettes and newspapers, and to smuggle out a couple of letters to Liliane. As the Allied troops toiled in the heat of August through the Norman bocage, Ronald Seth spent his days lounging naked on a rug in the garden. When he was not in the garden, he was writing his report in a foolscap notebook. It seems incredible that he was able to write this highly incriminating report in an SS hospital, but with the fall of Paris a matter of days away, the hospital staff and SS personnel clearly had no time to spare in watching a scabby Englishman who spent his days lolling around in the sun.

Seth's report, written in his inimitable discursive style, amounted to sixty-one foolscap pages. He managed to bribe one of the nurses to post it to M. Carnot Brulin on 11 August. By now, the Germans were making preparations to evacuate Paris: orders to evacuate the city for eastern France were issued to military occupation staff on 13 August. On the evening of the 16th, Seth claimed he was invited to drink coffee in the garden with 'Dr Fritz'. He had hardly finished his first cup when he began to feel drowsy and only just managed to drag himself to his room before collapsing into a deep sleep. The following morning, he was awakened by Dönhoff and told that they must make haste, as they were leaving the city. The entire hospital had been evacuated during the night, and 'Dr Fritz' had slipped Seth a Mickey Finn to make sure he did not escape in the confusion. Ronald Seth's sojourn in Paris was about to come to a sudden end, and, instead of being liberated by the Allies, he was to find himself conveyed eastwards with the retreating German forces, to an unknown fate.

Notes

1. Seth 2008, p.191.
2. The list is in File HS7/138.
3. Interrogation of Richard Delidaise, October 1944, KV2/307.
4. Seth 2008, p.205. Report of 5 October 1944, Paris, HS9/1344.
5. Interrogation of Yvonne Delidaise, November 1944, KV2/307.
6. *Ovid's Art of Love*. A new prose translation by Ronald Seth. Spearman and Arco, London 1953. Review by Richard Bruère, Classical Philology, 49/4, 1954, pp.280–1. Bruère found the translation

readable and lively, but noted that any reader familiar with Ovid's Latin would soon be distressed by the infelicities and mistranslations that occurred on every page.

7. Report 44, p.29. Captain Milton, true to form, remarked that he would be very interested to see the scar on Seth's right buttock. The good captain seems not to have invited Seth to drop his trousers in order to verify the incident.

8. Report 44, p.31.

9. Report 44, p.30. In his book, this young man becomes Dr Krauss, a former student of King's.

10. Details of the two codes in Report 44, pp.34–7.

11. 'Germany counter-espionage 15 April 1945', pp.6–7, HS9/1345. Hereafter Bern report.

12. MI5 report 3. p.16.

13. Report 44, p.31.

14. Report 44, p.32.

15. Report 44, p.32.

16. MI5 report 2, p.47. Seth 2008, pp.213–5.

17. '*Pardonne-moi, chèrie. Sais bien que n'importe quoi arrive je reviendrai te chercher. J'ecriverai toute de suite et souvent. Ne t'enquietes pas, chèrie : je suis bien sûr que tout ira comme nous voulons. Je t'aime terriblement à la folie. René*' (Ronny's less than perfect farewell letter seems to ignore entirely the fiction that he was supposed to be Sven, returning to the fatherland to fight the Russians). Bern report, p.8, HS9/1945.

18. Interrogation of Emil Kliemann/HS2/378. Colonel Garthe was a *Leiter* of the Abwehr station in Lyon, and had previously been a *Leiter* of the Luftwaffe section of the Paris Abwehr, so was presumably well acquainted with Kliemann. British security noted that he had an English mother, and was said to be pro-British, HS7/138.

19. Report 44, p.33. Dönhoff is not named in the report: he is merely Graf von (blank), who had lived for ten years in Kenya and spoke perfect English.

9 | 'Lately I have been in a depressed state of mind.'

Oflag 79, Brunswick, October 1944

S eth and his aristocratic companion left Paris in some style, in a Bugatti. From a third-floor window of the hospital, Seth had watched the neighbouring houses being stripped of their fine contents, which were hastily loaded on board a convoy of lorries. Nets were then thrown over the stacks of furniture and pictures, and branches of nearby trees were torn off and woven into the netting as camouflage. The Bugatti joined one such convoy that proceeded south-eastwards out of the city. It was an odd assortment of vehicles, ancient and modern, trucks, requisitioned lorries and civilian cars. The faster vehicles drove ahead and after 50km waited for the slower section to catch up. By nightfall, they had reached the village of Soncourt-sur-Marne, and on the following day, headed eastwards for the spa town of Vittel. Here they spent the next week lodged in rooms on the sixth floor of the Hôtel Beau Site, which the Political Department of the Security Service (Sicherheitsdienst, SD) had commandeered.

Over these seven days the two men worked on plans to get Seth into a prisoner-of-war camp, his cover story and details of the kind of information he was meant to gather, and how he was to pass this information on to Dönhoff. Seth was provided with two cover stories, one for any German intelligence officers who might interrogate him, the other for the British officers he would mix with in the camp. To any inquisitive German, he was to make no mention of Estonia, and was to present himself as a desk-bound army officer who had volunteered for a special mission in March 1944 as a French-speaker. Parachuted into France as a liaison officer on a sabotage mission, he had been forced to go into hiding after the operation went wrong, and was captured on 28 August. He was to tell his fellow officers the true story of his activities until his imprisonment in Frankfurt. He had then managed to escape in an air raid on the prison, had stowed aboard a train bound for France, and with help from the French resistance had made his way from Verdun to Paris, where he had lived until the Allied invasion in June. He had subsequently joined up with resistance fighters in northern France and had been taken prisoner on 28 August as he was attempting to cross over into the British lines. He was to inform the Senior British Officer in the camp of his real name, but he was to be officially entered as Captain John de Witt – a suggestion made by Seth, who claimed that it was an old family name and would easily be recognised by his wife.

On 27 August, accompanied by two SS non-commissioned officers, Seth and Dönhoff set off in a couple of cars for a large POW transit camp in Châlons-sur-Marne. They arrive amidst scenes of chaos, with communications virtually non-existent. Eventually they learned that the camp had already been evacuated, so they set off the next day for another camp at Charleville, on the Belgian frontier. This camp too was in process of being evacuated and the party accompanied its German officers as far as Sedan. After further reconnoitring and hasty retreats, they holed up in the Hôtel de la Gare in Arlon, on the border of Belgium and Luxemburg.

Seth asked his MI5 interrogators to note that during this meandering trek through north-eastern France, he had been given plenty of opportunities to escape 'with 100% chances of success', though he was unable to explain why he did not take advantage of these opportunities, other than that he was 'working on a hunch'.[1] He was, however, able to fire off another, mercifully much shorter report from the Hôtel de la Gare, together with a note in French asking for it to be handed over to the first British or American officer who arrived in the town. This found its way to London, via SHAEF, at the end of September.

Seth's short report has a few snippets of recent information, but its central feature was the story told by the condemned Russian agent in the cell in Tallinn Central Prison about Russian plans to occupy Norway. This piece of information was relayed by Air Commodore Archie Boyle, the man with overall responsibility for intelligence and security matters at SOE, to the Assistant Chief of the Security Service, Claude Dansey, at the end of September. Neither man attached much credence or value to it. Dansey's comment was that Seth's informant was 'a very dead man' who might never have existed. 'Under the circumstances he would naturally tell some story of great interest which might delay any process which would involve him following his dead friend'. Seth's averment that getting this story to the authorities in London had governed all his actions since his capture sounded to the 'bitterly cynical' Dansey like a very well thought out alibi. Boyle scribbled at the bottom of Dansey's reply that he regarded this piece of information 'as very definitely a German statement'.[2] Seth persisted in believing that he had secured information of first-rate importance during his stay in Tallinn, but he failed completely to persuade the top brass in London of its significance.

Seth also admitted in his brief report that he had had many chances to escape in the past two weeks but he believed the work he had been asked to do by the SD would be so important for the British side that he had decided to carry on. He claimed furthermore that he had so much vital political information that it was absolutely essential that he should be released immediately war was over. The report ends with a statement of Seth's achievements in Estonia and Paris (destruction of aircraft, naval emplacement and oil tankers, assassination of two German soldiers) and his successful endurance of seventeen hours of torture in Tallinn.[3]

Seth and his German escort resumed their odyssey on 2 September, proceeding via Luxemburg to Berncastel on the river Mosel, and, after an exhausted and poorly Dönhoff had rested a couple of days, they drove on through Coblenz to Limburg, where Seth was finally placed in a camp, Stalag XIIa, as Captain John de Witt. Four days later, 10 September, he was sent with five other British officers to another transit camp at Hadamar, and was finally transferred some time in October to Oflag 79 near Brunswick.

From the outset of his relationship with Count Dönhoff, Seth resorted to a tactic that had served him well in the past, and began dropping hints that he was extremely well connected. He enjoyed painting vivid descriptions of meals and chats with luminaries such as Anthony Eden and Stafford Cripps, and of course, of his intimate friendship with the Prime Minister.[4] In Limburg on 5 September, Seth laid it on even more thickly. Firstly, he made a confession to his new friend, the count. He had not been forced to undertake his mission, he said, but in fact had volunteered to go to Estonia, as the only person available with a knowledge of the country and the language. Seth pitched this version in such a way as to make it seem that he did so as a matter of personal honour, something which Dönhoff as an aristocrat would appreciate. He added that he was not such an insignificant person as he had made out initially. He was a member of an ancient family which held the hereditary office of page to the king; he was an expert in codeography, and a group captain in the RAF; furthermore, just before leaving England, he had been knighted. From the age of 16 he had been 'on terms of very intimate friendship' with the Duke of Windsor, who had spent long periods of time at the Lincolnshire property of Seth's aunt.

Seth then threw himself at the mercy of the count. If Dönhoff were to pass on this confession, Seth would be lost. But, as an ardent anti-Russian, keen to avert the disaster of a Russian occupation of Germany and convinced that Anglo-German friendship was the only way of preventing such a catastrophe, he no longer felt obliged to work for Dönhoff simply to save his life.

He then tried to steer Dönhoff in the direction of commissioning him as a suitable agent to be sent to England. Gathering information from men already out of touch with news from home and perhaps influenced by German propaganda during their long months and years of captivity was perhaps less important, Seth went on to suggest, than 'much more vital work' amongst his important political contacts in Britain. The key figure amongst these important contacts turned out to be none other than Seth's greatest friend (whom he had known whilst working at the BBC), Gilbert Harding, 'the one man in England with a comprehensive view of the relations between the Foreign Office and the various foreign provisional governments in London'.[5]

What Dönhoff really thought of these claims is a matter of speculation. We do know from SS *Obersturmbannführer* Otto-Ernst Schüddekopf, interrogated in September 1945, that Dönhoff had requested English newspapers, magazines and other material in the summer of 1944 to help him get up to date on current affairs in Britain as part of his preparation for the interrogation of a British prisoner of war. 'Source did not see Graf Dönhoff again until about the end of October or the beginning of November 1944 when the latter visited source ... in order to be briefed as to what information VI D 2 wanted to obtain through Seth's activities in the British PW camp near Braunschweig.'[6] This would seem to suggest that at this stage, Dönhoff was working with, if not for Amt VI D, the department of the Reich security service (RSHA) which was responsible for espionage in western European countries. Dönhoff also let it be known that efforts were being made to send him to Switzerland, to work there as an agent (*Vertrauensmann*) for Amt VI. The count was well connected, and able to pull many strings; in the aftermath of the failed bomb plot against Hitler in which many of his aristocratic acquaintances were involved, he probably thought it prudent to secure a passage out of the Third Reich whilst there was still time.

Seth evidently made a very favourable impression on Dönhoff, as can be seen from the translations of correspondence between Dönhoff and his contact in Oflag 79. On 17 November, Dönhoff writes that so far, he had been 'exceptionally pleased with the results of our mutual friend'. So impressed was he that he was inclined to take up Seth's 'new plan which he has probably talked over with you'. A month later, he declared that Ronny's reports had become 'an ever more important source'. His military and political reports were really good – and they had style.[7]

In subsequent interrogations, Seth intimated that the idea of sending him on a mission to England had been discussed by the two men even before he entered Oflag 79. This may indeed be the 'new plan' that Dönhoff was tempted to take up in November. If so, he gave no intimation of his plans to Schüddekopf, who was left with the impression that it was the count himself who was eager to go abroad.

What these plans might have been, and what motives may have driven Dönhoff to work with Seth will be taken up in the next chapter. Let us also leave Seth for the time being, about to enter the portals of Oflag 79, and return to London, where the sudden reappearance of Agent Blunderhead had prompted a flurry of inter-departmental correspondence. Major Soskice, to whom fell the task of analysing the lengthy report handed over to Air Commodore Jones in Paris at the end of August 1944, recommended that a strict watch be kept in case Seth should return to England as a double agent, but he also urged that if there were any possibility of freeing him from German hands, this should be treated as a matter of urgency, since his life would be in danger should the Germans decide they had no further use for him. Soskice found no reason to suppose that Seth was anything other than genuine in his repeated assertions that he fully intended to double-cross the Germans, and he was concerned that Seth might be in danger. Since Seth in all probability did not know the names of other agents, other than any he might have met in prison, Soskice concluded, he was unlikely to give anyone away, so his continued detention in German hands did not pose any threat to security.

Three days after Soskice completed his report, John Senter, head of the Security Directorate at SOE since August 1942, wrote to Commander Kenneth Cohen, the SIS Controller Western Europe, to seek his assistance. After outlining the bare details of the Seth case, he asked if Cohen, through his own channels or with the assistance of MI9 might be able to report on the likely whereabouts or fate of Seth. Senter had already alerted Colonel T.A. ('Tar') Robertson of MI5 to the possibility that Seth might now be working as a double agent. MI5 was quick off the mark in responding, forwarding on 9 September an extract from a field interrogation of an *Oberleutnant* who had stayed behind in Paris in August 1944. The unnamed prisoner was Wolfgang Krause-Brandstetter, the man who had wined and dined Seth at the Hôtel Claridge in Paris. His evidence, although confusing in that he claimed Seth had taught in Lithuania, not Estonia, before the war, contained sufficient detail to corroborate Seth's own report. A preliminary interrogation of Richard Delidaise at around the same time also has Seth as a member of the faculty of the University of Kaunas, Lithuania, and fluent in that language, which may suggest that Seth had tried to muddy the waters of his past existence.

SOE had not only to search for the whereabouts of their agent, but also to sort out the embarrassing question of his current status. He had been officially declared killed in action just before he resurfaced, and his putative widow had been unofficially told of this sad event. The wheels of bureaucracy had also been set in motion to remove Seth from the pay list and to produce a pension for his widow. Less than two months after Seth was declared dead, Air Commodore Boyle now decreed that the notification 'killed whilst on active service' should revert to the original 'missing'. Mrs Seth was once more unofficially informed of this 'so that no official notification at this stage need be sent to her'. Mrs Seth was now no longer entitled to a pension or any 'in action' gratuity to which an officer might be entitled, and would thus revert to the allowance paid to her before 1 August 1944. A letter sent to the Ministry of Pensions at the end of September, however, asked if the pension could be allowed to stand, since although information received made it fairly certain that Seth was still alive at the end of August 1944, 'the circumstances under which he is placed give no guarantee that he is likely to continue to remain so.'[8]

There was thus a lot of doubt about Seth's chances of survival in German hands, and none of his erstwhile acquaintances interrogated in France had any knowledge of his fate after he had been removed to the Cherche Midi prison. Mrs Seth did not hear from her husband until 15 November, when a series of letters written some two months earlier and posted to her mother's address in Keswick finally reached her at RAF Chivenor, near Barnstaple. Her mother had been puzzled to receive letters from a Captain John de Witt, currently held in a German prisoner of war camp, and these letters, addressed to 'My dearest Sepha' and signed 'Your affectionate brother, John', also puzzled the authorities to whom the letters were handed over by Mrs Seth. The language of these letters is of longing, as one would expect of a couple long separated. It is not the language of a brother to a sister. In his first postcard, sent from a transit camp, Captain de Witt sent his love to 'Hazel', and this mysterious person turns up again in subsequent correspondence. On 15 September, Sepha is urged to get in touch with 'Hazel' and ask him to pull every string he can, seeing Anthony (presumably Eden) if necessary to get him out immediately peace is signed. 'I must get home all at once, otherwise all my work will have been wasted.'[9]

Squadron Leader Hugh Park, SOE's head of General Security, identified 'Hazel' at the end of November 1944 as Lieutenant Colonel Hazell, the man largely responsible for training and despatching Seth to Estonia. As it was believed that Hazell had arranged a code with Seth, Park promised to show the letters to him on his return from France. There is no trace of any response from Colonel Hazell in the archives, and it was not until the beginning of April 1945 that decoders were able to offer the first clear evidence that the letters contained a coded message. They were fairly certain that the letters written in September contained no messages, and of the two coded messages sent in October, only one was clearly identifiable: 'AM POSTWAR SECRET CONTACT WITH HUN FO'.[10] In other words, Seth was clearly trying to convey the message that he was involved in dealings with the German foreign office, but he failed to say what these were.

Whatever Ronald Seth believed his mission to be as the autumn descended towards winter, his attempts to send coded messages in his correspondence with his wife failed entirely to gladden the hearts of any would-be recipients. His assumption of a false name, the reluctance of 'Captain de Witt' to reveal his regiment, and an obscure obsession with contesting the Ely constituency served only to heighten suspicion of him. MI9, the arm of the secret services that was responsible, amongst other things, for communications with British prisoners of war, was also picking up strange messages from its sources. One from Oflag 79, dated 10 October, shortly after Seth's arrival at this camp, has him claiming that he joined Bomber Command in 1940, had been promoted to the rank of group captain, and had been awarded the KCB. Seth was evidently spinning the same story to his fellow officers in the POW camp as he had spun to Dönhoff during their journey through north-eastern France.

The information coming out of the camps about de Witt was sufficiently concerning to bring together senior representatives of the different branches of the secret service at a meeting in Broadway Buildings, the headquarters of SIS, on 7 December. Squadron Leader Park was asked by Major Banks of MI9 what evidence he had that de Witt was actually Ronald Seth. Park replied that he was 'reasonably certain' that the handwriting in the letters to Mrs Seth was that of their agent, and he personally could see no point in the Germans producing a man who knew all about Seth, calling him de Witt, and planting him in a POW camp. MI9 remained unconvinced and asked if Seth had any outstanding physical features that might be used to check his identity. It was, however, decided, in view of the frequency with which Seth seemed to have been moved around, and the fact that, as SOE admitted, 'a large part of what he says is fabrication', that a warning be sent to all POW camps to be gravely suspicious of Captain John de Witt.[11]

Seth had in fact aroused suspicions from the moment of his arrival at Oflag 79, according to two officers subsequently questioned on their return to England. Captain Geoffrey Kennard-Egger, interviewed in February 1945 after repatriation, declared that 'Ronald de Witt (Seth) is almost certainly acting as a stool pigeon'. The British security officers in the camp in fact considered him so dangerous that they were seriously thinking of having him killed. It was widely believed that more than one British officer had vanished from the camp as a result of de Witt's machinations.[12]

The most authoritative account of Seth's stay in Oflag 79 was provided by the Senior British Officer (SBO), Colonel W.D.E. Brown of the Royal Artillery, writing on 3 April 1945 to the Under-Secretary of State for War. Brown declared that Captain John de Witt had caused great difficulties in that he apparently belonged to no unit and could not provide particulars of any mutual acquaintances with any other officers in the camp. He had claimed that his real name was Group Captain Sir Ronald de Witt Seth, KCB, and that he had joined the RAF in 1939 as a pilot officer; in other words, Seth had not been able to resist the temptation to inflate his own importance within the cover story devised by the Germans, and he had confused the SBO by mixing up his real name and assumed cover name. Seth had also recounted his adventures in Estonia, including the march to the scaffold and the last-minute failure of the trapdoor, and claimed that he had been recaptured in July whilst attempting to join the Allied forces in France. He told Colonel Brown that his army captain uniform had been given to him by the French resistance. The colonel was persuaded to send the message about Russian designs on Norway, signed 'Blunderhead', but he did so in a more detailed message, which gave particulars of de Witt Seth, and urgently requested 'credentials and descriptions'. This message was sent in mid-October, but not received in London until two months later.[13]

In camp, the colonel continued, Seth drew attention to himself by telling all and sundry incredible and divergent stories about himself. He was also particularly friendly with the German welfare officer, *Sonderführer* Ackermann, 'a nasty piece of work', according to Captain Kennard-Egger. Although officially designated as interpreter to the German security officer, the elderly Major Werner Hoffmann, Ackermann was in fact in charge of the section of the German security service that dealt with political matters. In civilian life an academic with a doctorate in philology, Ackermann had been introduced to Seth by Count Dönhoff a few days after he entered the camp. Contact between Seth and Ackermann was to be set up by a request from Seth, in the presence of other British officers, for piano sheet music. This would allow Ackermann to invite Seth to the *Kommandantur*, ostensibly to consult catalogues, but in reality to hand over his reports on opinions expressed by his fellow officers. Seth wrote some eight reports between 19 October and 20 December. Under interrogation in London, he claimed that he invented around three-quarters of the material, which dealt with topics as diverse as the prospects for Labour, the Beveridge Plan and Australian views of America, and which he thought would be the sort of thing Dönhoff would find agreeable.

Seth told MI5 that he did not believe at the time that his fellow officers suspected him, though later developments made him wonder how much they knew. His situation became precarious, however, towards the end of 1944, as a result of the sudden removal from the camp of a Lieutenant Webster. Webster had arrived in the camp in mid-November, and had subsequently given a lecture in which he had been rather indiscreet about future Allied military operations in Europe. Seth had attended this lecture, but claimed he left early, horrified by Webster's loose talk. When Webster was removed from the camp soon afterwards, suspicion fell on Seth as an informant. Seth himself asked Ackermann the reason for Webster's removal, and was told that he had been taken for further interrogation because he had revealed such a lot of interesting information. When Seth asked how Ackermann knew this, he was told that the Germans had other contacts in the camp besides him.

Doubts as to Seth's loyalty were tempered by worries about his state of mind. In his book, Seth claimed that he had sought to create the impression of insanity from the very beginning of his period in the POW camp. Carefully selecting a number of officers who lived in his barrack, he gave out that he was a millionaire, thanks to a generous bequest from an uncle in Australia, and he proposed after the war to invest this money after the war in a chain of shops across Britain, selling Estonian meat pies. The men he took into his confidence were offered jobs. As Seth frankly admits, at any other time, they would not have believed a word of what he was saying, but bored stiff by inactivity and confinement, they took to the idea enthusiastically.

Other accounts of life in Oflag 79 lend some credence to this story. The pummelling meted out to Germany by Allied bombers also meant a drastic decline in the standard of living of the inmates of the camps. Rations were reduced, heating was feeble and sporadic, and the disruption of communications meant that the lifeline of Red Cross parcels was virtually cut off. It became more difficult to sustain the high level of activity of earlier years: the post-Christmas pantomime had to be called off after only two performances, bringing to an end what had been a lively dramatics club. The prisoners took less exercise, and spent more time on their bunk beds trying to keep warm: everyone yearned desperately for the end of the war, for food and being able to go home. In such circumstances even the most fantastic schemes for making money when peace came were a welcome distraction from hunger and the cold.

The meat pie scheme was only one of Seth's ruses to create the impression that he was somehow unhinged. He continued to elaborate on his close friendship with the Duke of Windsor and the prime minister. To a few officers, he confided that he was in touch with certain high officials in the German foreign office, who were planning a coup against Hitler. He also began to spread the idea that the senior officers of the camp were antagonistic towards him. There was more than a grain of truth in this, though Seth himself did more than enough to annoy the senior officers. He was summoned to see the Senior British Officer in November on account of a letter written to Liliane, to which he had attached the monogram of his signet ring as a kind of personal security check. Colonel Brown accused him of sending a coded message, against camp regulations: Seth denied this and protested about his correspondence being held up. The interview ended with them 'both rather heated'.[14] Seth frankly admitted that he felt a very strong antipathy towards substantive captain, temporary full colonel Brown, 'an irritatingly bombastic little man of 32', and he did not think much either of the camp security officers ('amateurs at this game').[15] He certainly put the noses out of joint of 'C and D' (Cloak and Dagger, the collective name given to the security officers in the camp) by insisting on going over their heads directly to the Senior British Officer, and he seems also to have irritated Lieutenant Colonel Thompson, the camp medical officer, by revealing details of his relationship with the Germans and asking for drugs to enable him to keep up his stamina.

Seth claimed that he had embarked on a carefully planned campaign to establish in the minds of his fellow officers that he was mad in order to qualify for repatriation, and that this had been suggested by Dönhoff whilst they were together in Limburg as the best way for him to be released and returned to England – where he would of course fulfil the mission entrusted to him by the Germans. At the beginning of January, Dönhoff reappeared at the camp. Seth was arrested on a pretext, and taken to the *Kommandantur*, where he was briefed by the count. Dönhoff told him that his reports on opinions expressed by the officers in the camp had been read with great interest in Berlin. As a result, it had been decided to send him on a mission to England. Dönhoff added that a new German offensive was due shortly, and that messages between London and Moscow deciphered by German intelligence showed that the British were begging the Russians to start a new offensive. In Dönhoff's opinion, the war would last another eighteen months.

As we have seen, however, Dönhoff had been tempted in November 1944 to take up Seth's 'new plan'; writing the reports may have been a test of Seth's reliability and willingness to work for the Germans, or it may have been simply a way of keeping him occupied whilst plans were hatched to send a British POW to England to open up a line of communication for those seeking to secure a separate peace deal for Germany. When the two men met on 4 January, the German army operation Wacht am Rhein was little more than a fortnight old, but it had already punched a huge hole through the Allied forces in the Ardennes. On 1 January 1945, the Wehrmacht launched what was to prove to be its last major offensive of the war, Operation North Wind against the overstretched lines of the American Seventh Army. Although the Allies managed to regain most of the terrain lost in this 'Battle of the Bulge' by the beginning of February, there can be little doubt that Dönhoff at the beginning of January had good reason to feel that Germany was still strong enough to hold out on the Western front, and that the war-weary British might be persuaded to listen to the kind of peace offer that he and his friends were prepared to make.

Seth was instructed to intensify the symptoms of his insanity in preparation for the repatriation board due to meet in March. But on his release from detention matters took a different course. Reporting to Colonel Brown in accordance with camp routine, Seth was surprised to be told that the senior British officers were worried that the Germans were beginning to get suspicious of his true identity as a British agent. The following day, Seth was again interviewed by the SBO, who proceeded to tell him 'that it had been suggested that Seth should be thrown out of a top storey window and his death represented a suicide; that the padres had reported that Seth had been telling them queer stories; and that Seth had written a very curious letter to Lieutenant Colonel Thompson'.[16] In conclusion, Colonel Brown said that the Medical Officer believed Seth to be mentally deranged, and he was therefore arranging for him to be held in protective custody, in other words, he was not to leave his room without an escort. Seth replied that he was not mad, and that he was in touch with the German foreign office and was to be removed from the camp. He flatly refused to reveal any further details.

Although he had prepared himself to be labelled insane, it seems that Seth was deeply shocked when he was placed in protective custody for his own safety. In his letters to his wife, he had complained of being depressed; there can be no doubt that the strain of maintaining a multiplicity of identities over a period of two years, far removed from family and familiar circumstances, was immense. On the other hand, his ability to spin unlikely tales helped in creating genuine alarm about his mental health. To that extent, he was probably relieved, as he says in his book, that his mental illness was taken seriously.

Seth's mental state now came under serious scrutiny, though he was unsure whether this was at the instigation of the Germans or the senior British officers. On 16 January, escorted by a guard, he tramped 5 miles from the camp to the Inselwald hospital in Brunswick. This visit proved abortive because of an air raid, but when Seth returned to the hospital two days later, he was asked by the specialist to translate into French a note from the British Medical Officer. This detailed some of the extravagant financial schemes proposed by Seth, whom it was claimed was suffering from delusions of persecution. Colonel Thompson concluded that he was suffering from paranoid schizophrenia. The German specialist carried out a physical examination, and asked a few questions, but felt unable to offer a diagnosis on the basis of a cursory examination, and recommended Seth be sent elsewhere for further observation.

This was not what Seth had hoped for. His situation in the camp was now extremely awkward, the more so because of the tension caused by rumours of informers in the camp. On his return for the second visit to hospital, he managed to see Ackermann and warned him that because he was suspected of being an informer and under protective custody, he would not be able to contact him any more. He pressed Ackermann to contact Dönhoff at once.

Seth made a third visit to the hospital in February, and there met Ackermann, who said that Dönhoff would be coming to Brunswick early in March, and intended getting Seth to Berlin as soon as possible. Seth told his interrogators in London that this news surprised him; he imagined that Dönhoff's department would be in the process of evacuating Berlin before the Russian assault on the city, and hence too disorganised to worry about him. It was clear that repatriation was now out of the question, and Seth had no alternative suggestions to make as to how he might be removed from the camp.

The record of Seth's interrogation gives the date of the meeting with Ackermann as Thursday, 22 February. In his book, however, Seth has it as 2 February, and adds that it was a further five weeks before he heard from 'Cristopher', during which time he believed it was often touch and go whether he would remain sane.[17] Hungry, deprived even of narcotic comfort (the supply of cigarettes had run out weeks before), Seth, in common with his fellow prisoners, spent much of his time lying on his bunk. He was so engaged on Sunday, 11 March when he was summoned to the *Kommandantur*. Here he found Dönhoff, accompanied by a man in civilian clothes from the Brunswick Gestapo and two SS officers. The Senior British Officer was also summoned, and questioned by these three men in an adjoining room. The purpose of this charade was to leave the impression that the Senior British Officer's report on Seth's mental state had aroused the suspicions of the Gestapo, whose subsequent enquires had identified Captain de Witt as the escaped British agent, Ronald Seth.

Seth had revealed to Colonel Brown that he had been sent on a mission to Estonia, but he seems to have muddied the waters so thoroughly thereafter that Brown had difficulties in knowing what to believe.

Seth was taken from the camp to the Hotel Deutsches Haus, Brunswick, given a change of civilian clothing for his tattered uniform, and treated to a very welcome dinner. He was also interviewed by a regional security officer, who had a list of information about the secret organisation within the camp, including details as to existence and location of a camera, dark room and secret radio set. This information, according to Dönhoff, had been given to the Germans by a Captain Berneville-Claye.

Berneville-Claye's name had cropped up on an earlier occasion, when Seth met Ackermann on his return from hospital in February. Ackermann told him that the situation was now very awkward, because 'the other one' who 'does it voluntarily' was frightened by the rumours flying around about informers. This 'other one', Seth revealed to Captain Milton, was Douglas Berneville-Claye, who was removed from the camp on 26 February.[18]

This particular gentleman far outshone Ronald Sydney Seth in the self-promotion game. Indeed, Seth later observed that the stories he told were even more fantastic than his own. Son of a staff sergeant in the Royal Army Service Corps, Berneville-Claye had managed to clock up one bigamous marriage and convictions for fraudulent deception and impersonating an officer before he enlisted as a private in the West Yorkshire regiment in 1940. Claiming to have been educated at Charterhouse, Oxford and Cambridge, Berneville-Claye, or as he now styled himself, the Honourable Douglas St Aubyn Webster Berneville-Claye, was promptly sent off for officer training, and was commissioned as second lieutenant in October 1941. He managed to brush off another charge of fraud, claiming to be a barrister and successfully defending himself at court martial, before finally being captured during an operation in Tunisia, and eventually ended up in Oflag 79. Here he fell under suspicion of being an informer, and was removed by the Germans for his own safety after the Senior British Officer warned that the prisoners were planning to try him, and would carry out an execution were he found guilty.[19]

During the discussions in Brunswick, Seth claimed that he had never met Berneville-Claye, and that the information put to him by the regional security officer about the secret organisation within Oflag 79 was new to him, and he was therefore unable to confirm its accuracy. But when

Dönhoff asked the regional security officer if Berneville-Claye was the man who had given Webster to the Germans, he replied 'Yes – and him', pointing to Seth.

Seth makes no mention of Webster or Berneville-Claye in his book, but it is clear that the 'certain piece of information' that had reached the Germans in December, indicating the presence in the camp of an informer, refers to the Webster incident. Seth claimed later that he tried to reveal the presence of an informer in the camp by drawing suspicion to himself, but if this was the case, he seems only to have succeeded in drawing attention away from Berneville-Claye, who was later found to have in his kit incriminating evidence of the whereabouts of the concealed camera and dark room.[20]

What then of Seth's reports on opinions regarding current affairs, which had apparently made such a good impression in Berlin? Seth claimed that he invented most of the material, and skewed it so as to appeal to Dönhoff. A couple of these reports were added as appendices to his interrogation file. The first concerns reactions to the communiqué issued after the Yalta conference, the second is a summary of a discussion involving four named officers of Britain's future status in the world. What is striking about both is a strong sense of British patriotism, and considerable suspicion of the motives and ambitions of Britain's allies. Although most officers considered the division of post-war Germany into three spheres of control good in principle, there was considerable criticism of the zone allotted to Britain. This 'Northern Region' included one or two ports and the North German plain, but the Americans would take the rich industrial areas of the Saarland and Ruhr, and the Russians would have Silesia. It was likely that the Germans from the other two regions 'would flock into the British controlled region as long as they were allowed to do so ... and this would undoubtedly be a good thing if Great Britain used this opportunity wisely, of cementing a lasting agreement and friendship between the two nations.' The reason why the Germans would flock to the British zone was that, even after all that had happened, they would realise that the British were the best of the three. Interestingly, though, the general opinion was more understanding of the Russian needs than those of the Americans, who, it was feared, would be able to utilise their great industrial strength to drive everyone else out of world markets. French demands merely aroused great indignation that a nation that had done little to help itself or the Allies should 'have the audacity to come forward and lay unproportionate [sic] claims to German territory'.[21]

The significance of Seth's reports may have lain less in their details and more in Dönhoff's willingness to believe that somehow Britain offered the best option for the survival and revival of a post-war Germany. Like his supposed agent, Dönhoff was suffused with self-belief: it may have been this that bonded the two men in the chaos and destruction of a collapsing Germany. As the Red Army advanced inexorably upon Berlin from the east, Seth and the count took the train from Brunswick to the shattered capital of the Third Reich. The final and most fantastic episode of Agent Blunderhead's wartime career was about to begin.

Notes

1. MI5 report 1, p.3.
2. V.C.S.S. (Dansey) to A/CD (Boyle), 9 October 1944, HS9/1344. The characterisation of Dansey by Kenneth Cohen, a senior wartime colleague in SIS, is quoted in Jeffrey 2010, p.314.
3. The two-page report, dated 2 September 1944 is in HS9/1344.
4. Seth 2008, p.241. MI5 report 1, p.10.
5. MI5 report 1, p.10. Gilbert Harding achieved fame and a degree of notoriety as a broadcaster in the post-war years, but at the time Seth knew him, he was a humble staff member of the Monitoring Unit, having tried several careers unsuccessfully since graduating from Cambridge. One can only wonder what the notoriously rude and outspoken Harding would have thought of Seth and his story.
6. Interrogation of Otto-Ernst Schüddekopf, KV2/2646. Schüddekopf was the expert on British affairs in Amt VI, section D, the office in the RSHA that dealt with espionage in western European countries. He was to enjoy a distinguished career as a historian in the post-war years.
7. KV2/378. The original letters were left behind when the contact – Sonderführer Ackermann – left the camp for Berlin some weeks before Oflag 79 was liberated.
8. Correspondence in HS9/1344.
9. Letter of 15 September 1944, HS9/1345.
10. Major G. Follis, for Commandant Group B to Park, 5 April 1945, HS9/1345.
11. Park to Wilson (MI5), 8 December 1945, HS9/1344.

12. Interview with Captain Kennard-Egger, 7 February 1945, KV2/377.

13. Col W. Brown to Under-Secretary of State, 3 April 1945, KV2/379.

14. Seth 2008, p.263. The postcard was picked up by British security at 3 rue de Lincoln, and found its way into Seth's file, HS9/1345. In it, Seth declares that he was thinking of nothing else but Liliane, whom he loved madly. The only coded part is a reference to 'Rose', the code-name for Richard Delidaise, but this is only to ask him to look after Liliane. The little drawing under the signature is very clearly a monogram.

15. Seth's handwritten report, Bern, April 1945, KV2/378.

16. MI5 report 1, p.17. Seth 2008, pp.270–2.

17. MI5 report 1, p.19. Seth 2008, p.276.

18. MI5 report 1, pp.20–1.

19. KV2/626, 627 for details of Berneville-Claye's wartime escapades.

20. MI5 report 1, p.13. Seth 2008, p.264.

21. Appendix 3 to MI5 report 1, pp.1–2.

10 | 'An occupation for gentlemen of high social standing.'

Berlin, Easter 1945

As Seth and his companion travelled eastwards towards Berlin, the massed forces of the Red Army were less than 40 miles away from the capital. Seth had lived through the darkest days of the war for British citizens; now he was to see and experience devastation and despair at a level far worse than the Blitz. 'Bewildering' was the apt word he chose to describe the extent of the damage wrought by two years of incessant Allied bombing. Whole quarters of the city had been laid waste. Hundreds of thousands had been made homeless. Seth noted in his account that Berliners never knew whether they would have a home to come back to when they went out to work or to look for food and fuel, so they always carried their most essential possessions with them in a rucksack or suitcase. The daily routine of normal life no longer had any meaning. Lack of soap and a regular water supply obliged people to go without washing or shaving. Foraging, for wood to provide some meagre comfort from the bitter cold, or to afford the possibility of a hot meal, and for whatever food might be available, was now the normal routine. Seth, who was still hungry though on triple rations, could not imagine how ordinary citizens coped on rations less than those of an officer on leave. Nevertheless, in a note on morale in

Berlin which he wrote in the comfort of a Swiss hotel a fortnight after he had left the German capital, he admitted:

> The Berliners, in fact all Germans in large towns, gained my profoundest admiration. Berlin is little more than a heap of rubble, yet the Berliner still laughs, food is to be got, public services are not bad. The two weeks in Berlin showed me why the German civil population has not cracked. There is no apathy. There is a certain fatalism. I believe the average German still hopes in his heart for something to be pulled out of the bag; but he does not mind if he loses the war as long as it is over.[1]

Equipped with a written confirmation (*Bescheinigung*) stating that he was a released prisoner of war, permitted to wear civilian clothes, and that he was an employee, or collaborator (*Mitarbeiter*) of the RSHA Amt VI, Captain de Witt was lodged in his friend's flat at 125 Hohenzollerndamm, in the leafy and affluent south-western suburb of Grünewald. The house was fortunately undamaged, though most of the furniture and fittings of the flat had been removed to the Rhineland during the evacuation of the Dönhoff family. The two men made themselves as comfortable as they could in the circumstances, and whilst the count busied himself with his plans, Seth kept house, doing the shopping, cooking and cleaning. Every night at nine-thirty, they had to pack their suitcases and rush to the air-raid shelter. Seth later recalled spending an uncomfortable few hours squashed together with the high and mighty in the elite Hotel Adlon during a daytime raid. Another time, he was hustled into the vast shelter near the zoo, built to accommodate thousands of civilians as well as house many of the treasures of the city's museums. With walls 10ft thick and towering 120ft above the ground, it also served as a platform for heavy anti-aircraft guns.

In addition to his household chores, Seth received instruction in radio operation and codes from a man attached to the Havel Institute, the German wireless school. He was also trained in secret writing, and later gave his British interrogators a detailed description of the process. The main thrust of his mission, however, was worked out over two days of discussions with Dönhoff in mid-March. He had three main objectives. Firstly, he was to report on the subjects he had covered earlier at Oflag 79, in particular, the relationships between the British political parties, the likelihood of Mr Eden succeeding Winston Churchill, and Mr Eden's position in political circles. Secondly, he was to use his political contacts to promote the idea of Anglo-German collaboration against Communism. Finally, he was to ask Stanisław Mikołajczyk, whom Seth claimed as a personal friend, how Germany could help the London Poles to oppose the Lublin committee.[2]

The Polish question was something that had not cropped up in previous discussions of Seth's mission, and it is likely that it was brought up by Dönhoff's superior in Amt VI, Theodor Paeffgen. Paeffgen, the head of section D, concerned mostly with espionage in the Americas, had apparently given permission for Mr Mikołajczyk to be told that as pledge of the Germans' good faith, his wife would be released from captivity. The Germans were, however, rather adrift of developments in regard to Poland. The so-called Lublin committee, the Polish Committee of National Liberation, had been officially proclaimed as the provisional government of Poland on 21 July 1944. By declaring itself the only legitimate government of Poland, this Soviet-backed committee rejected the London-based exile government, of which Stanisław Mikołajczyk had been the prime minister since July 1943. In spite of his considerable reservations about the provisional government in Poland, Mikołajczyk resigned his office in November 1944, and joined the Lublin Committee of National Liberation, which in January 1945 was transformed into the Provisional Government of the Republic of Poland. As a result of the talks between the wartime Allied leaders at Yalta, this became a government of national unity in June 1945, and Mikołajczyk became one of the two deputy prime ministers of that coalition. In other words, by the time Seth was receiving his instructions to offer German help in combating the Lublin committee, that committee had been installed in Warsaw as the provisional government of Poland, and Mikołajczyk was no longer a member of the government in exile in London – and was indeed bitterly denounced as having sold out to the communists.

Seth was to be guided across the German–Swiss frontier, and having given himself up to the Swiss authorities, he would be repatriated to England. His cover story for the British authorities would take up from where he had left off at Oflag 79. In other words, he was the British agent captured by the Germans in Estonia, who had managed to conceal his identity until removed from the camp by the Gestapo as a consequence of the camp medical officer's report. He had then been incarcerated in jail in Brunswick for a fortnight, and had then been passed to a camp near Berlin, and thence transferred south on a military train. This train had been attacked by Allied airplanes, the passengers had scattered and Seth had made good his escape. He had then managed to make his way by a series of trains to Feldkirch, on the Swiss frontier, where he had managed to crawl under the wire under cover of darkness.

The two men also devised means of communication, and here, Liliane was to be allotted a key role, at Seth's suggestion. On Seth's return to England, he was to seek permission to visit Liliane in Paris and persuade her to return to her Swiss homeland because of the troubled political climate and the food shortages in France. She was to be told that she would be working for the British secret service, and that she would also be paid an allowance by Dönhoff. On arrival in Zurich, she was to put an ad in the *Neue Zürcher Zeitung*, seeking the services of a French-speaking dressmaker, and giving her name and address. This would enable Dönhoff, who had been appointed vice consul in Zurich, to collect Seth's letters. Dönhoff, who had known very little of Seth's relationship with Liliane until then, seemed happy to go along with this plan, though he gave Seth the address of another woman in Zurich as a back-up in case the Liliane plan fell through.

Dönhoff would also arrange for Seth to have a small two-way radio set, which he would smuggle to him in a box of chocolates, together with four crystals, spare valves, three tablets of secret writing materials, 6,000 French francs and 400 Swiss francs. Coded messages would also be sent at 2100 hours GMT on Wednesdays and Saturdays, using the permanent call sign 'Ron' and the code to be used in Seth's own transmissions. Messages written with the secret ink were to be sent to Captain de Witt at Oflag 79, purportedly from a friend. Finally, the two men resorted to one of the hoariest methods of the spy manual, advertising in *The Times*. Liliane, rather fancifully, became an ocelot coat; the last two figures of a price sought in the sale of such a coat would indicate how long it would take her to return to Switzerland, whilst an ad expressing a wish to buy a fur coat would mean that her return to Switzerland could not be arranged. A gentleman willing to sacrifice a fur coat would mean that everything had gone wrong. For some reason, Seth was to collect the text of these messages in Switzerland. They were to be written in French, so that if the package were intercepted, he (presumably acting the part of the linguistically challenged Englishman) could deny ownership.[3]

Why did a man with close connections in high places and a long record of working in a senior position within the apparatus of the Nazi state spend two days drawing up this laughably amateurish plan, as his fatherland was collapsing around him? Was Dönhoff so taken in by Seth, so mesmerised by his charms, that he ended up trying to out-Seth himself? Seth was at pains later to stress how close and intimate their relationship had been, and the letters written by Dönhoff to Ackermann do seem to reveal a man who was very positively inclined, indeed, almost enthusiastic about Seth's abilities to deliver the goods. It may well be of course that, with the war lost and the German leadership falling apart, any throw of the dice was acceptable, and that any scheme to establish some sort of link with Britain was worth trying.

Dönhoff was not, however, simply indulging in a wild and private fancy. During his interrogation after the war, *Brigadeführer* Walther Schellenberg, head of the foreign intelligence arm of the SD, revealed that he had drawn up a plan with the connivance of a senior SS leader, *Obergruppenführer* Gottlob Berger for the release and repatriation of twenty British officers 'in order that a true picture of the situation in Germany might be brought before the Allied governments'. Theodor Paeffgen had already chosen these officers when Schellenberg's bitter rival, the head of the Reich security office Ernst Kaltenbrunner, got wind of the plan and told Hitler. Berger, who headed the main office of the SS in Berlin and also had responsibility for POW camps, had earlier tried to win over Hitler by saying that all these British officers had helped their prison guards escape from the advancing Russians. The Führer was disinclined to swallow this story, dismissing it as nonsense and vetoing the plan.[4]

Only one year older than Seth, Walther Schellenberg had joined the SS in 1933 after graduating with a law degree. A soft-spoken man with a considerable degree of boyish charm, Schellenberg also possessed a quality rare in the hierarchy of Nazi Germany: an ability to win and retain the trust of his superiors. He worked closely with Reinhard Heydrich in the counter-intelligence section of the security service (SD), his most spectacular achievement occurring at the beginning of the war, when he masterminded the capture of two British agents at the Dutch frontier town of Venlo. In 1942, thanks largely to Heydrich, he was made head of Amt VI, which he described at the Nuremberg Trials as 'the political secret service of the Reich [that] worked principally in foreign countries'.[5] With the final absorption of the remnants of the Abwehr into Amt VI in the aftermath of the failed July bomb plot against Hitler, Schellenberg acquired full command of the espionage network of the Reich security service.

There is an interesting insight into Schellenberg's views on espionage in the record of an interrogation of *Oberleutnant* Arntz, who had been present at a meeting in November 1944 at the officers of Amt VI. In Britain, Schellenberg claimed, 'espionage is considered to be an occupation for gentlemen of high social standing, whereas in Germany the worst and most corrupt elements are recruited as agents'.[6] This he blamed on his predecessor as the head of the Abwehr, Admiral Canaris. He now proposed a new approach, which would take and train men of good repute and thereby place espionage on a higher social footing. If this is a true representation of the views of Schellenberg and others of his same age and educational background, it may go some way to explain why Seth, and others who played on their connections with high society in Britain, were able to succeed in winning the Germans' confidence.

Schellenberg had also been trusted by Heinrich Himmler, the head of the SS, as his general plenipotentiary, and it was in this capacity that he played a decisive part in the last months of the war. He was used by Himmler as an intermediary in the negotiations over a possible peace agreement with the Western Allies, conducted through the Swedish Count Bernadotte in April 1945, and he himself negotiated with the former Swiss president Dr Jean-Marie Musy for the evacuation of a number of Jews from Germany to Switzerland – a plan blocked by Kaltenbrunner and Hitler. How far he was involved in, or initiated moves to oust Hitler and seek a separate peace with the Western Allies is open to question. He said tantalisingly little on this matter during his interrogations, but sufficient to indicate that opening a line to the British in the hopes of securing a more favourable peace was high on his agenda. If Schellenberg is to be believed – and there is no reason to disbelieve him on this detail, at least – the key figure in the plan to send British officers back to Britain was Dr Theodor Paeffgen. A lawyer by training, Paeffgen had been recruited into the security service in 1938. When Hitler launched his attack on the Soviet Union in the summer of 1941, SS *Sturmbannführer* Paeffgen was the man responsible for tracing and recording the movements of the SS task forces (*Einsatzgruppe*) charged with rounding up and liquidating Jews and communists. After further service in Tilsit and Białystok, he was appointed leader of the D section of Amt VI, mainly responsible for espionage in the Americas. It was these activities, rather than his role as information liaison officer in 1941, that most interested his American interrogators after the war, and there is some suggestion that he may have been taken up by the CIA as an expert on Latin America.

It is not easy to ascertain the importance of *Obersturmbannführer* Paeffgen (he was promoted in 1944). A tall, blonde man with a very small head, he is generally characterised as a colourless bureaucrat, good at obeying orders but totally lacking in charisma or dynamism. Seth, however, felt that Paeffgen was always treated with a respect beyond his rank by all who had dealings with him.[7] According to Schellenberg, it was Paeffgen who trained Dönhoff, and who authorised the mission to England of a British prisoner of war who had been working for the British Intelligence Service in Estonia – clearly, Ronald Seth. Schellenberg claimed that he had met Dönhoff only once, as the count was about to leave Berlin to take up the post of vice consul in Zurich – which he had managed to get thanks to his close friendship with the Secretary of State at the Foreign Office, Gustav Adolf Steengracht van Moyland. 'I gave Dönhoff a fairly exact notion of my political ideas', Schellenberg told his interrogators in August 1945, 'and asked him to work roughly along those lines.'[8]

Seth claimed that he was introduced by Dönhoff to the Secretary of State at the Foreign Office at the Hotel Adlon on Thursday 15 March. The son of a Dutch nobleman who had taken German citizenship in 1902, Gustav Steengracht von Moyland was one of the many young men who flocked to join the Nazi party after it came to power in 1933. He was widely regarded as one of the protégés of the Foreign Secretary Joachim von Ribbentrop. A man with the right aristocratic credentials, he was generally dismissed within the party as something of a pen-pusher, a mediocrity with no power base of his own. In the words of his defence counsel at his trial in 1949, he was 'a man who filled the gap in a hopeless situation'.[9] He did, however, have a wide circle of acquaintances amongst the German aristocracy, some of whom were involved in the opposition to Hitler. Freya von Moltke, the widow of one of the leading figures behind the July 20 bomb plot, testified after the war that Steengracht had put his own neck on the line in trying to save his student friend Peter Yorck von Wartenburg and her husband James, and he seems to have enjoyed the confidence of a number of members of the opposition.[10]

Speaking at the trial of the former Foreign Minister Joachim von Ribbentrop, Steengracht von Moyland declared the Foreign Office and its officials were detested by Hitler, and that foreign policy in its traditional meaning did not exist in Nazi Germany. He asserted that efforts by his boss to persuade Hitler to adopt a more moderate and conciliatory policy were contemptuously rebuffed. 'Experts and decent people who tried to influence Hitler to their way of thinking were engaged, in my opinion, in an altogether vain task', Steengracht told the court. 'On the other hand, irresponsible creatures who incited him to take violent measures, or who voiced their suspicions, unfortunately found him extremely accessible.'[11] This picture of an impotent Foreign Ministry whose 'expert and decent' officials sought in vain to modify Nazi policy has been significantly challenged by revelations about active complicity in some of the worse excesses of Nazi activities in occupied Europe. The German Foreign Ministry did not escape the corruption of values wrought by the Nazi regime, even though it undoubtedly was increasingly sidelined as the war progressed. The best that can be said is that those who ran the Foreign Ministry, men such as Steengracht von Moyland, were conscious that the institution had existed long before the Nazis came to power and it represented the hope of continuity into the uncertain days ahead. In other words, in whatever plans were being hatched for contacts with the Allies lay the idea of German survival after the final collapse of the regime.

Why did the Secretary of State of the German Foreign Office choose to lunch with a British prisoner of war in Berlin's most prestigious hotel, as bombs rained down on the city (Seth claimed that the lunch was interrupted by a raid, forcing guests at the hotel into cramped shelters)? We have no means of ascertaining whether or not this or subsequent meetings did actually take place. Captain Milton thought Seth might 'just possibly' have met 'Steengrath, Paeffgen and Vonsschulenburg' [sic] or heard of them through Dönhoff, but he still found it hard to believe that they would have chosen Seth as their courier.[12] In the report he prepared in Bern, Seth wrote the names of Steengracht and Schellenberg phonetically, which would suggest that he heard these names, either from Dönhoff or when these people were introduced to him. The one name he does spell correctly is that of the man he learnt on 19 March was Dönhoff's immediate superior, SS *Obersturmbannführer* Dr Paeffgen. The fact that he learnt of this name, and the precision with which he gave his titles (and correctly spelt a difficult name), may mean it was written down in some form or other – perhaps Paeffgen politely offered him his card when the two men met?

In Bern, Seth reported only that he received from Steengracht 'the special commission to the Prime Minister in person which I cannot give here and can only do so in a personal interview'. In the version recorded on his return to London, Steengracht proposes that he return to England with a personal mission to Mr Churchill, details of which would be given to him later. The reason why Seth has been chosen for this special mission is that he claimed to be closely acquainted with Churchill. In his book, Seth elaborates further, making it clear that the purpose of the mission was to sound out the prospects of an Anglo-German rapprochement against Russia. When he asked Steengracht why he had been chosen, he received a somewhat evasive answer. Prisoners known to be close to the highest echelons of the establishment were not approached because they would have been suspicious, and would in any case have been unlikely to accept such a mission. Let us assume, the Secretary of State went on, that one of their representatives, a Colonel Hertzog, had talked to Seth in Oflag 79 and recommended him, and that he was removed from the camp, brought secretly to Berlin and helped to escape. This inconsequential explanation seemed to Seth just another clumsy piece of German security, which became even more complicated when Steengracht told him that he must not reveal the mission to those training him as agent 22D for operations in England.[13]

The day after the interrupted meeting at the Hotel Adlon, Friday 16 March, Dönhoff set off for Hamburg to collect his family before leaving for Switzerland to take up the post of vice-consul. He returned empty-handed on the Monday, and set off again that evening. Seth thought he had some difficulties with the Gestapo, who were reluctant to allow his wife to leave with him, but that he managed to get to Zurich after a few days.

Seth was now alone in the flat with his minder, a young SS officer called Dick (or Willy) Tiesler. He recorded no further meetings until Good Friday, 30 March, in his Bern account, but in London, he detailed a series of meetings at the flat with Paeffgen between 20 and 30 March. The purpose of these meetings was to prepare Seth's mind for his mission, mainly through endless repetition of the line now thought likely to save Germany. Germany had never wanted to fight England, but only to expand eastwards. Germany must be led, but the younger generation deplored the violence excesses of the leadership, and wanted to get rid of them and 'make the Nazi Party merit respect abroad'. The SS under Himmler was the only institution in Germany capable of maintaining control; without them, civil war would ensue.[14] This process of indoctrination, delivered in stentorian tones by Dr Paeffgen, was completed on Good Friday with the final rehearsal of Seth's instructions. Steengracht and Paeffgen were present, as was Schellenberg.

The terms to be conveyed to Churchill were as follows:

Germany had no claims on any colonies or overseas territory;
Ley, Goering, Goebbels, Ribbentrop and others named by the British government would be handed over to the British by Himmler;

The fate of Hitler would be subject to negotiations between the British
government and Himmler on account of Hitler's popularity;

The Nazi Party would be dissolved and replaced by a New German Socialist
Party, led by Himmler. It would contain all the best elements of Nazism and
was to be recognised by the Allies;

All fighting against the Allied armies would cease and the SS would cooperate
with the Allies in maintaining order in Germany;

In exchange for these concessions, the Allies would cooperate in building up
a strong Germany to preserve central Europe from Communism;

A lasting Anglo-German friendship on this basis was to be sought.[15]

Seth was to reveal these proposals to Churchill, whom the Germans knew
to be fiercely anti-communist. He was not to reveal them to the Foreign
Secretary, Anthony Eden, whom the Germans saw as their bitter enemy. If
the British government was minded to take up the proposals, Seth was to
suggest himself for the role of intermediary. Furnished with a diplomatic
pass, he would return to Switzerland and contact Dönhoff, who would
then arrange any further meetings between the British government and the
sponsors of the proposals.

In view of the Allies' stated insistence on unconditional surrender, and
the parlous situation Germany found itself in at the end of March 1945,
these proposals seem fanciful at the very least. However, we have other
evidence to indicate that they do represent thinking within leading SS
circles at the time. According to Otto Ohlendorf, a leading SS official
interrogated by the British in July 1945, the creation of a new government
led by Himmler that could make a separate peace with the western Allies
was seriously discussed in April. Men such as the SS generals Felix Steiner
and Richard Hildebrandt 'who were sober enough in all other respects, still
believed they had a sporting chance against the East'.[16] The British chargé
d'affaires, reporting from Stockholm on talks between a high-ranking
official of the German Foreign Office and a member of the American
legation in April 1945, gained a distinct impression that certain Germans
were endeavouring to establish some kind of contact with the Allies, with
a view either to prepare the way for unconditional surrender or to let the
Allies know that there were persons in Germany prepared to collaborate in
the reconstruction of a new Germany.[17] Various approaches had been made
to the western governments in previous years, and Walther Schellenberg
had played a central part in most of them. However, since even he was

unable to read Himmler's intentions, it was unlikely that the West would have taken up the chance of driving a wedge between Himmler and Hitler. Schellenberg's admission under questioning that it was exceedingly difficult to detach Himmler from the idea of continuing the war, even though he had been willing as early as 1942 to consider a peace plan that would have restored the pre-war western frontiers of Germany, and the evidence he gave of Himmler's unwillingness to consider moving against Hitler, only confirms this view.

Seth's Easter weekend in Berlin was crowned on Easter Monday with a visit from a most eminent person. In the published version, which sets the event on Easter Sunday, Seth is alone in the flat, attempting to peel some wizened carrots for lunch, when the doorbell rings. Believing it to be his minder, returning home without his latch-key, Seth abandons the carrots and goes to open the door, only to find four men in uniform standing there. He recognises Paeffgen and Steengracht, and discovers subsequently that the third man is Schellenberg (which casts some doubt on his earlier accounts, in which he definitely claimed to have already met Schellenberg). The fourth man is SS *Reichsführer* Heinrich Himmler.

Having built up to such a momentous climax, one might have expected Seth to pull out all the stops at this point but the dialogue between himself and Himmler is somewhat inconsequential, and after the party had left, he felt 'unutterably depressed'. Reading between the lines, it is hard to avoid the conclusion that this was because, as Seth put it, 'the highest authority was doubtful'. Paeffgen praised his political acumen; Steengracht his connections with the prime minister; but it was Schellenberg who had the last word: 'We know of no-one else and time is short.'[18]

In 1945, Seth also downplayed the significance of Himmler's visit. It did not produce anything new, and Himmler only talked in general terms.[19] That the *Reichsführer* and senior figures in the SS and Foreign Office should make the trip out to Grünewald to speak to a British prisoner of war seems highly implausible, though it is also odd that Seth should make so little of this episode if it were merely a figment of his imagination. It is also worth noting that on Monday, 2 April, the Swedish representative Count Folke Bernadotte had a four-hour meeting with Himmler at Hohenlychen, some 100km to the north of Berlin, a meeting which in Bernadotte's own words suddenly carried his humanitarian activities in Germany along an entirely new route. Schellenberg, who was also present, took the opportunity of Himmler's temporary absence from the room to ask the Swedish count if he were prepared to go to General Eisenhower, C-in-C of Allied forces, to discuss the possibility of a German surrender on the western front.[20]

Significantly, it was Schellenberg and not his master who pressed Bernadotte to act, although Schellenberg intimated that the *Reichsführer* was considering the idea of approaching Eisenhower. A Swedish aristocrat with easy access to his government was undeniably a far better option than a somewhat discredited British prisoner, but Schellenberg was well aware of how easily his rivals in Berlin could gain the ear of Hitler and shoot down his efforts to open up contact with the West. In this regard, the words attributed by Seth to Schellenberg have the ring of truth: time was indeed running out, and all previous efforts to establish meaningful contact with the western governments had run into the sand. Ronald Sydney Seth, the British agent who had managed to survive through his ability to spin a plausible tale since his capture in Estonia, was in April 1945 one of the few assets still left in German hands. How far the Germans believed in Seth's vaunted connections in high places is open to doubt, though they do seem to have been particularly susceptible to his easy manner of parading his intimate knowledge of well-born folk. At this stage of the war, they had may have had little option but to pin their faith in what little they had, and trust Seth to carry out his mission.

Notes

1. Seth's handwritten report, Bern, April 1945, KV2/378.
2. MI5 report 1, p.25.
3. Bern report, pp.10–1. MI5 report 1, pp.25–9.
4. Final report on Walther Schellenberg, KV2/99.
5. Nuremberg Trial Proceedings, Vol.4. Twenty-Sixth Day, Friday, 4 January 1946., Morning Session, p.374. http://avalon.law.yale.edu/imt/01-04-46.asp
6. Interrogation of POW *Oberleutnant* Arntz, KV2/94. See also Trevor-Roper 1952, p.34.
7. Seth to Hugh Trevor-Roper, 22 December 1946. Lord Dacre of Glanton papers, Christ Church Oxford.
8. KV2/97. According to the Final Report on the interrogation of

Schellenberg, Dönhoff was surprised by the frankness with which Schellenberg expressed his views. Doerries 2003, p.318.

9. Opening statement of Steengracht's defence counsel, Trials of War Criminals before the Nuernberg Military Tribunals, Vol.12, p.253.

10. 'Gegen Hitler und gegen Goerdeler', *Frankfurter Allgemeine Feuilleton*, 27.2.2011.

11. Nuremburg Trial Proceedings, Vol.10. Ninety-First Day, Tuesday, 26 March 1946, Morning Session, p.109, http://avalon.law.yale.edu/imt/03-26-46.asp. 'All Blame Put on Hitler', *The Times*, 27 March 1946.

12. MI5 report 3, p.24.

13. Bern report, p.12. MI5 report 1, p.30. Seth 2008, pp.292–3.

14. MI5 report 1, pp.30–1.

15. MI5 report 1, pp.31–2. Seth 2008, p.299 makes no mention of colonies, and has as the first point the seizure of control in Germany by the SS under Himmler, whose new government the Allies are asked to support.

16. Interrogation of Otto Ohlendorf, http://www.archives.gov/iwg/research-papers/ohlendorf-irr-file.html.

17. Himmler Negotiations, FO188/526.

18. Seth 2008, pp.296–7.

19. Bern report, p.13. MI5 report 1, p.33.

20. Bernadotte 1945, p.62.

11 | 'Seth is mental.'

Bern, April 1945

Seth left Berlin on the night of 3 April. The train that pulled out of the ruined Anhalter Bahnhof that evening was jam-packed with soldiers headed south to the southern redoubt. Seth and his companions were unable to find a seat, and spent the night perched on their suitcases in the corridor. Leaving the train at Dachau, they travelled on to Munich, where they arrived in the early hours of the morning. From the station they went straight to SS headquarters at Franz-Joseph Strasse 38 to receive final instructions for the mission.

Seth found the city to be as devastated as Berlin, though food was good and plentiful. Given yet another identity, this time as a Dutchman, Jan de Fries, he was to remain in Munich for a further week, waiting for Dönhoff, who failed to appear. His attempts to send a practice radio transmission to Berlin were equally fruitless. Finally, on Monday 9 April, orders were received from Berlin that he was to cross the Swiss frontier at once. The Americans were rumoured to have reached Augsburg, some 75km north-west of Munich, and were moving rapidly eastward. Seth found that the railways were even more chaotic than they had been a week previously, but, accompanied by his minder, Willy (or Dick) Tiesler, he was still able to reach the meeting-point at Bregenz, after a nightmare journey lasting almost twelve hours.

Having received final instructions for crossing the frontier, the pair travelled by train to the village of Götzis, arriving shortly before one o'clock on the afternoon of 11 April. They spent the rest of the day here, lunching at the inn and enjoying the hospitality of their contact man, an elderly manufacturer of embroidery called Hans Ender, whose proud boast was that he had once entertained James Joyce in his cottage.[1] They boarded the train again shortly after midnight, travelling the short distance to Feldkirch, where they were met by a captain and a lieutenant of the frontier guard. These two officers drove Seth to the frontier, where the captain distracted the guard and the lieutenant escorted Seth along a rough track to a deserted farmhouse. The captain now reappeared and took Seth further along the track to a gate in the frontier fence, which had been kindly opened by the lieutenant. The two men shook hands with Seth, wished him good luck, and he crossed out of Greater Germany into the tiny principality of Liechtenstein. The last stage of his journey to freedom was a night-time walk downhill to the village of Ruggell, where he surrendered to the Swiss guards as Captain John de Witt, an escaped British prisoner of war.

To the end, Seth sought to maintain his role as an agent – in fact, as a truly double agent. To give veracity to his German cover story, as agent 22D, he had not washed or shaved since leaving Munich, and he was determined to be as hungry as possible, so that the Swiss guards would believe that he really was an escaped prisoner of war. But as agent Blunderhead, he had managed to preserve Richard Delidaise's wireless codes, to which he had added not only notes on his operation written since January but also copies of the radio plan, procedure and call sign for his work as agent 22D. These documents were stored in a special bag he had made, and stitched into the lining of his army greatcoat.

By his own account, the Swiss seemed to have believed him. He was escorted from Swiss army-patrolled Liechtenstein, across the river Rhine, into Swiss territory, and held for a day at the town of Buchs. The following day, Friday, 13 April, he was sent on to Bern, where he announced himself at the British legation and told his story to the military attaché, and later that day, to the British minister, Clifford Norton. He spent his first night at the Hotel St Gotthard, but for the remainder of his stay in the federal capital of Switzerland was lodged at the rather more luxurious Hotel Bären.

In his published account, even though he was unusually restrained on the contents of the proposals entrusted to him by the top echelon of the SS leadership, Seth wrote that he stressed the urgency and importance of his mission to the legation personnel. What he fails to mention is that he was not the only man slipped across the frontier by the Germans. The papers in his file, however, show that he was not only aware of this man, but that he seems to have made a deliberate attempt to smear him by alleging that he looked unusually fit and well for an escaped prisoner, and that his description 'entirely fitted' that of the infamous Douglas Berneville-Claye. It is hard to avoid the conclusion that the self-proclaimed loner, believing himself within a whisker of becoming an intermediary in a massive diplomatic endgame, did his best to queer the pitch of a man he saw as a rival.

This other man was Lieutenant John Boucicault de Suffield Calthrop. The son of a famous stage and screen actor, Donald Calthrop (himself the nephew of the Victorian dramatist Dion Boucicault), he had been captured in May 1940, whilst serving in France in the Royal Sussex regiment. His subsequent adventures in internment were as colourful as those of Ronald Seth, and there are indeed a number of close resemblances in the activities of the two men. Socially, temperamentally and politically, however, they were rather different. Dismissively characterised by his MI5 interrogators as a conceited playboy, Calthrop described himself as a theatrical and film producer, with an address in Chelsea. He had also been an active supporter of Oswald Mosley in the early 1930s, during the period in which Mosley broke with the Labour Party and founded his New Party. Calthrop, however, claimed that he broke with Mosley in 1932 when the New Party merged with various minor fascist groupings to create the British Union of Fascists.

In captivity, he passed through several prisoner-of-war camps. In the autumn of 1941, he tried to join a team to work with film apparatus, which, he told his Senior British Officer, would give him a chance to glean intelligence. In his statement, given in May 1945, Calthrop claimed that the Senior British Officer (who subsequently died in captivity) agreed to this. In order to win the Germans' confidence, he gave them to understand that his sympathies lay with the right, that he was anti-communist and thought the distances between Britain and Germany were 'not incompatible'. His efforts, however, seemed to fall on stony ground, and it was not until July 1943 that the German security service attempted to get in touch with him. He was ordered to an unknown destination along with two other officers.

They were taken to a camp at Zehlendorf, midway between Potsdam and Berlin. There were twenty-seven officers in this camp, Stalag IIID/999, where conditions were much better than in ordinary POW camps. The camps at Zehlendorf and nearby Genshagen (this intended primarily for other ranks), seem to have been the brainchild of the German foreign office. Men thought to be suitable potential recruits for the British Free Corps were singled out and sent to these 'holiday camps'. Calthrop was contacted at Zehlendorf by an official of the German foreign office who had been a press attaché at the German embassy in London before the war; but further contacts seem to have been disrupted by Allied bombing and the forced evacuation of the camp. Contact with the German foreign office was resumed at Genshagen, to which Calthrop was moved in April 1944.

During interrogation in London, Calthrop claimed that he was the only officer at Genshagen and as such assumed charge to carry on valuable welfare work and in order to put himself in a position 'where in due time I could render valuable service by passing back to the British authorities information of various kinds'.[2] Up to that time the man in charge had been Quarter-Master Sergeant John 'Busty' Brown. Brown had also been captured in France in 1940, and had subsequently used his pre-war association with the British Union of Fascists to ingratiate himself with the Germans. An accountant at Truman's Brewery in civilian life, Brown had also been active in welfare work in the YMCA, and continued to work with the International YMCA during his captivity for the benefit of his fellow prisoners of war. Unbeknown to his fellow prisoners, however, he was also spying for British intelligence, giving guidance on targets for bombing raids in coded letters and keeping a watchful eye on German attempts to recruit POWs for a British Free Corps detachment.

Brown was sufficiently well in with the Germans to be able to visit Berlin freely, dressed in civilian clothes, and it was not long before Calthrop secured the same privilege. The two men also had connections with a British-born opera singer, Margery Booth, but whereas her relationship with the devout Christian John Brown appears to have been limited to the business of collecting information on possible British traitors, with John Boucicault de Suffield Calthrop the lass from Wigan had a full-blown affair. In a post-war statement, John Brown expressed his disgust that the couple flaunted their affair, openly kissing and cuddling during Marjorie's visits to the camp. In his own statement, Calthrop admitted that he was aware that he might be being used, though he was convinced this was not so. Rather like Seth with his Liliane, the love-starved lieutenant defiantly proclaimed and defended his passion under questioning back home.[3]

Calthrop was transferred to Oflag 79 in August 1944. He soon aroused suspicion here because of his close association with the camp welfare officer, Dr Ackermann, and his extravagant boasts that he had a pass signed by Himmler and a car to take him to Berlin whenever he wanted. Like Seth, he claimed to be 'involved in mysterious negotiations with certain German individuals', and he was also hurriedly removed on a pretext from the camp in early spring, 1945.[4] His high-level handler was General of Waffen-SS, Gottlob Berger, the man in charge of POW camps, and it was Berger who suggested that he might be returned to Britain to stand for Parliament on a platform of reconciliation with Germany and a joint front against communism. Calthrop arrived in Munich at more or less the same time as Seth, and was also subjected to delay, though he believed this was caused by another person waiting to cross the frontier. From overheard talk, Calthrop concluded that this person was de Witt, who had been at Oflag 79 at the same time as himself. 'I knew that de Witt was a suspicious character', Calthrop declared in the statement he made back in England, 'who had been put under arrest by the SBO at Brunswick on suspicion of having given information to the Germans'.[5]

In view of General Berger's order that he be put across the frontier at the earliest opportunity, it was decided to give Calthrop precedence. The fact that Calthrop crossed into Switzerland before him was to have fateful consequences for Seth. In the eyes of the British secret service, who now took over the investigation of his activities, the precedence accorded to Calthrop in the matter of crossing the frontier might well mean that his mission was more important than he cared to admit, whilst Seth's was less important than he claimed.

This indeed seems to have been the conclusion already arrived at by the British minister to Switzerland. Seth tried to impress upon the minister the urgency of his mission, but he had the feeling that the minister deemed it less important than Seth himself believed it to be. Seth agreed with the minister's dismissal of the German peace terms as unlikely to impress Churchill, but wrote later that if only he could have had an audience with the prime minister, he was certain that Churchill would have made some use of the situation.[6]

In his telegrammed report to London, the minister was of the opinion that Seth appeared to be sane and answered questions freely. The proposals detailed by the minister do not differ in substance from those delivered to Seth in Berlin, but the way in which they are presented does place considerable emphasis upon the Russian threat to the future of democracy and stability in Europe. A healthy Germany is seen as necessary for Europe and Great Britain. Russia intends to communise Europe through a defeated and desperate Germany. The only force capable of countering this threat is the SS under Himmler, which can and would form a moderate government with British support. Prominent Nazis would be seized: Hitler 'must not be made a martyr', but can be held.[7]

The minister's report is carefully neutral, in the best diplomatic manner. The same cannot be said for the messages sent to London by the secret service personnel at the legation. Although interrogation of Seth proceeded on the assumption that his story was credible, his interrogators found it 'difficult to avoid the suggestion that he is a paranoic [sic] type as diagnosed by the camp doctor at Brunswick'. 'Seth is mental', was the blunt opinion of one of the team (name carefully blanked out), to which a more sympathetic note added that, if he actually went through the experiences he described after his capture, this was hardly surprising.[8] The secret service also found distinctly odd Seth's requests to be met by Hazel or Major Hamilton-Hill at the aerodrome to help him clear customs, and to book the bridal suite at the Howard Hotel, Norfolk Street, and decorate the room with pink roses. They were clearly foxed by the mysterious Hazel, as had been their colleagues in London. They also wondered why Seth should wish to make a big splash at the Howard, since he had apparently been told in Oflag 79 by an officer who knew him that his wife had re-married, Seth having been posted missing, presumed dead.

It is pleasing to note that, less than a week after these withering comments were sent to London, a double room had been booked for a week at the Eccleston Hotel, at the War Office's expense, for Ronald Seth and his wife. The War Office, however, jibbed at paying for Mrs Seth: SOE tactfully suggested that a sum still owing to Seth be used to cover the costs of her stay at the Eccleston. Whether or not the room was decorated with pink roses we do not know, but as many men returning from the war to their wives and sweethearts discovered, the reunion might not have been as blissful as expected.

Seth left Bern in the early hours of the morning of 18 April, and arrived back in Britain three days later, after a wearisome journey across France. In Switzerland, he had been allowed 400 francs with which to buy presents for his family. When he arrived back home, he found that his pay had already been debited the equivalent sum of £20, prompting him to comment later that the transmission of messages was not so slow when it was a matter of really vital importance.[9]

Of Dönhoff, he heard no more, but there was one final twist to the tale of their relationship. In his final instructions, Seth had been told that he should go to a certain café in Bern immediately upon arrival there. Here, he would be recognised from a photograph by a German agent, and the wireless transmitter set would then be delivered to him at the legation in a parcel from the shop where he had been shopping. However, this plan had broken down since he was never given the address of the café. On 16 April, in an attempt to procure the wireless set, Seth wrote a letter to the Gräfin Dönhoff (Christoph Dönhoff's wife, not his sister Marion), asking if she would have the goodness to inform 'Cristof' or his friend that '*la voiture est arrive* [*sic*] *et tout marche très très bien. Je vais faire des courses demain, mardi, et on m'a dit que provisionellement je pars le jeudi soir.*' (The vehicle has arrived and everything is going well, really well. I shall go shopping tomorrow and they've told me that provisionally I shall be leaving on Thursday evening.)[10] The 'vehicle' left Bern two days later, and he never learnt whether or not the wireless set was ever delivered.

On 19 April, however, the day after Seth's departure, a parcel addressed to him and containing books and chocolates arrived at the legation. There was also a rather sad note, addressed to '*chère amie*', which regretted that the writer could not send either the portable gramophone (i.e. W/T set) or the drugs (the tablets for making invisible ink): the first did not work, and the second had not even arrived. '*Mes affaires en général vont mal*' (Things are not in general good with me) confessed Seth's once intimate friend, Count Dönhoff. Things were now so bad that he did not think it worth the trouble to start any new 'transactions', though he gave Seth the address of a new contact in Geneva.[11]

Dönhoff's sojourn in Switzerland was to be soon cut short. In spite of his protestations that he was not an agent of German security, the Swiss Federal Council decided otherwise. On 8 May, the Council decreed that he should be expelled. He was handed over to the American military authorities in northern Italy at the end of June. The count now passes out of the story, denying all knowledge of Seth under interrogation in Italy, and managing to make some sort of career for himself in post-war Germany writing pseudonymous articles for the journal *Die Zeit*, of which his sister Marion was a co-founder. But Seth was able to see an even more intimate friend on his return journey through France. His route took him through Paris, and here he took the opportunity to phone the apartment at 3 rue Lincoln, where Liliane had lived with the Soulier family, and where she had earlier entertained 'Ronny'. The phone was answered by a hysterical Mme Soulier, who urged him to go there immediately. On arriving at the once-luxurious apartment, Seth found it a shambles. Mme Soulier was waiting for him in her outdoor clothes, and the two set off by a circuitous route to avoid being followed to a shabby apartment at Square Carpeaux, in the working-class suburb of Clichy.

Here he found Liliane, frightened and penniless, her only protection a Spanish bartender at American headquarters, called José Escribano. Together, the two women told Seth their story. Shortly after the liberation of Paris, Mme Soulier's son Jean, Liliane's former lover, had turned up at 3 rue Lincoln. In a fit of jealousy, 'chiefly on my account', Seth noted, Jean denounced Liliane to the Paris police as a German agent. She was arrested but soon released, as Jean retracted his accusation. During the autumn, she was visited several times by a 'Captain Jimmy' who asked her questions about Seth. Liliane was again arrested and thrown into a concentration camp on information laid by Mme Soulier's elder son, Pierre, a ruthless communist ex-resistance fighter alienated from his family and intent on revenge. According to the two women, Liliane was released from the concentration camp on March 3. Since then, she had been in hiding, mortally afraid of the evil Pierre, 'who has threatened that when the communists have won the Paris elections, he will have her imprisoned once more, after he has possessed her'.

Seth wrote up his account of his visit to the scruffy flat in Clichy just over a week later. He was evidently hoping to secure permission to return to Paris to lay depositions with the juge d'instruction that might free the rearrested Jean Soulier and close the file on Liliane. He also sought permission to bring Liliane back to England where he would take responsibility for her until her ex-husband could be contacted, and financial arrangements be made for her. Seth was certain that he could immediately find a job for here and that she would be able to support herself.[12]

Were permission to return to Paris granted, Seth hoped to meet up with 'Captain Jimmy' or some other British intelligence officer. If the unsigned reports sent back to London in October 1944 emanated from the mysterious 'Jimmy', then it is very likely that Seth would not have found a very sympathetic voice in his quest. This officer had interrogated Liliane 'discreetly', and described her as having one lover after another, entertaining them in the apartment of the Souliers. His report, filed on 5 October 1944, pins the responsibility for Liliane's first arrest on Mme Soulier, who denounced her as a German spy to the fearsome FFI (Forces françaises de l'intérieur), which was enthusiastically pursuing suspected collaborators in the Paris region. She was taken to Drancy concentration camp, but released after seventeen days, interrogated and then released. An attempt by this unnamed British intelligence officer to stage a confrontation between the two women was frustrated when Mme Soulier ran away.[13]

The records do not reveal whether the order for the arrest of Mme Soulier was successful, nor do they mention her ruthless elder son, Pierre. Jean, however, was rounded up in December 1944, after the FFI had managed to prise Richard Delidaise from the hands of the American and British secret service. Together with the principal members of the Delidaise coterie – Richard, his sister (and Kliemann's mistress) Yvonne, his wife Louise and her sister, Liliane, née Beucherie, married name Renggli – Jean Soulier was to stand accused of collaborating with the Germans.

It is unlikely that Mme Renggli was the ardent patriot willing to risk her life as a hostage for Seth's good behaviour as a German agent, as he insisted in his reports and letters to London. She was intimately involved in the sleazy world of the black market and lubricious collaboration, and she clearly knew how to win favours from her men friends. But she had perhaps a sounder appreciation of her faults than did the romantic Ronald Seth. Writing to him five days after he had left Paris for England, she confessed that during his long absence in Germany, she had not always been the model woman which she would have wished to be, though she attributed this to the necessity to survive in a world that had now turned hostile. In the event, Seth's plea to be allowed to return to Paris to rescue his fair maiden fell on unsympathetic ears. In a note of 9 May to Colonel V.H. Seymer, Hugh Park, SOE's man with responsibility for liaising with MI5, assumed that MI5 would not wish Seth to be allowed to go to Paris. 'I am certain too, that no one here would desire that he should interest himself in Mme Renggli's welfare. We have, however, an office in Paris and if your department approves we can no doubt arrange for Mme Renggli's circumstances to be investigated.'[14]

By 9 May, the war in Europe was over. A month earlier, however, as Ronald Seth crossed into Switzerland on his special mission, Himmler and his agents were still hopeful of reaching some sort of accommodation with the Western allies which would allow Germany to continue to fight the advancing Russians. Indeed, this determination to fight on against the Russians survived right up to the end. Himmler's offer of unconditional surrender to the Western Allies at the beginning of May included the proviso that fighting against Russia would continue, whilst Admiral Dönitz, on assuming the powers of government entrusted to him by Adolf Hitler, declared that saving the German people from annihilation from the advancing Bolshevik enemy was his first task, and that by continuing the war, the Anglo-American forces were merely contributing to the victory of Bolshevism in Europe.

During the last weeks of the war, the main conduit for negotiations over peace was the Swedish Count Folke Bernadotte, who held a series of talks with Schellenberg and Himmler in Sweden and Germany. The tenor and progress of these talks was well known to the British. The sudden reappearance of an SOE agent, claiming to have important peace proposals which he insisted could be shown only to the prime minister, caused a momentary flurry in London in mid-April. The first instinct of MI5 and the security directorate of SOE was to try and clamp the lid firmly on the situation. In a series of meetings and exchange of letters between SOE and MI5 on 16 April, at which the news of the 'sensational' peace proposals conveyed to London by the British minister in Bern was discussed, the undesirability of this news leaking out was agreed by both sides. Seth on his return was to be treated as a 'side-door' case, that is, he would be interrogated discreetly. Guy Liddell of MI5 noted in his diary that John Senter, SOE director of security, was worried by this turn of events and wanted to know more about the peace mission. All concerned believed that close tabs should be kept on Seth, and that his case should not be allowed to slip into the hands of higher authorities – which presumably meant that the secret service would obstruct any attempt by the Foreign Office or even the prime minister's office to find out the details of the German peace proposal which had been entrusted to Seth.[15]

Yet there is no evidence of interest from higher authority in such proposals: the separate peace offer transmitted to the western allies via Sweden on 25 April was rejected out of hand by Truman and Churchill. Seth may have been miffed in August 1945 that Count Bernadotte had been 'allowed to make public his role in the Himmler affair', whilst no publicity had been given to his mission, which had occurred two weeks earlier, but it has to be said that Seth himself made little or no effort to carry out his mission once he had divulged its contents to the British minister and the military attaché in Bern.[16] It is hard to avoid the conclusion that he himself had little faith in the mission, even though we are led to believe that he had been entrusted with conveying the message personally to the highest authority, the prime minister himself. For a man who had spent the best part of three years in a state of uncertainty, whose experience of captivity had ranged from good dinners and comfortable accommodation to watery soup and skin infection in fetid prison cells, the realisation that for him, the war had actually ended, that he was a free man, in a neutral country with clean trains and feather beds, and no air raids, must have been overwhelming. It is clear from his rather extravagant desire for a rose-filled double bedroom that he was longing to reattach himself to life as he had known it before the disruptions of war. As we have seen, Ronald Seth was a man suffused with his own self-importance; but even the prospect of a top-level tête-à-tête with Winston Churchill seems to have paled against that of seeing his wife again.

Notes

1. The evidence for this encounter is discussed by Andreas Weigel, 'James Joyces Österreich-Aufenthalte', in the journal *Praesent* 2006, p.100.
2. Calthrop's statement, 1 May 1945, KV2/439.
3. KV2/439. Married to a German, Margery Booth's career took off in Nazi Germany, where she appeared in leading roles at Bayreuth and the Berlin State Opera. She was allowed to sing to the POWs in the 'holiday camp' at Genshagen, and was alleged to have smuggled sensitive documents out of the camp in her underclothes. She was eventually arrested by the Gestapo, but refused to divulge any information. She managed to make her way to the Allied lines in 1945, and returned to London, where, as a suspected collaborator, she was unable to find work. Margery Booth died of cancer in New York in 1952.
4. Statement of Colonel Brown, 19 April 1945, KV2/439.
5. Calthrop's statement, KV2/439.
6. Seth 2008, p.321.
7. Norton to Foreign Office, 14 April 1945, HS9/1345.

12 | 'I clean buttons very well.'

Barnstaple, June 1945

Ronald Seth's reunion with his wife at the Eccleston Hotel was fated not to last long. On 26 April, the couple travelled north to be at the bedside of Seth's dying mother-in-law. He was instructed to return to London on 30 April for further interrogation. His wife's compassionate leave was due to expire on 4 May, by which time it was hoped that the interrogation process would be finished. Whether Seth himself would then go on leave or remain in London would depend on what MI5 decided to do with him. He had been kitted out with a new uniform and supplied with money and the necessary papers, including a ration card. SOE had managed to lose some of the clothes he handed in before his departure for Estonia, and he had been advised to put in a claim for compensation. On a matter of great importance to Seth, the finance section of SOE was looking for guidance as to the sums of money to which he was entitled during his absence. Should it be proved in a court of law that he had by his conduct endangered the war effort, this might well affect the amount to be paid.

Money worries continued to plague Seth. The £50 he had been given on his return had soon been spent on clothing and the fees paid for medical care for his mother-in-law. He also had expensive school fees for his son and daughter to take care of. Reading between the lines, it seems clear that the marriage itself was in danger of going on the rocks. Faced with these troublesome issues, Seth seems to have taken refuge in the world he had come to know well. On 6 May, he wrote a long letter from the Imperial Hotel, Barnstaple, to Wing Commander Redding, whom he seems to have chosen as his confidant in SOE. He enquired if the Wing Commander had been able to do anything about Liliane and the Souliers, over which he was losing sleep, since he had been distressed about the state in which he had found them. Picking up on a remark uttered by Redding on their last meeting, that 'these chaps might soon be working for us', he raised the prospect of Dönhoff becoming one of 'these chaps'. The count had many close contacts with leading figures in the German hierarchy, and would know the plans and whereabouts of leading Nazis:

> If I could see Dönhoff immediately I am certain I could get him over to us, and through him, the others. I believe that only I could achieve this with the fullest confidence of these men. Knowing them as I do, I am 100 per cent certain that if any other Englishman made the same suggestions as I should make – no matter how highly placed he might be – their answer would be no, because of the suspicions they would have.

Seth therefore proposed that he be authorised to go at once to Zurich to meet Dönhoff. Having won him over, he might then be able to lead the Allied authorities to the others, if they were still at large. If, however, they had already been caught, 'I suggest I should be the person to see them and talk to them first'.[1]

Seth boundless belief in his own abilities was evidently not shared by higher authority, and he was not allowed to rush to Switzerland or Sweden to interrogate Dönhoff or Schellenberg. It is interesting that the idea of persuading leading figures of the fallen regime to work for the British secret service – if that is what Redding had in mind – may already have been afloat even before the final surrender was signed. But this was to be strictly the business of the top brass of SIS, not of a junior officer still under suspicion of unsavoury dealings with the enemy.

The ebullient tones of Seth's letter to Wing Commander Redding do not indicate a man troubled either by pangs of remorse or guilt, or by worries of condign punishment for treacherous activities. But he was clearly keen to get away, perhaps from a rather sticky marital crisis. Concluding his letter with regrets that Redding was about to depart for India, he asked, rather wistfully, that if his scheme to contact Dönhoff failed, 'I don't suppose you could take me with you as a batman? I clean buttons very well'. On VE Day two days later, he wrote yet again to Redding, putting his name forward for consideration for the Allied (or, as Seth mistakenly thought, the RAF) Control Commission to be sent to Germany.

How seriously in trouble was Flight Lieutenant Ronald Seth? That he was under suspicion for having in some way or another colluded with the enemy had been known since the autumn of 1944. When news that he had resurfaced in Switzerland reached London, a hurried conversation was arranged on 14 April between Colonel Seymer of MI5 and the head of SOE's directorate of security, John Senter. The two men agreed that Seth should be permitted to see his wife and given freedom of circulation in London, and that he was to write up his adventures in a report. Once this report was to hand, it would be decided what type of interrogation was called for, and whether it should be conducted by SOE with MI5 coming in at a later stage should his account prove unsatisfactory, or whether it should be a joint investigation from the outset.

This agreement was confirmed at a joint meeting of MI5 and SOE security directorate representatives on 16 April. After the meeting, Air Commodore Boyle, who was now in overall charge of security and intelligence at SOE, passed Senter the telegram from the British minister in Bern. The somewhat sensational 'peace proposals' therein alluded to put a different perspective on the Seth case. Acting on instructions from Boyle, John Senter spoke twice that evening to MI5's Guy Liddell, 'explaining our inability to check that story in any way, and suggesting that as it would undoubtedly have excited interest, it would be desirable that a Department with the necessary expert knowledge should interrogate him on that without delay'.[2]

Reading between the lines of John Senter's carefully worded résumé of 18 April, SOE had been forced by Seth's proposals to allow MI5 to take the lead in his interrogation. Seth was to report daily to the London Reception Centre, housed in the Gothic hulk of the Royal Victoria Patriotic School in Wandsworth. It was here that MI5 processed aliens. The 'side-door' approach suggested by Guy Liddell was designed to conceal or downplay Seth's purported mission.

The two reports on Seth's activities were written up in admirably short order by Captain Milton, and signed off on 27 April. Milton now embarked upon a detailed analysis, filling twenty-five typed pages. This analysis, delivered on 16 May, was dismissive of most of Seth's story. Milton clearly thought Seth was possessed of an over-active imagination, which had allowed him to invent the vast majority of the incidents he claimed had happened to him. Nearly half of the analysis dealt with Seth's actual mission to Estonia, and Milton was merciless in his dismantling of Seth's story.

The hypothetical explanation offered by Milton at the conclusion of his analysis was that, during his pre-war sojourn in Estonia, Seth absorbed the Estonian dislike of Russia. Towards the end of his training, he realised the enormity of the task he had taken on; he also thought his preparation for the mission was inadequate. In consequence, he entered the field in a pessimistic frame of mind, although his vanity stopped him from backing out. Milton concluded that Seth hid with his friend Martin Saarne until his money ran out, possibly spent largely on trying to bribe fishermen to obtain a boat to get to Sweden. He was either denounced or surrendered to the Germans, who captured his gear, though possibly an essential part of his radio equipment was missing, since they did not use the set themselves. He was not maltreated or condemned to death because he agreed to work for the Germans. His information of Russian intentions bore no substance in reality, but was the product of his own 'megalomania' and anti-Russian feelings, which had been inflamed by stories of the Russian occupation of Estonia told to him by his friend Saarne.

Captain Milton thought the length of Seth's stay at the interrogation centre for captured Allied airmen at Oberursel was significant. Seth claimed that he was confronted with a copy of British Air Ministry lists which showed him to be an intelligence officer. Milton believed it unlikely that the Germans would have in their possession such a highly sensitive document, and he suspected that Seth might not only have revealed his identity as an intelligence officer to them, but might also have given them information on Bomber Command.

Milton was dismissive of Seth's account of his stay in Paris. He shot no German soldiers, as he claimed, nor did he steal any Abwehr radio codes. Mme Delidaise's trust of Seth, to whom she entrusted the keys to a cupboard supposedly containing confidential papers 'is remarkable'. Richard Delidaise may have been half-German, but his mother tongue was French. The errors in the code Seth claimed to have filched from the cupboard were unlikely to have been made by a native speaker, but 'seem to me those which an Englishman might make'. Milton was inclined to believe that the code supplied by Seth in his Paris report was in fact his own translation into French of an Abwehr code given to him for the purposes of his own mission.

Having noted that Seth was transferred successively between the army and air force branches of Abwehr intelligence, and finally ended up with Amt VID of the Reich security services, Milton declared bluntly that 'For VID he carried out a mission as stool pigeon in Oflag 79 reporting on military as well as political matters and knowingly giving information valuable to the Germans which they considered very important' and concluded that 'since Seth's chances of leaving Germany depended on Berlin's reception of the reports from the Oflag he had a strong inducement to give important information'.

In conclusion, Milton admitted that, although he found it hard personally to see Seth as a suitable choice for courier for such an important mission, he could not decide whether he had so deceived the Germans to the extent that that they were willing to entrust him with the task or whether the mission was yet another invention consistent with his megalomania. He recommended that every attempt be made in Germany to locate material and witnesses from Oflag 79, Amt VID and the German Foreign Office, and when such evidence was available, to recall Seth for further interrogation to determine whether or not he had behaved discreditably as a stool pigeon in Oflag 79, and whether he had a long-term mission on behalf of the German security services which he had not yet revealed.[3]

As summer approached, the men charged with investigating the case of Ronald Seth began to realise that recovering information from witnesses would be no easy task. In the meantime, Ronald was getting restive, firing off letters to Wing Commander Redding from Barnstaple, where he was enjoying a period of leave. At the end of May, he wrote to say that, should his leave be extended, he would have difficulty in finding accommodation since all the lodgings in the town and surrounding countryside were fully booked up. His suggestion that he might be posted as a temporary supernumerary to RAF Chivenor, where his wife was a station officer, sent a quiver of nervousness through the men in London. This might lead to 'many complications', Squadron Leader Park informed him on 7 June. Seth meanwhile had managed temporarily to solve his accommodation problems, but he continued to nag his erstwhile employers on the matter of his pay. Whilst admitting that the finance department at SOE was quite right to argue that if Seth were proved to have been working for the Germans, he would be disentitled to his pay, Park was also aware that the conclusion of investigations would take a very long time. He therefore suggested that Seth be paid what was due to him, and 'if there is subsequent proof that he is a traitor', the money should either be recovered from him, or if this were not possible, simply written off.[4]

This seems to have been the conclusion arrived at by Air Commodore Archie Boyle, who also issued instructions that Seth be outposted by the RAF. The Air Ministry, however, took a rather dim view of this idea, pointing out that administrative jobs were scarce. Wing Commander Spencer intimated that the Ministry would look favourably upon early release from the service if Seth managed to find himself a job at the BBC or as a schoolteacher, whilst the most Group Captain Porrie could offer was a posting to Airport Control.

The frustration of those charged with handling the Seth case is evident in Roland Bird's response to this news:

> I realise that it is not a very good talking-point in your negotiations with the Air Ministry to stress the fact that Seth is a returned German agent whose security case is by no means clear as yet. On the other hand, it is surely a new doctrine that such a character should be granted unconditional liberty in preference to many thousands in the services whose loyalty has never been in question. As for the suggestion that he might be a suitable candidate for Airport Control, I can only say that this office has no intention of providing Seth with what would undoubtedly be the apotheosis of his career.[5]

Bird therefore urged Park to persuade the Air Ministry to change its mind on this matter, since it would be most unwise to allow such an unstable character as Seth to enjoy 'untrammelled opportunities of line-shooting' once free of the discipline and control of military life.

The Air Ministry finally agreed to outpost Seth as administrative officer, and he seems to have been moved around various RAF stations for the rest of the year. The problem of what to do with him continued to bother Park and Bird throughout the summer. Park was now the recipient of Seth's letters – three in four days in mid-July, dealing with matters as diverse as securing employment for a German internee with a good knowledge of languages, Seth's entitlement to medals, and a proposed application for the post of Chief Constable of Wiltshire. This last-named idea quickly fell to the ground, since – as Seth informed Park on 19 July – it was no use applying unless he could state he was married. Seth's marital problems had clearly reached a crisis point, and in 1945, divorcees stood no chance of becoming part of the police establishment.

For Seth himself, there remained the problem of his wartime mistress, Liliane. The ardour with which he had initially pressed his superiors to be allowed to return to Paris to rescue her from the vengeful Pierre and bring her back to England soon cooled. He wrote to Park on 23 May from the Imperial Hotel, Barnstaple, returning Liliane's letter of 24 April. He did not want it back, nor did he clamour to be allowed to hasten to Paris in response to a couple of telegrams from Mme Soulier, summoning him to the aid of a sick Liliane. In fact, he himself suggested that *RONNIE MALADE NE PEUT VENIR* (Ronny ill cannot come) should be sent in reply to Mme Renggli. Seth now accepted completely that he could not be allowed to go to Paris at the moment, and that he was entirely in the hands of his investigators for the future.

If Ronald Seth no longer wished to renew his acquaintance with Liliane, the French legal system suddenly found his attendance in France a matter of great urgency. At the end of June, a letter from the office of R. Auric, juge d'instruction, marked 'très urgent', found its way to Wimpole Street, the holding address for Seth. M. Auric was about to conduct his examination of Jean Soulier, Lucienne Beucherie, Richard Delidaise and others accused of consorting with the enemy, and he believed Seth's testimony was indispensable for the uncovering of the truth. This prompted some head-scratching amongst Seth's handlers, though they assumed that this was a subpoena, when in fact Auric only asked politely if Seth envisaged a brief return to Paris in the near future. In any event, MI5 and SOE were firmly against any such trip, on two grounds: firstly, that Seth might try to escape, and secondly, there was no guarantee that he would tell the truth. In these circumstances, MI5 proposed that a certified copy of the relevant parts of the statement made by Seth at the London Reception Centre be sent to the juge d'instruction with commentary on its accuracy or otherwise provided.

This communication seems never to have been passed on to Seth: MI5 simply took it upon itself to interfere with the course of French justice and offer to provide a carefully redacted version of Seth's statement. The urgency of M. Auric's note may have had something to do with his wish to go off on holiday, for on 23 July, SOE's security officer in France, Colonel

Richard Henry Atkinson Warden, one-time jockey and racehorse trainer, wrote that he had been unable to get in touch with Auric as he was away on holiday until mid-August. His clerk had, however, been helpful, giving him a list of nine people currently held at Fresnes prison. According to the clerk, 'all were highly suspect, and at least three will be shot. Their general excuse for behaving as they behaved is that they were really playing a double game without the Germans knowing it.'[6]

Seth was to be one of the chief witnesses for the defence, and the clerk repeated the request that he be allowed to go to France to be interrogated and to confront the prisoners. Warden told him that regrettably, Seth could not be allowed out of Britain since he had not yet been cleared by the authorities. He also made sure that the French were left in no doubt that the British investigators had found Seth 'extremely untruthful'. In addition to promising the French the redacted copy of Seth's statement, Seth would be asked to state what he knew of the nine persons listed by the clerk.

Seth responded to this request on 31 July. Five of the nine persons mentioned he did not know. His comments on François, also known as Richard Delidaise were distinctly unfavourable. He described him as a member of Major Kliemann's intelligence service, consulted on radio matters, and earning the greater part of his livelihood on the black market. He had little good to say either about his wife Louise or his sister Yvonne, the mistress of Major Kliemann. He was, however, effusive in his support for Jean Soulier and Mme Renggli (charged under the name Lucienne Beucherie). He retold the story of Liliane offering to act as hostage for his good conduct as a German agent charged with a mission to Britain, and made great play of the assistance she and Jean Soulier gave him in his abortive attempt to escape to England via Brest in the summer of 1944. He had confided in Soulier in the spring of 1944 that he was a British agent since he was convinced he was an anglophile, as was his mother.

Seth's unequivocal support for Jean Soulier is somewhat surprising, especially in view of Liliane's revelation to him in April that it was Jean who had initially denounced her as a German agent. In a seven-page memorandum, written in mid-August, he reiterated his support for the couple, and provided more details of his commitment. Whilst in Paris in the months before D-Day, he had given both of them written promises that, should they ever need assistance, they should get in touch with the British authorities. He had subsequently written to Jean Soulier in Fresnes prison, repeating his undertaking to do all he could for him. Since then, he had faced nothing but low-level obstruction in his attempts to respond to the juge d'instruction's request to give evidence. His proposal for dealing with what he calls 'the French situation' is pure Seth. Since 'no one is more subservient to RANK than the French' and 'as a Flight Lieutenant with the RAF I should carry little weight with the juge d'instruction' he proposed that he be given the temporary rank (and pay) of Air Commodore. This would enable him to persuade the juge d'instruction to drop the charges against Jean Soulier and Mme Renggli as well as to gain the 'little necessary cooperation of senior service officers', from whom nothing but obstruction could be expected.[7]

Seth accompanied this memorandum with a campaign to attract the attention of members of the recently formed Labour government. He managed to persuade Squadron Leader Asburey of his wife's RAF station at Chivenor to write to Herbert Morrison (who referred the matter to the Foreign Office), and he himself contacted John Strachey, Under-Secretary of State for Air. Bird and Park moved swiftly to counter these moves. Lucienne Beucherie was Seth's mistress between November 1943 and July 1944, whilst he was undergoing training by the Germans for an intelligence mission against this country, Roland Bird told T.E. Bromley of the Foreign Office, and there was no reason to believe the French would be in any better position than MI5 to confirm or refute Seth's claim that Lucienne Beucherie (aka Liliane) saved his life. In any event, information compiled by Seth had been handed over to the juge d'instruction, so there were no grounds for anticipating a miscarriage of justice owing to Seth's absence from court. Wing Commander Rose of the Air Ministry was able to inform Hugh Park at the end of August that he had spoken to the Under-Secretary of State's office, and there was nothing to fear from that quarter.

Back in Paris, M. Auric was still seeking further clarification from Ronald Seth. A series of follow-up questions were transmitted to Hugh Park from Ensign Hack, one of Colonel Warden's staff in the French capital. Auric also wanted to know to what extent Seth could be considered to have been a loyal British agent whilst in Paris, and how far his statements could be considered reliable. Park's own opinion on this was brutally frank. Seth could not be considered a loyal agent whilst in Paris, since he was in fact not an agent at all; and his interrogators in England had formed the view that he could not be considered reliable. Captain Desmond Vesey of MI5 concurred entirely with these views.

Seth duly obliged the juge d'instruction with another lengthy digest of his knowledge of the Delidaises and Jean Soulier. Once again, he could find nothing positive to say about the Delidaises, though he did throw some new light on their relationship with Emil Kliemann. His additional comments on the Delidaises and Jean Soulier, and MI5's comments as to his reliability, were passed on to M. Auric, and Ensign Hack was able to report to London at the end of September that the juge d'instruction appeared to be satisfied with them. Ronald Seth, however, was not so easily satisfied, and he seized the opportunity provided by the return to England of his old boss, George Odomar Wiskeman, to widen his campaign against those whom he considered to be deliberately concealing his past achievements and blighting his prospects through their obstructive tactics.

Wiskeman had left SOE in autumn 1944 to work for a large timber firm, and had since taken up residence in Stockholm. He remained in touch with his old colleagues, however, even offering to do the odd spot of work for them (an offer not warmly welcomed, it has to be said). Some time towards the end of the summer of 1945, he got to hear of the investigation into Seth's activities, and wrote that, unless it was intended to bring charges against the officer in question, he should be helped by the organisation. That letter was evidently passed on to Major General Gubbins, the executive director of SOE, for on 12 September, 'CD' (i.e. Gubbins) wrote to 'Archie' Boyle, asking to be informed about the position as regards Seth. 'I understood that he was very much suspect and gather than he is now at large. Has he left this Organisation yet and been signed off or is a case still being prepared against him, or what?'[8]

Boyle's reply was careful to place the responsibility for the Seth case fairly and squarely at the door of MI5. MI5 had recommended that every effort be made to gather more information in Germany, from the staff of Oflag 79, Amt VID and the German Foreign Office, and when such evidence was available, Seth would be interrogated once more. MI5 had not so far discovered such evidence, but were still hopeful of obtaining material from German officers still to be interrogated. At MI5's request, Seth was kept on SOE's books until a posting which complied with MI5 requirements was found; such a posting was found in August, and Seth had been duly assigned to RAF Andover as an administrative officer.

This posting was an additional source of complaint for Seth, since he had been returned to the rank of Flying Officer. This apparent demotion was included in a package of grievances, all meticulously documented, which were sent to Wiskeman. Accompanying the précis was a manuscript, which Seth urged his old boss to read first. This was the manuscript of a book, entitled 'Blunderhead British Agent or the Failure of Another Mission' which had already found its way to the desk of the Under-Secretary of State for Air.

In his letter to Wiskeman, Seth listed nine things that continued to puzzle and worry him. Why would the British authorities not allow him to go to Paris to give evidence? Why was nothing being said about his report or his operation? If his operation had not been a success, why had he not been told? 'Being susceptible to atmosphere', Seth observed, 'I feel that there is something wrong somewhere'. If something was wrong, he ought to be allowed the opportunity to clear himself. Even if there were insufficient evidence on which to rest a case, he felt that he ought to be court-martialled, so that a public announcement could be made to that effect. If a case could not be brought, then the authorities should take some action, such as the award of a small decoration, which would ensure that he was cleared of suspicion of treachery in the eyes of the 2,500 officers who had been at Oflag 79. If this were not possible, he should at least be allowed to publish his book, which he was prepared to alter if and where advisable, in order to defend himself. Seth also wanted to know who issued the warning to treat him with the gravest suspicion to the Senior British Officer at Oflag 79, his old enemy Colonel Brown. Finally, he was also particularly unhappy that Count Bernadotte 'had been allowed to publish all the facts of his relations with Himmler, whereas no announcement at all has been made of mine'.[9]

This was not the end of Seth's long diatribe; the unsuspecting Wiskeman was urged to consider yet another letter, fired off to John Strachey, Under-Secretary of State for Air, listing in minute detail his complaints about the lack of promotion and the unsuitability of his posting to an RAF maintenance depot.

Whether or not Wiskeman met Seth in London is unclear, though the fact that the précis and the manuscript were handed on to Group Captain Redding, now returned from India with a promotion, would suggest that Wiskeman deemed it prudent not to get involved any further. Redding, who seems not to have annoyed Seth as much as certain other figures in SOE (as Seth frankly admitted), had for some weeks previously been the recipient of a series of letters from the aggrieved administrative officer, Seth's complaints (which were usually detailed in itemised paragraphs in his letters) fell under three main headings: his desire to give witness in the French courts (and the obstacles placed in his path by certain individuals); his concern about his impugned honour; and a tangled knot of personal matters, ranging from his entitlement to medals to lost kit and clothing. This last generated a series of memoranda and notes that swelled his personal file. The correspondence on his lost kit is particularly hilarious. Seth was apparently claiming that there was a particularly valuable sealskin-lined overcoat, riding breeches and coat in the suitcase he had entrusted to Colonel Hazell before his departure to Estonia: the finance department at SOE rather peevishly replied that without prior notice, they could not be expected to guess that such articles had been deposited. They were therefore unwilling to accept liability for the loss, but were prepared to offer £45 plus fifty clothing coupons as a contribution towards the loss of his service and civilian kit. Seth snapped up the offer, but could not refrain from insisting that Hazell was fully cognisant of the fact that his suitcase contained only civilian clothes and had indeed suggested that Seth leave it in store with his section. With this 'bitter little note', the protracted wrangling over the lost riding outfit was brought to an end.

Seth continued to pester Redding (as he himself acknowledged) into the late autumn. On 6 November, he had good news: the British Council had offered him a job in Istanbul at a salary of £1,500 a year, on condition that he could be released immediately from the service. Redding replied encouragingly that he though it highly probable that Seth would be released by the end of the year. If, however, he hoped that at long last he would see the back of the irrepressible Seth, he was mistaken. He should have known better than to say that since Seth had invoked higher authority in his pursuit of justice, the matter was now out of his hands. He may have wished this was the case, but that did not spare him from a further outburst of self-justification, interspersed with heartfelt thanks for the way in which Redding had treated his wife during his absence.

What of the job in Turkey, which Seth seemed confident was his (and which he clearly hoped to combine with a bit of information-gathering on Soviet-Turkish relations)? On 14 January 1946, Group Captain Jackson of the Appointments Department of the British Council wrote to the Air Ministry seeking a confidential report as to the suitability of Flight Lieutenant Seth for the post of Publications Officer in Istanbul. As he would be taking up the appointment very shortly, the Group Captain would be grateful for the earliest possible answer. Four days later, however, Group Captain Jackson sent a copy of this letter to a Major Mott at 14 Kendrick Place, Dorset Street, London W1, seeking a reply, and asking if he should regard it as the official one. Major Mott was one of those still holding the fort as SOE was being wound up, and he passed the matter on to Air Commodore Boyle, the man who had been in charge of security, intelligence and personnel at SOE since 1943.

Boyle had never met Seth, but he had become acquainted with him through the Paris report in 1944, and, as he told Jackson, he knew a great deal about his case. Boyle made no bones about it: Seth did not possess the qualities suitable for employment with the British Council. Though brave and well suited to 'an irregular type of war time work', Seth was possessed of an over-vivid imagination and lacked a sense of balance. His case contained so many contradictory aspects that doubts had been expressed about the veracity of his story. Nonetheless, Boyle did have the goodness to admit that 'no definite proof of collaboration with the enemy has come to light and I think it is unlikely that any further evidence will emerge from the muddled and contradictory stories in circulation'.[10]

Having effectively destroyed Seth's chances of obtaining employment with the British Council, Boyle ended his letter by pushing the final responsibility for any judgement as to Seth's suitability on to the Air Ministry, on the grounds that they had been responsible for Seth since his return to England. SOE had one further parting shot for their hapless ex-agent before their ways finally separated early in 1946. On 20 March, ex-Blunderhead Ronald Seth, now returned to civilian life, wrote a short letter to Major General Sir Colin McVean Gubbins, CMG, DSO, MC, congratulating him on his recent honour, and asking politely if any decision had yet been made about his final report. A pencilled note on the letter suggests that the ineffable Major Mott was deputed to speak to Seth. The major general was in process of proceeding abroad, but he did ask Mott to let the Air Ministry know that in his view, publication of Seth's book was not desirable either on account of specific objections already discussed or on account of its general tone, and he would be grateful if the men at the ministry could use all their endeavours to prevent publication.[11] And with that, the SOE file on Ronald Seth, alias Blunderhead, comes to an end.

Notes

1. Seth to Redding, 6 May 1945, HS9/1345.
2. Senter to Liddell, 18 April 1945, HS9/1345.
3. MI5 report 3, pp.21–5.
4. Park to Seth, 7 June 1945, and minute by Park, same date, HS9/1345.
5. Bird to Park, 19 June 1945, HS9/1345.
6. Warden to Lt Col Roche, 23 July 1945, HS9/1345.
7. 'Minute regarding the position of M. Jean Soulier and Madame Lilyane Renggli', 16 August 1945, HS9/1345.
8. Memo from CD, 12 September 1945, HS9/1345.
9. 'Precis of events regarding Blunderhead's arrival in U.K. and subsequently', 1 October 1945, HS9/1345.
10. Boyle to Jackson, 21 January 1946, HS9/1345.
11. 'Manuscript submitted for censorship by Ronald Seth', 22 March 1946, HS9/1345.

13 | 'An extremely serious business.'

Reading, Christmas 1946

Ronald Seth did not get the job in Istanbul. In February 1946, he received a letter from the British Council, informing him that 'for reasons outside our control' it was not possible to proceed with the appointment. When Seth took the matter up personally at the British Council headquarters, he was led to believe that the reason for their decision was the refusal of the Passport Office to renew his passport. This of course produced an eloquently furious letter from Seth to MI5, declaring that a passport was the right of every freeborn Englishman, and demanding that he be allowed to clear his impugned honour in a court of law. When the Home Office also began to ask for clear proof as to why he should be denied a passport, MI5 was forced to admit that there was no evidence to show that Seth 'would continue to be disloyal' if given a passport.[1]

After he was finally demobbed from the RAF, Seth managed to find employment with the Ministry of Works, later moving on to teaching on the island of Guernsey. He was never charged with any offence, but neither was he ever officially exonerated. Like many others whose actions during the war were scrutinised by the British security services, he was to remain in the shadowlands. He was, however, determined to justify his actions publicly, and he had the talent, ability and sheer persistency to do this. As we have seen, he had managed to write up his account into book form during the time he was waiting for his case to be resolved. At the end of 1946, we find him writing to Hugh Trevor-Roper, whose investigation into the last days of Hitler was just beginning to reach the British public through press articles, and sending him a few chapters of his manuscript. He tells Trevor-Roper that it is 125,000 words in the telling, without frills, and that he had just been given permission to publish by the security department of the Air Ministry.[2]

Seth does not give a name to his book, and when it finally appeared six years later, it bore the rather enigmatic title *A Spy Has No Friends*. The subtitle is perhaps more revealing: *To Save His Country, He Became the Enemy*. In 1945, he had provisionally entitled his book Blunderhead British Agent or Failure of Another Mission. The published title may owe a great deal to the persuasive abilities of an editor, and the contents may not have changed greatly over the intervening period; however, bearing in mind the increasingly tetchy relationship between Seth and higher authority in 1945, it is probable that Blunderhead British Agent had rather more to say about the failings of the British security services than was contained in the book brought out by Andre Deutsch in 1952.

The subtitle of the published book alludes of course to the double agent role Seth claimed that he had taken on. The fact that his mission to Estonia had been explicitly defined as sabotage, and intelligence-gathering had been excluded from his brief, rather weakens his claim to have been a British agent, but Ronald Seth was never one to allow such restrictions to cramp his style. And it might be argued that, had SOE really wished merely to blow up Estonian shale-oil installations, they would have fared better with a well-equipped, resourceful commando unit. The exact nature of the mission to Estonia, and the consequences of its failure, will be examined in greater detail later. Here, I want to consider a number of questions pertaining to Seth's activity from the time of his capture and imprisonment in Estonia to his return to England in April 1945.

In *A Spy Has No Friends*, Seth presents his willingness to work with the Germans as part of a scheme, the 'vague lines of action' of which had been sketched out in discussions with his SOE mentor, 'Major Larch' (i.e. Hazell). Essential for this scheme to work was access to a microphone, which would allow Seth to use a secret code and thus transmit information to Britain.

This in turn meant that he had to appear to be pro-German, and to tell a plausible story which contained sufficient misleading elements to confuse the enemy.[3]

Whether such discussions took place is open to question. What was said and discussed in SOE's offices, meeting places and training stations was undoubtedly far more interesting and revealing that the rather bland, guarded language of official correspondence, which is what a researcher has to rely upon. One can assume that operatives and their handlers did talk about what might happen if something went wrong and the operative fell into enemy hands. Not everyone could or would wish to swallow the cyanide pill with which agents were supplied. We have the tantalising evidence of John 'Busty' Brown, the man who was said to have been given training beforehand as a double agent: was Seth also programmed to act as a 'stooge', prepared to work for the Germans but secretly spying on them? Or are we yet again faced with a subtle piece of invention designed either to add to Seth's own importance or – as many in MI5 tended to think – to cover up his failings?

Another way of looking at this problem is to see it through German eyes, and to consider Seth's value as a potential recruit. He was a published author, and had worked for the BBC, both of which showed that he had a way with words and was familiar with the media. Like John Calthrop, who tried to get work in the German film industry, he seems to have been put on hold by the German intelligence service, filed away as a person of possible interest, but in the meantime shunted across Europe from one prison to another, until someone picked him up and sought to train him as a possible agent.

Another person who also had a talent that might conceivably have been useful to the Germans was John Renshaw (Robert, or Bob) Starr. Partially educated in France, where he worked before the war as a jobbing artist, his fluent French made him an asset for SOE, and he was eventually recruited into the French section. Starr carried out one successful if uneventful mission in 1942, but was captured in Dijon on his second mission. He made two unsuccessful escape attempts, but eventually opted to work with the Germans. Under interrogation in 1945, he confessed frankly that he chose to do so in preference to imprisonment, though he also claimed that he hoped to gain advantage from this by finding out what the Germans knew. Hans Kieffer, the head of the Gestapo in Paris, was apparently impressed by Starr's talents as an illustrator – much as Dönhoff seems to have admired

Seth's skills as a reporter – and this undoubtedly gave him a degree of protection and privilege.

Starr was one of several SOE agents in France who were to come under suspicion for consorting with the enemy and the French section of SOE was severely censured by MI5 for the laxity of its security procedures on several occasions. There was a constant conflict between SOE, which felt a responsibility and loyalty towards its agents, and MI5 with its overriding concern for national security. MI5 tended to assume in cases where treachery could not be immediately proven that this was because the necessary evidence was not yet available; that an agent might in fact be innocent was something MI5 investigators were often unwilling to consider, as we have seen in the case of Ronald Seth.[4]

Most of the problems over security occurred from 1943 onwards, as SOE developed into a major organisation with scores of agents operating across the world. For every one who managed to survive successfully, there were many who were far less fortunate. Given the hazardous nature of the work, it was inevitable that some agents would crack and succumb to pressure once captured, though not all who did so were 'turned'. This leads to a difficult question: can one discern identifiable traits in certain individuals that might have marked them out as likely candidates for co-option to the 'other side'? An anonymous author of a critical report on the practices of SOE's French section was in no doubt that the 'wild man' who drifted from job to job and had no basic loyalties or ideals was not the kind of person likely to keep faith with either his employers or his country. The work of the secret agent, in the opinion of this veteran of the service, whether he was a political intelligence agent or a saboteur, was an 'extremely serious business' which no man should take up unless prepared to make very considerable social sacrifices.[5]

Did organisations such as SOE attract the kind of people possessed 'of a natural predilection to live in that curious world of espionage and deceit, and who attach themselves with equal facility to one side or the other, so long as their craving for adventure of a rather macabre type is satisfied'?[6] Was the anonymous reviewer on the right tracks when he hinted that the 'rolling-stone type' could not be relied on?

The pioneering historian of SOE, M.R.D. Foot, discerned two distinguishing characteristics of the organisation from the start: a lack of thorough preparation, necessitated by having to improvise at very short notice, and an overweening obsession with personality.[7] The paramount need to get agents into the field as soon as possible may well have persuaded those in charge of recruitment and training to go for those with flair and imagination, for the unconventional, even wayward type, rather than the solid, unspectacular safe pair of hands. What to an MI5 officer would immediately raise the possibility of a security risk – a fondness for alcohol and the company of women, for instance – was not generally seen as a serious obstacle by those in SOE seeking to recruit agents for overseas missions. Indeed, it was sometimes seen as an advantage, enabling the agent to establish valuable contacts and to procure information. The possibility that Ronald Seth might have a girlfriend in Estonia was not seen as an obstacle to his recruitment, or it was overlooked by the evident fact that he had 'guts' in proposing his risky venture. And some of the distinguishing features of his personality, which were later to attract the most consistent criticism, were often seen by his handlers and trainers as his greatest asset.

Seth never had the chance to become a radio operator in German captivity, and this drastically reduced any hopes he might have had of becoming a double agent. Radio was the crucial element in deception. The right double agent (ideally able to move relatively freely and thus meet handlers on the 'other' side) was an invaluable asset – although, as many studies have shown, also a liability. In the initial stages of the war, the Abwehr scored some notable successes with its radio deception, or *Funkspiel*, but by 1943, British intelligence was demonstrably ahead in the game. In part, this was a consequence of the desperate overstretching of German resources brought about by the occupation of huge swathes of Eastern Europe and Russia; but it was also the case that the Allies had more options at their disposal. Allied agents, for example, were able to get help from local resistance networks: German agents sent to Britain had no such extensive networks at their disposal to provide them with food, shelter, transport, or equipment. The fate of those who did manage to get to Britain was almost invariably to be captured in short order, and either imprisonment or further employment under British control. Sabotage, certainly on the scale as practised in France or Norway, for example, was virtually impossible, simply because Britain was not occupied and hence had no resistance movement eager and willing to fight the occupier. Double agents such as Juan Pujol ('Garbo') fed the Germans reams of intelligence purportedly gathered by a vast network of his agents across Britain, but in reality, concocted in his own imagination, carefully assisted by his MI5 handlers. The stark truth was that, certainly by 1943, Germany no longer had any effective means of gathering reliable intelligence on the ground in Britain, whereas the British had ample opportunity to do so in occupied Europe.

There is a further aspect to be considered, and that is, the relationship of the intelligence-gathering services with each other and, more importantly, with the state. That SOE and SIS were rivals even to the point of obstruction of each other's efforts was well known, and was the subject of earnest enquiry and discussion in high official circles. Other intelligence-gathering agencies, such as MI9 or the various service departments also pursued their own course and were often reluctant to collaborate. But (*pace* the part played by secret agents of the Soviet Union) there was no question of their loyalty to the state, which was old, established, conservative and conventional. The Nazi state was almost the complete antithesis, a new, monstrous, aggressive and destructive force, which relied for its momentum on a breathless kind of divide-and-rule principle. Dozens of grotesque fiefdoms competed for the favours of the Führer and sought to do down their rivals at the same time. The kind of loyalties which British security services regarded as essential in a trustworthy agent were in Nazi Germany suborned to the *Führerprinzip*, unconditional obedience to the dictates of the leader. Those whose love of country could not accommodate the excesses of Nazi policy, particularly once the tide of war had turned in 1943, were perforce drawn into some form of opposition, either silent or active. This was particularly the case in the regular army, the Wehrmacht, and its intelligence-gathering Abwehr. Important top-secret information was leaked by Abwehr operatives to Allied intelligence, and a number of top people in the organisation had close links to the opposition to Hitler that began to grow apace after Stalingrad. The Abwehr was dissolved and effectively absorbed in 1944 into Himmler's empire, the RHSA; however, as we have seen, there were also high-ranking figures in the SS who were prepared to contemplate moving against Hitler. Keith Jeffrey has revealed that in December 1944, a well-placed and experienced intelligence officer from the RSHA contacted the newly opened British embassy in Paris, saying that he had been sent by his superior on a special mission to make contact with the British government. The proposal he outlined bears some resemblance to those floated by Schellenberg and others in 1945, namely some sort of co-operation with Britain to avoid the destruction of Germany and its absorption into the Russian sphere of influence.[8]

Opening up lines of communication with the enemy through the medium of an agent was a risky business. On the other hand, handling a potential agent conferred a kind of power which some must have found attractive. It also seems to have allowed the handlers considerable freedom to entertain lavishly and to dispose of money, which to a bon viveur such as Emil Kliemann was irresistible. And it also offered scope to pursue an agenda at variance with official policy: this seems to have been the case in the Third Reich once the war had turned decisively in favour of the Allies. For the Allied agent or serviceman who fell into the hands of the enemy, and who had the wit and ability to discern these nuances of loyalty and to play upon them, there was clearly scope to play an active, if dangerous game of deception.

At the risk of oversimplification, then, it would appear that the person willing to become an agent of the Germans had firstly to possess something of obvious value: an expertise in radio signalling, an ability to communicate fluently and persuasively, and an intimate, preferably native knowledge of Britain and British society. Equally vital was a kind of peculiar chemistry that bonded the potential agent with his handler. On several occasions, Seth waxed eloquent on the intimacy of his relationship with Christoph Count Dönhoff, and he also seems to have got on well with Emil Kliemann. Berneville-Claye and Calthrop also seem to have found it easy to establish relationships with the Germans. We have the testimony of a senior SS general, Felix Steiner, to illustrate Berneville-Claye's talent to amuse and win over those he encountered. In the last days of the war, Berneville-Claye ended up at Steiner's headquarters in the Mecklenburg town of Neu Strelitz. He himself later confessed that he 'expected to crash', but was received with open arms and given a set of papers explaining he was one of the 'honourable Englanders' who had elected to fight side-by-side with Germany in its race war. Steiner told his interrogators that Berneville-Claye, who was dressed in the field-grey uniform of a Panzer captain, made a good impression; he understood German quite well, gave witty replies and seemed sincere in his desire to fight Bolshevism, even though Steiner told him he believed the war was lost.[9]

A professed eagerness to fight Bolshevism was also an important ingredient in forging a relationship between the German security services and the would-be agent or collaborator. In Berneville-Claye's case, it seems to have precipitated him in front of a bunch of disconsolate individuals, the final forlorn remnant of the British Free Corps. He argued subsequently that he continued to play the role assigned to him by Steiner, and played 'the part of a rat to the full'. He was later to achieve notoriety as having strutted about in public wearing the uniform of an SS captain (which it seems was given to him by Steiner), but by appearing eager to serve the Nazi cause even at its last hour, he was able to persuade the SS to let him have a vehicle, in which he eventually managed to reach the American Sixth Independent Airborne Brigade.

Like Berneville-Claye, John Boucicault de Suffield Calthrop also played the anti-Bolshevik card for all it was worth. In the dying days of a lost war, however, those Germans with whom such men came into contact seem to have had no very clear idea of how they might use them. In the case of Berneville-Claye, Steiner might have been hoping that this ebullient person who had landed up at his headquarters would be able to breathe some life and enthusiasm into a group of foreign recruits who might conceivably be drafted into the Panzergrenadier Division Nordland for the defence of Berlin, though he seems to have been more amused at the man's audacity than impressed by his fighting qualities. Calthrop, who had crossed paths with Seth in Oflag 79, was eventually brought into contact in March 1945 with a man called Vivian Stranders, born British but taking German nationality in 1933. Stranders had broadcast anti-British propaganda, and as a *Sturmbannführer* in the SS, had been active in recruiting members of the British Free Corps. According to Calthrop's statement during interrogation in London, Stranders had no clear idea of what to do with him, and asked him if he had any suggestions. General Gottlob Berger, the man eventually responsible for despatching him across the Swiss frontier on a mission to stand for Parliament, sought at an earlier stage to get rid of him by asking him to command the British drivers of some Swedish trucks at Lübeck, which were intended to carry food parcels to prisoner-of-war camps. The history of Ronald Seth also shows that the Germans had no very clear idea of what to do with him, either.

❖ ❖ ❖

Let us now turn to the original mission as proposed in 1941 by Ronald Seth and taken up in 1942 by SOE. The unofficial history of the Polish minorities (*sic*) section of SOE, written after the war, concluded that Seth's motives remained obscure. 'Perhaps he saw himself as a modern Lawrence, only of Esthonia, not Arabia!' was the rather jocular observation of the history's anonymous author.[10] Seth's own post-war explanation, that he heard by chance that the Germans had managed to get the shale-oil mines working again, and this prompted him to come up with a plan to destroy them which, much to his surprise, was taken up by Intelligence, is weakened by the fact that he seems to have attempted to return with official backing to Estonia before the Germans attacked the Soviet Union. The explanation that he gave the Germans, that he had been virtually blackmailed into undertaking the mission, that he did so only for the sake of his family, and that he had no intention of carrying out the operation, but would surrender at the first opportunity and offer to work against the Russians, whom he had always hated, clearly ran contrary to what stands in the official record, i.e. that he himself initiated the mission. It is also very much against character: Seth was notoriously reluctant to work with others or under others' dictates.

There can be no doubt therefore that the Estonia project emanated from the fertile mind of Ronald Seth, or that it remained very much his own right up to his arrival in the country. However, in one respect what he told his German captors in Estonia bears the ring of truth, although he was perhaps alarmed, rather than disgusted by the whole business. There had been a number of serious hitches along the way, not least the last-minute worries about his radio equipment. Writing up his report in Bern in 1945, he claimed that SOE had little or no information on the state of affairs in Estonia, and what little there was turned out to be entirely false. The enormity of what he was undertaking finally struck him during the last hour of the flight in the Halifax bomber, he admitted, and he prayed fervently for something to happen which would render the operation impossible at the last minute.[11] This probably flashed across the mind of all agents as they realised a point of no return had been reached, but in Seth's case, he found himself alone and without any hope of a supportive network.

As we have seen, Captain Milton of MI5 was highly sceptical of the veracity of Seth's story. However, his own sources were not always reliable either. He relied heavily on the information supplied by Wolfgang Krause-Brandstetter, who had met Seth some time in the early weeks of 1944 in order to assess his reliability and suitability for employment as an agent. The two men had enjoyed a bibulous lunch at the Hotel Claridge. Milton concluded that Seth possibly 'told the truth on this occasion under the influence of drink'.[12] Seth's own opinion of Krause-Brandstetter was that he was a most unsuitable agent, and the evidence, such as it is, would tend to support his view. Krause-Brandstetter was one of the first wave of German intelligence officers rounded up and interrogated, and he seems to have talked quite willingly. He admitted that he had revealed his real name to Seth, and he also consistently placed Seth's mission in Lithuania. This may have been an error on his part, but it might also have been part of Seth's cover story. Krause-Brandstetter also said that Seth had told him that he had forged a cheque in England, which had allowed the authorities to put pressure on him to undertake the mission. Seth had told this story earlier, in Frankfurt, as part of his cover. It is highly likely that by the spring of 1944, he had become so used to living with his own fantasies that it was impossible to separate truth from fiction, indeed, the story he had devised and elaborated had now become the truth for him.

Captain Milton is careful to say that it was Seth who thought SOE's preparations were inadequate, though he has the grace to admit that some essential part of the radio set might have been missing. This is something that Seth himself complained about – that the vital crystals had not been packed in any of his containers. When he raised this matter during interrogation in London, the subject was abruptly changed, clear evidence, he thought, that his suspicions were well founded.

As M.R.D. Foot pointed out, the failings of SOE should be seen against the fact that they had to improvise at very short notice, which gave their operations the stamp of haste and inadequacy of preparation. In Ronald Seth's case, the improvisatory nature of planning was further hampered by difficulties in obtaining maps, documents and basic information about the target of the operation. Very little thought seems to have been given to the question of how a man on his own was supposed to survive the onset of winter, even if he were fortunate enough to find and unpack the three containers dropped into the woods and bogs of northern Estonia.

It is hard on this evidence to avoid the conclusion that the soubriquet 'Blunderhead' attached to the mission was a mocking comment on the entire show. But, if SOE can and should be criticised for the shortcomings of this operation, some responsibility also lies with Ronald Seth, whose idea it was in the first place. His earlier attempt to persuade the War Office to sponsor a surveillance operation during the Russian occupation of the country may indicate a burning desire to do something to help a country to which he had evidently become attached, but he seems not to have appreciated subsequently that for many Estonians the experience of Russian occupation meant that the Germans were seen, initially at least, as welcome liberators. His claims to be an expert in the country and its language no doubt convinced those in SOE who seem to have suffered from a common upper-class English assumption that nothing was beyond the ability of a gentleman with an Oxbridge degree. Seth was indeed one of those people whose sublime self-confidence persuades them – and others – that they are verily all that they claim to be.

His self-belief also made him self-willed. Although he was reminded on more than one occasion that intelligence-gathering was not part of his brief, his subsequent career in Nazi-occupied Europe was, in his own words, devoted to that task. In his own eyes, Ronald Seth was a spy, not a saboteur. To give him his due, however, the precise nature of his operation was never properly defined by his handlers. Sabotage was not mentioned in his initial proposal to the Air Ministry in October 1941, though it was explicitly declared to be the object of the operation for which SOE sought Moscow's blessing a month later. The draft project of mid-December 1941 also listed sabotage of the shale-oil mines as an objective, but it also spoke of other forms of sabotage and passive resistance that the organiser might be able to accomplish once he arrived in the field. The organiser was furthermore 'to organise and foment disaffection amongst the Estonian population and friction between them and the occupying Germans'. This seems most closely to accord with Seth's own views, both at the time and later.[13] Reflecting on his mission on 22 April 1942, some six months after he first proposed the idea, he concluded that he should concentrate for the first two or three months of his mission on underground propaganda, which would give him an idea of what might be achieved by more active measures. He explicitly rejected sporadic or isolated acts of sabotage in favour of bands of saboteurs, up to 100-strong, who might carry out simultaneous attacks on rail communications, enemy aircraft and shale-oil installations.

The lion's share of the estimate of expenses meticulously drawn up by Seth in September 1942 was to be paid to locally recruited Estonians, organised in cells for surveillance operations and acts of sabotage. In other words, as the autumn deadline for the operation loomed, Seth was still thinking of organising teams of saboteurs, rather than preparing himself for a one-man operation to blow up the shale-oil installations. This assumption was not challenged. Commenting on Seth's estimate of expenses, his handler Major Hazell admitted that 'it is, of course, very difficult to give any indication as to what he will be able to do when he reaches his destination', but he supported his application for the equivalent of £1,500 so that SOE could at least feel it had done all it could to make the operation a success.[14]

In the end, the remarkable thing about Seth's story is not the hapless Estonian adventure but his subsequent survival thanks to an ability to play upon the snobbish susceptibilities of his captors. What were recognised by those responsible for his training in England as his chief assets – his abundant self-confidence and an overwhelming tendency to dramatise everything he did – proved to be his salvation. Ronald Sydney Seth was a social outsider in Britain, a man from a humble background who went down prematurely from Cambridge and left the country in a state of bitter confusion in 1936. His time at the BBC in the early months of the war seems also to have left him with a sense of resentment. During the time he spent in the employ of SOE, he wrote numerous letters pressing his case for promotion, and his grievances against the service mounted up after his return to England in 1945. In captivity, however, he found himself free to create the kind of character for himself that he had never been able to be in civilian life. How far his German interlocutors believed him to be a man who moved easily in the highest circles of British society is of course open to question. *Obersturmbannführer* Heinrich Bernhard, who met Seth in 1944 and saw him again in April 1945 on a train in southern Germany, believed him 'to have been a member of one of England's most prominent families', and it may well be that Seth's fantasies caught the imagination of men working under stress, perhaps desperate to claim some success in recruiting a new agent.[15]

Against this, however, must be placed the evidence that those higher up the chain clearly did not wish to use him. According to Emil Kliemann, Seth had been sent to Paris on the instructions of Major Walter Brede, a Berlin-based *Gruppenleiter* in the Luftwaffe section (1L) of the Abwehr; but within weeks of his arrival in Paris, 1L in Berlin was telling Kliemann that he was not be used as an agent, since he was considered unsuitable. The responsibility for Seth was transferred to the army section (1H) on the orders of Colonel Rudolph, the head of the Paris Abwehr, some time around the middle of February. Shortly after D-Day, according to Kliemann (Seth's own account gives May as the time), he was approached by 1H and told they did not want Seth, having no faith in him, and, in any event, seeing little opportunity of sending him to England.

Neither branch of the German military intelligence, therefore, believed Seth to be of any value as a potential agent. Seth was again lucky in falling under the care and protection of Christoph Graf Dönhoff, for Dönhoff worked for the security services (SD) which were about to take over entirely the functions of the disgraced Abwehr.[16] We do not know if Dönhoff was acting under instructions when he and Seth embarked on their jaunt through eastern France, but there is certainly no evidence at this stage that Seth was to be anything other than a stool pigeon, reporting on the views and opinions of his fellow inmates in the prisoner-of-war camp to which he was finally confined. Dönhoff was impressed by the quality of Seth's reports, and this evidently persuaded him and, one must assume, his superior, SS *Obersturmbannführer* Paeffgen, that here was a man who might be entrusted with a mission to England. This mission, however, was rather more modest in scope than that which Seth presented to the astonished British minister to Switzerland in April 1945. Seth was to report back on British political developments, and was to work for the promotion of an Anglo-German rapprochement to counter the threat of Soviet Communism. This was pretty much the same sort of task entrusted to Calthrop, the other British POW smuggled across the frontier into Switzerland.

How then did Seth come to acquire the peace proposals which he revealed at the British legation in Bern? We know that attempts, largely at the instigation of Walther Schellenberg, were being made at the time to contact the western Allies, and that the German peace proposals were roughly along the lines outlined by Seth in Bern. There is also evidence to suggest that circles within the German Foreign Office were prepared to use a POW with supposedly close connections to the British prime minister to transmit a peace message. Major John Bigelow Dodge, distantly related by marriage to the British prime minister, and held in a variety of POW camps since 1940, was suddenly released from Sachsenhausen concentration camp at the beginning of February 1945 and asked by two senior officials of the German Foreign Office to undertake a peace mission. The offer was similar to that emanating from SD circles, namely, surrender on the western but not the eastern front. Dodge was caught up in the Dresden air raid, but managed to cross over the frontier to Switzerland and make his way to Britain, where he relayed the German peace offer to Churchill and the American ambassador on 6 May.[17]

There is, however, no documentary evidence that can unequivocally support Seth's claims to have been entrusted with a special mission. He says that he committed the proposals to memory, but as we have seen, Ronald Seth was more than capable of concocting a plausible story from his own fertile imagination. On the other hand, the contents of the proposal do go beyond the basic offer of capitulation on the western but not the eastern front, as conveyed to the western allies by the Swedish government at the end of April. They are predicated upon the idea that Himmler would be in charge of a purged and reformed German state, which chimes in with contemporary notions within the top echelons of the SS leadership that they were the only force capable of maintaining order and of avoiding the catastrophe of a communist takeover in Europe. This at the very least would suggest that Seth had been exposed to such ideas, even if no concrete proposals were ever given to him for delivery.

What then of the supposed meeting with the Nazi top brass on Easter Monday? It is perhaps significant that this event as described by Seth occurred after he had separated from Dönhoff, and in the absence of his minder. There was thus no independent witness, and none of the men subsequently detained and interrogated at length by the Allies admitted to any such meeting. Furthermore, why would a man charged with the task of conveying German peace proposals to the highest authorities - Prime Minister Churchill no less, as Seth insisted – need a clandestine radio set? Dönhoff's last message to Seth, which accompanied the books and chocolate sent to 'chère amie', c/o the British legation in Bern, regretting that he could send neither the portable gramophone nor the drugs, was not only the last episode of a rather risible cloak-and-dagger story concocted by the two men: it also showed that the count at least believed Seth's task was simply to gather and transmit intelligence.

Seth's revelations to the British minister in Bern caused a momentary flurry in London, and SOE and MI5 moved quickly to ensure his speedy return for interrogation, but they were unable to prevent his interrogation by SIS officers in Switzerland. These men concluded that the peace proposals 'took anti-Bolshevik brotherhood line and are cover for political espionage mission on behalf of SS'.[18] Both branches of Military Intelligence made great play of Seth's anti-Russian attitude. MI5 even described him in May 1945 as 'rabidly anti-Soviet, to such an extent that all his actions and loyalties are subordinated to this ruling passion'.[19] Captain Milton clearly believed that Seth had been largely motivated by his dislike of Russia, though it would be fair to say that his unwillingness to accept Seth's account was based primarily on his conviction that Seth was suffering from megalomania.

In his book, Seth says that, during his fortnight-long interrogation by MI5, no mention was made of him seeing the prime minister. He did not know whether Churchill ever heard of him and his mission, and at the end of his interrogation, he did not greatly care. He did, however, have a brief moment of triumph when reports of Bernadotte's negotiations with Himmler were revealed in the press at the end of April.[20] These revelations hit the headlines after the completion of his interrogation and the writing of Captain Milton's first two reports on his activities (though not his final report). In mid-April, MI5 was keen to ensure that, as Guy Liddell wrote in his diary, 'the one thing to be avoided was that the case should get into the hands of the high-ups before it had been properly sifted'. Only after Seth had been thoroughly investigated would the security services be able to judge 'whether any attention at all should be paid to his rather sensational disclosures of peace terms'.[21] In other words, MI5 made sure that the proposals never saw the light of day during the final days of the war. Two months later, however, one of the men entrusted with the task of shepherding Seth on his arrival in London, Roland Bird, freely admitted that Seth's story 'sounds less fantastic today in light of Himmler's other approaches to the Western Allies'.[22] Hugh Trevor-Roper, who had been in correspondence with Seth, was also inclined to think his story was true.[23]

Seth's obsessive tendency to exaggerate his own role, and the lack of substantive evidence from those on the German side who were in a position to know, make it almost impossible to deliver a balanced verdict on his mission. What can be said with some certainty is that a small circle of high-ranking Nazi functionaries, believing that the British might be persuaded to conclude a separate deal with a Germany no longer under Hitler's control in order to stem the advance of communism in Europe, were prepared in the final hectic weeks of the war to employ British prisoners as their intermediaries. Ronald Seth was a very minor cog who found himself caught up in a monstrous machine that was rapidly running out of control. He himself later admitted in a letter to Trevor-Roper that the machinations in Berlin during the last days of the war were such that one could not be certain of anything. His own interpretation was that Schellenberg's immediate inferiors, led by him, were determined to seize power even without Himmler, and he singled out Paeffgen as one of the driving forces of this movement within the SS.[24] The peace proposals Seth outlined to the British minister in Bern were in line with those conveyed by other intermediaries such as Count Bernadotte, and it is unlikely that they were of his own invention. One can only speculate what might have happened in Germany had these peace proposals been revealed to the wider world at the time. Himmler would undoubtedly have been forced to show to him by a group of refugees – is confused. Steiner was sceptical about his claim to have been a parachutist in the Coldstream Guards, and asked jokingly how a parachutist could become a Panzer man. Berneville-Claye's reply, that he could learn, was rather typical of his brash self-confidence, KV2/627.

10. HS7/184.

11. Seth's handwritten report, Bern, April 1945, KV2/378.

12. MI5 report 3, p.22.

13. Draft project for Operation Blunderhead, 15 December 1941, HS9/1344. In a letter dated 5 December 1945, Seth wrote that he had been sent to Estonia 'to organise a resistance movement in that country', KV2/380.

14. Memo, 23 September 1942, HS9/1344.

15. Interrogation of Bernhard, 11 January 1946, KV2/380.

16. This is confirmed by Bernhard, who stated that Seth was saved from being returned to Frankfurt for execution by the intercession of Dönhoff, an 'honorary member' of Amt VI, KV2/380.

17. Carroll 2012 for the life and career of Major Dodge. Dodge also had dealings with Paeffgen.

18. Cipher telegram from Bern, 16 April 1945, HS9/1345.

19. MI5 Minute Sheet, 17 May 1945, KV2/280. The SIS officers in Switzerland believed he convinced the Germans by his 'partially genuine anti-Russian attitude', HS9/1345.

20. Seth 2008, pp.324–5.

21. Liddell's diary entries, 16–17 April 1945. West 2005, pp.285–6.

22. Memo by Bird, 11 June 1945, KV2/380.

23. Note concerning Trevor-Roper, 17 January 1947, KV2/380.

24. Seth to Hugh Trevor-Roper, 11 December 1946, Lord Dacre of Glanfield archives, Christ Church, Oxford. Interestingly, there is no mention of Dönhoff in this correspondence.

25. Ibid.

14 | 'Still drawing considerably on my imagination.'

Kiiu Aabla, September 2014

On a glorious late summer day in 2014, accompanied by an Estonian friend, I set off to explore the Kolga peninsula, the site of Ronald Seth's failed operation in autumn 1942. The coastal road was virtually devoid of traffic, and there were few signs of life in the neat cottages and gardens we passed. Just as we drove past the sign indicating that we were in Kiiu Aabla, we spotted an elderly lady leaning on her bicycle by the side of the road. 'Let's ask her if she knows anything about Ronald Seth and Martin Saarne,' suggested my friend, pulling up alongside and winding down the car window. The lady listened to my friend's question, and then replied that of course she knew the story and would be pleased to tell us, if we chose to join her for coffee. We followed her a few metres back down the road to a brightly painted cottage facing the road and the seashore beyond. This, she told us, was the cottage where Seth, his wife and two children had stayed. As we sat in the kitchen drinking coffee and eating the delicious open sandwiches which our hostess insisted on making for us, we heard the story. Her description of Mart – the Estonian version of Martin – corresponded well with Seth's portrait of 'Juhan', a jolly bachelor who preferred to spend his time playing the accordion. When Seth turned up at the beginning of November, his friend advised him that the situation was hopeless and that there was no boat available to take him to Sweden. He then accompanied Seth when he went to surrender to the Germans, but was himself arrested and imprisoned with the Englishman.

After coffee, we walked back through apple trees to see the house of Mart's sister, Amanda Eslon. Amanda's husband Johannes had been a sea captain and spoke English, which is why Seth came looking for help. He was the elderly infirm man of Seth's story. Johannes in fact died some weeks later, on 6 February 1943; his wife survived him for a further twenty-six years. A more substantial building than the cottage, the house lies empty, surrounded by an encroaching belt of trees. A path leads off directly into the forest behind. The sauna where Seth hid no longer exists, but has been replaced with a new house now owned by the elderly lady's son.

Armed with this knowledge I went in search of further evidence in the archives. The lady was insistent that Seth had come down at Pedaspea, a couple of miles further south. The records of the Estonian militia units, the Omakaitse, revealed that it was there, 10km south of Loksa, that a suspicious armed man speaking Estonian with a Russian accent made an appearance on 1 November 1942. He asked for something to eat, but was refused and an attempt was made to detain him; the man ran off into the woods. A week earlier, on 25 October, it was reported that one or more parachutists had come down in the Kolga peninsula, 10km south of Loksa, and that four packages containing food and explosives had been found. The parachutist[s] had not been caught, but suspicious persons had been spotted moving around the district.[1] This summary of district reports from Omakaitse units makes no mention of any arrests being made, which would seem to support the idea that Seth went along with Saarne to give himself up to the Germans. There is no mention either of any sabotage activity on the Kolga peninsula, though curiously, on 4 November, there is a report of two bombs being dropped 6km west of Loksa.

Records of prisoners released from custody or transferred to other authorities also show that on 16 November 1942, a Martin Saarna, born 15 April 1899, was released from custody. Ronald Zath, born 5 June 1911, was handed over to the Germans on 12 January 1943. I was unable to find any record of Anton Prokhorov, but there is mention of Laine Kass, a 19-year-old handed over to the German Field Police on 4 December.[2] During his interrogation in London, Seth spoke of a fellow inmate of this name at the central prison in Tallinn, about 20 years of age, who had been captured and turned by the Germans, and who was used to transmit false information to Russia. In his published account, she becomes Eva Kass, parachuted by the Russians over Narva, whom his captors offered to him as a cell companion.[3] It is therefore likely that Seth may have gleaned some information from her, which, drawing considerably on his imagination as he later wrote, he was able to transform into his own account of his activities.

What then really did happen during those twelve days of freedom, which Seth described so vividly? Using the material available, and taking into account the significance of evidence which is lacking, especially concerning acts of sabotage, I would make the following tentative conclusions. Ronald Seth was dropped perhaps a couple of kilometres south of the spot originally chosen, in the vicinity of Pedaspea. The local militia, based at the nearby village of Loksa and numbering 332 men in total, was made aware of the drop, though suspected that there was more than one parachutist. The cylinders containing his supplies and explosives were almost immediately discovered. The story of an escape from an incompetent German patrol was without doubt an invention, as were the acts of sabotage – though the remains of wartime gun emplacements can still be seen on the northern tip of the peninsula, so Seth must at least have been aware of them. The forests on the peninsula are dense enough to conceal a man without him having to climb a tree, but as in all isolated rural areas, a person lurking on the fringes of the woods soon rouses suspicion. Seth tried to obtain food from a farmhouse, but was refused and had to retreat under fire into the woods. Some time later, he managed to find his peacetime acquaintance Martin Saarne in his cottage at Kiiu Aabla, and was persuaded by him to give himself up. Both men were arrested and imprisoned, but Saarne was lucky enough to be released. He died in 1969, and is buried in the parish of Kuusalu, a few miles from his birthplace in Kiiu Aabla.

Seth was carrying with him a significant amount of money. What happened to it? Seth's accounts differ on this point. According to his published story, he handed over the money, with his wife's address, to the sick old man who was alone in the house. He was subsequently brought back to the house, where the frightened old man surrendered the money to his captors. This is substantially the same story he wrote down for MI5 in 1945. But his Paris report merely says that he was taken back to the house where his story was verified and Saarne was arrested. Interrogated by the Germans in 1943, Seth had said that he had buried some of the money in the woods.[4]

As we sat drinking coffee in the kitchen of Martin Saarne's cottage, however, we heard a different story. After the war, we were assured, Martin and his sister lived very well, and everyone in the village believed they were living off Seth's 'treasure'. Now, this may be nothing more than the sort of rumour that flourishes in small communities, but I would like to think that it is a story which would have left Ronald Seth with a feeling that one small part of his mission had been accomplished, even if the money did not end up financing resistance activities.

Ronald Seth never returned to Estonia, and died before that country regained its independence following the collapse of the Soviet Union in 1991. In 1945, Captain Milton had begun his third and final report in May 1945 by listing the various aliases of Ronald Seth, some nine in total. In the post-war years, Seth was to add at least one other name to that list: Dr Robert Chartham. In addition to being a prolific author of popular histories and children's books, he developed a new career under that name as a sexologist. His sex advice manuals now have a rather dated feel, and his method of penis enlargement ended up in a lawsuit in the United States and still provokes debate in cyberspace. The story of Dr Robert Chartham is rather more difficult to uncover than that of Agent Blunderhead/22D, but it bears the same hallmark: the easy assumption of expertise, a fluency of style and a certain persuasive quality that makes one want to believe him, even if one is not always quite sure why.

Notes

1. Omakaitse fortnightly digests of events, nos 19, 20. ERA-R.358.2.9.
2. ERA-R.64.1.101.
3. MI5 report 2, p.18. Seth 2008, p.77.
4. Seth 2008, p.45, 50. Seth's 1945 report, KV2/378. Report 44, p.9. MI5 report 2, p.11. Intercepted interrogation report, HS9/1344 and KV2/380.

Bibliographical Note

The details of Ronald Seth's adventures have been gleaned primarily from his own published story and SOE and MI5 files released by the National Archive at Kew. For an agent whose mission was a failure, Seth managed to create a surprising amount of paperwork: two thick SOE files (HS9/1344, 1345) and four MI5 dossiers (KV2/377-380), which consist for the most part of poor-quality photostats of original material. There is also more correspondence on Seth in HS4/240.

Evidence of Seth's activities after his capture can be extracted from various interrogation reports, of which those of Wolfgang Krause-Brandstetter (KV2/160), Richard Delidaise (KV2/307), Otto Schueddekopf (KV2/2646-48), Walther Schellenberg (KV2/94-99) and KV2/278 (Emil Kliemann) proved to be the most useful. The subject of KV2/439 is John Boucicault de Suffield Calthrop, whilst Douglas Berneville-Claye is honoured with two files, KV2/626-7.

Diplomatic papers concerning Estonia are in the Foreign Office archives at Kew (FO371), as is material relating to the German occupation of Estonia (GFM33).

Material on Seth's sojourns in Estonia is in the Estonian State Archives (ERA) and Tallinn Town Archives (TLA).

I am indebted to Dr Philip Pattenden of Peterhouse, Cambridge, for providing me with materials from the college archives, and Professor Blair Worden of Christ Church, Oxford, for Seth's correspondence with Hugh Trevor-Roper, now in the Lord Dacre of Glanton papers.

Bibliography and Sources

Books

Allen, M., *Himmler's Secret War: The Covert Peace Negotiations of Heinrich Himmler* (Robson Books, 2005)

Bailey, R., *Forgotten Voices of the Secret War: An Inside Story of Special Operations during the Second World War* (Ebury Press, 2009)

Baumann, U. & Koch, M., *"Was damals Recht war": Soldaten und Zivilisten vor Gerichten der Wehrmacht* (Be-bra Verlag, 2008)

Bernadotte, F., *Sidste Akt Mine humanitære Forhandlinger i Tyskland Foraaret 1945 og deres politiske følger* (Gyldendal, 1945)

Birn, R.B., *Die Sicherheitspolizei in Estland 1941–1944: Eine Studie zur Kollaboration im Osten* (Schöningh Paderborn, 2006)

Carroll, T., *The Dodger: The Extraordinary Story of Churchill's Cousin and the Great Escape.* (Mainstream Publishing, 2012)

Clark, F., *Agents by Moonlight. The Secret History of RAF Tempsford During World War II* (Tempus Publishing, 1999)

Collinson, Patrick, *History of a History Man* (Boydell and Brewer, 2011)

Cruickshank, C. *SOE in Scandinavia* (OUP, 1986)

Diamant, A., *Gestapo Frankfurt-am-Main* (Sebstverlag des Autors, 1988)

Doerries, R. *Hitler's Last Chief of Foreign Intelligence. Allied Interrogations of Walter Schellenberg* (Cass, 2003)

Doerries, R. & Weinberg, G., *Hitler's Intelligence Chief: Walter Schellenberg* (Enigma Books, 2009)

Dorril, S., *MI6: Fifty Years of Special Operations* (Fourth Estate, 2000)

Foot, M.R.D., *The Special Operations Executive, 1940–1946* (Pimlico, 1999)

Geck, S., *Dulag Luft: Auswertestelle West: Vernehmungslager der Luftwaffe für westalliierte Kriegsgefangene im zweiten Weltkrieg* (Peter Lang, 2008)

Jeffrey, K., *MI6. The History of the Secret Intelligence Service 1909–1949* (Bloomsbury, 2010)

McIntyre, B., *Double Cross: The True Story of the D-Day Spies* (Bloomsbury, 2011)

Murphy, C.J., *Security and Special Operations: SOE and MI5 during the Second World War* (Palgrave Macmillan, 2006)

O'Sullivan, D., *Dealing with the Devil: Anglo-Soviet Intelligence Cooperation during the Second World War* (Peter Lang, 2010)

Schellenberg, W., *The Schellenberg Memoirs* (trans. Louis Hagen) (André Deutsch, 1956)

Seth, R., *Baltic Corner. Travel in Estonia* (Methuen, 1939)

Seth, R., *A Spy has no Friends* (André Deutsch, 1952: reissued by Headline Books, 2008)

Stafford, D., *Secret Agent. The True Story of the Special Operations Executive* (BBC Worldwide Publications, 2001)

Statiev, A., *The Soviet Counter-insurgency in the Western Borderlands* (CUP, 2010).

Trevor-Roper, H.R., *The Last Days of Hitler* (Pan Books, 1952)

Tyas, S. & Witte P., *Himmler's Diary 1945: A Calendar of Events Leading to his Suicide* (Fonthill Media, 2014)

West, N. (ed.), *The Guy Liddell Diaries, Vol.2, 1942–1945* (Cass, 2005)

Wildt, M., *An Uncompromising Generation: The Nazi Leadership of the Reich Security Main Office* (University of Wisconsin Press, 2009)

Other sources

Ansell, E., *Admissions to Peterhouse, in the University of Cambridge, January 1931–December 1950* (Peterhouse, 1971)

Breitman, R., 'A Deal with the Nazi Dictatorship? Himmler's Alleged Peace Emissaries in Autumn 1943' (*Journal of Contemporary History* 30/3, 411–30, 1995)

Foot, M.R.D., 'Was SOE any good?' (*Journal of Contemporary History*, Vol.16, No.1., 167–81, 1981)

Hiio, T., Maripuu, M. & Paavle, I. (eds), Estonia 1940–1945 (Reports of the Estonian International Commission for the Investigation of Crimes against Humanity, 2006)

Verhoeyen, E., *Spionnen aan de achterdeur: de Duitse Abwehr in België 1936–1945* (Governance of Security Report Series, Vol. IV. Antwerpen – Apeldoorn, 2011)

Wheatley, B., 'MI5's Investigation of Ronald Sydney Seth, SOE's Agent Blunderhead and the SD's Agent 22D: Loyal British Agent or Nazi Double Agent?' (*Journal of Intelligence History*, Vol. 13. Issue 1, 41–61, 2014)

Index

If you enjoyed this book, you may also be interested in…

Take Budapest
Kamen Nevenkin

Kamen Nevenkin tells the fascinating story of the 'Market Garden'-like operation to knock Hungary out of the war in October 1944, thereby bringing the Red Army as far as Munich, using a number of never before published German and Russian archival documents, including German papers exclusively held in the Russian military archive. The dynamic, detailed text is accompanied by previously unpublished photographs and uses first-person accounts to render a human tale of all-out war.

978 0 7524 6631 6

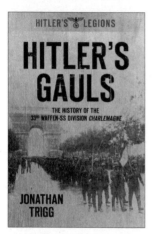

Hitler's Gauls
Jonathan Trigg

Hitler's Gauls is an in-depth examination of one of Hitler's foreign legions, the Charlemagne division, who were recruited entirely from conquered France. The men in Charlemagne, often motivated by an extreme anti-communist zeal, fought hard on the Eastern Front including the final stand in the ruins of Berlin. This definitive history, illustrated with rare photographs, explores the background, training, key figures and full combat record of one of Hitler's lesser known foreign units.

978 0 7524 5476 4

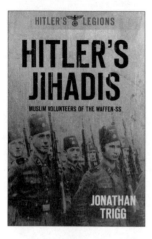

Hitler's Jihadis
Jonathan Trigg

Jonathan Trigg analyses some of the most intriguing and controversial of Hitler's foreign volunteers – the thousands of Muslims who wore the SS double lightning flashes alongside their erstwhile conquerors. Herein lies an insight into the pre-war politics that inspired these Islamic volunteers, who for the most part would not survive. Using first-hand accounts and official records, *Hitler's Jihadis* peels away the propaganda to reveal the complexity that lies at the heart of the story of Hitler's most unlikely 'Aryans'.

978 0 7524 6586 9

Visit our website and discover thousands of other History Press books.

www.thehistorypress.co.uk

The History Press